# European Business Systems

## Firms and Markets in their National Contexts

*Edited by*

Richard Whitley

SAGE Publications
London • Newbury Park • New Delhi

Chapters 1 and 12, Introductory material and editorial
arrangement © R. Whitley 1992
Chapter 2 © K. Räsänen and R. Whipp 1992
Chapter 3 © C. Lane 1992
Chapter 4 © Ad van Iterson and R. Olie 1992
Chapter 5 © P. Kristensen 1992
Chapter 6 © K. Lilja, R. Räsänen and R. Tainio 1992
Chapter 7 © J. Marceau 1992
Chapter 8 © B. Hellgren and L. Melin 1992
Chapter 9 © D. Knights, G. Morgan and F. Murray 1992
Chapter 10 © J. O'Reilly 1992
Chapter 11 © J. Nishida and S. G. Redding 1992

First published 1992
Reprinted 1994

First paperback edition 1994

SAGE Publications Ltd
6 Bonhill Street
London EC2A 4PU

SAGE Publications Inc
2455 Teller Road
Thousand Oaks, California 91320

SAGE Publications India Pvt Ltd
32, M-Block Market
Greater Kailash – I
New Delhi 110 048

**British Library Cataloguing in Publication Data**

European Business Systems: Firms and Markets in Their
National Contexts
  I. Whitley, Richard
  338.7094

  ISBN 0–8039–8732–3
  ISBN 0–8039–7815–4 (pbk)

**Library of Congress catalog card number 92–056428**

Typeset by Mayhew Typesetting, Rhayader, Powys
Printed and bound in Great Britain by
Biddles Ltd, Guildford and King's Lynn

# Contents

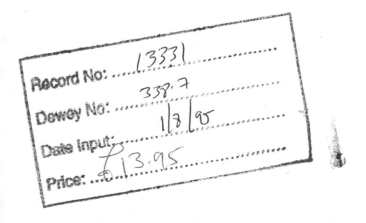

# European Business Systems

# Notes on Contributors

**Bo Hellgren** is Assistant Professor at the Department of Management and Economics, Linköping University. His current research interests concern strategic change processes and complex decision processes in networks of organisations.

**Ad van Iterson** is Assistant Professor in the Department of Organisational Studies in the Faculty of Economics and Business Administration at the University of Limburg, Maastricht. His past research has included a study of aspects of labour control in early factory systems.

**David Knights** is Reader in Organisational Analysis and Director of the Financial Services Research Centre, Manchester School of Management, UMIST. His recent publications include *Labour Process Theory* (co-edited with C. Smith and H. Willmott, 1990) and *Managing to Discriminate* (with D. and M. Collinson, 1991).

**Peer Hull Kristensen** is Associate Professor at the Institute of Organisation and Industrial Sociology, Copenhagen Business School. He has published widely and is the co-editor (with Finn Borum) of *Technological Innovation and Organizational Change: Danish Patterns of Knowledge, Networks and Culture* (1990).

**Christel Lane** is a Lecturer in the Faculty of Social and Political Sciences and a Fellow of St John's College, University of Cambridge. She is the author of *Management and Labour in Europe* (1989), and of many journal articles on aspects of business organisation and labour in Europe.

**Kari Lilja** is Professor of Business Management at the Helsinki School of Economics. In 1987/88 he was a visiting professor at the European Institute for Advanced Studies in Management, Brussels. He is a member of the Coordinating Committee of the European Group for Organisation Studies (EGOS). His publications include *Managerial Processes and Managerial Divisions of Labour*, a special issue of the *International Journal of Sociology and Social Policy* (edited with A. Teulings, 1989).

**Jane Marceau** is Professor of Public Policy at the Australian National University. Her recent publications include, *A Family Business? The Making of an International Business Elite* (1989) and *Reworking the World: Organisations, Technologies and Cultures in Comparative Perspective* (edited, 1992) as well as numerous reports and chapters in books on technological change and organisational issues.

**Leif Melin** is Professor of Strategic Management at the Department of Management and Economics, Linköping University. His current research interests concern strategic change processes in organisations and structural change in industrial fields.

**Glenn Morgan** is a Lecturer in Organisational Behaviour at Manchester Business School, Manchester University. He is the author of *Organizations in Society* (1990).

**Fergus Murray** is a Research Fellow at the Manchester School of Management, UMIST. He has published widely on the Italian industrial system. He is currently researching the role of information technology in the European financial services industry.

**Judith Nishida** is a Senior Lecturer in the Department of Management, Hong Kong Polytechnic. She is currently completing a doctoral thesis on firm development in the Japanese, Korean and Hong Kong textile industries, which follows on from an M.Phil dissertation on the Japanese influence on the pre-war Shanghainese textile industry and the implications for the Hong Kong textile industry.

**René Olie** is Assistant Professor in the Department of Organisational Studies in the faculty of Economics and Business Administration at the University of Limburg, Maastricht. He is currently working on a thesis on integration difficulties in international mergers, especially Dutch–German mergers.

**Jacqueline O'Reilly** is Lecturer in Human Resource Management at Royal Holloway & Bedford New College, London University. Her current research interests include comparative research on training, labour markets and women's employment in Europe.

**Keijo Räsänen** is an Associate Professor in the Department of Business Management at the Helsinki School of Economics. In 1988/89 he was a visiting professor at the European Institute for

Advanced Studies in Management, Brussels. His publications include, *Breaking History and Making History*, a special issue of *International Studies of Management and Organization* (edited with Grieco and Whipp, 1991).

**Gordon Redding** is Professor of Management Studies, and Director of the University of Hong Kong Business School. His publications include *The Spirit of Chinese Capitalism* (1990) and *Managers for Asia/Pacific* (1991). He also acts as an adviser to companies, particularly in Hong Kong.

**Risto Tainio** is a Professor in the Department of Business Management at the Helsinki School of Economics. In 1981 he was a visiting professor at the European Institute for Advanced Studies in Management (EIASM), Brussels and from 1985 to 1986 a visiting scholar at Stanford University. His article in the *Journal of Applied Behavioural Science* on management in different societal and cultural contexts (with T. Santalainen) won the Douglas McGregor prize in 1983.

**Richard Whipp** is Professor of Human Resource Management and Deputy Director of the Cardiff Business School, University of Wales. He has specialist interests in the automobile, ceramic and book publishing industries, financial services and the National Health Service. His most recent publications are *Patterns of Labour* (1990) and *Managing Change for Competitive Success* (with A. Pettigrew, 1991).

**Richard Whitley** is Professor of Organisational Sociology at the Manchester Business School, Manchester University. His publications include *The Intellectual and Social Organisation of the Sciences* (1984) and *Business Systems in East Asia: Firms, Markets and Societies* (1992).

# Preface

This book developed from a small workshop on dominant economic agents organised by Kari Lilja and Risto Tainio in Helsinki at the end of August 1990. Although participants came from a variety of intellectual backgrounds, it rapidly became clear that we shared a strong interest in the different patterns of economic organisation which have developed in Europe and their connections to dominant social institutions. This interest seemed an appropriate focus for a group to pursue at the 10th Colloquium of the European Group for Organisational Studies held in Vienna in July 1991 and most of the chapters in this book were presented in preliminary versions at that Colloquium. Revised papers were discussed at a meeting organised by Peer Kristensen on the island of Møn in Denmark in September 1991 and the final versions are published here. I am very grateful to the organisers of these workshops for providing opportunities to discuss the similarities and differences between forms of economic organisations in Europe and elsewhere and, of course, to the authors for bearing with editorial requests and meeting deadlines so efficiently.

The timeliness and significance of the topics discussed in this book are highlighted by the changes taking place in the European Community at the end of this year and, more dramatically, in Eastern Europe. Because of the considerable differences in how each country is establishing a market economy, and variations in their cultural and institutional inheritances, the former Eastern bloc states constitute ideal economies in which to compare and identify the processes by which major social institutions structure configurations of firm–market relations. The importance of the comparative analysis of firms and markets in Europe has recently been recognised by the European Science Foundation's establishment of a new Programme on European Management and Organisations in Transition which will bring together work on these topics being carried out in different European countries. The chapters in the present volume represent a start towards such collaborative research and will, I hope, provide a useful contribution to the new ESF enterprise.

Richard Whitley,
Manchester 1992

# Introduction

## Richard Whitley

Current attempts to remove trade barriers between European countries and facilitate the growth of Europe-wide firms and markets have highlighted the continuing importance of national differences in how economic activities are organised across Europe. Despite the increasing internationalisation of some industries over the past four decades, there is considerable evidence that national institutions remain quite distinct in Europe and that they reproduce systems of economic organisation which vary significantly between countries. The structure and operation of firms and markets, in, say, Britain differ in many important respects from those in Germany, and these differences clearly stem from variations in dominant social institutions such as the state and the financial systems. As long as such national institutions continue to be more influential in structuring systems of economic organisation than pan-European ones, these differences will remain significant and the development of pan-European forms of firms and markets remains unlikley.

This book explores the ways in which important social institutions have generated different sorts of economic and business organisation in a number of European countries, and shows how they continue to structure firms' strategic choices. Economic structures and outcomes are conceived here as *socially* constructed, such that major differences in dominant institutions result in different kinds of leading firms becoming established and following different growth patterns in different European economies. For example, differences in the level and type of diversification pursued by Finnish and Swedish paper and pulp firms cannot be understood without linking patterns of firm growth to variations in land ownership and in the structure and operation of the political and financial systems in these countries. Similarly, large British and German firms have followed quite different paths of development because of major differences in their political, financial and labour market institutions. There is, then, no single best way of organising firms and markets in Europe, and a central task for the analysis of market economies and effective forms of business organisation is to understand how variations in major social institutions constrain, guide and reproduce distinctive ways of structuring firms and markets. The chapters in this volume constitute an initial contribution to such an understanding.

The two chapters in the first part deal with the general theoretical framework for comparing systems of economic and business organisation. Richard Whitley discusses the nature of business systems as distinctive configurations of firms and markets which become established in different institutional contexts and considers the critical background and proximate institutions which structure these. The ways in which institutional variations affect business system characteristics are also briefly analysed. This broad framework is then discussed by Keijo Räsänen and Richard Whipp from an industry sector perspective, drawing on their comparative studies of industries in Britain and Finland. They suggest that distinctive ways of organising economic activities are largely sector-based and that these compete for domination of national economies.

The second part contains five chapters which focus on national business systems in Europe and how these are related to major institutions. Christel Lane shows how firms and markets in Britain and Germany follow divergent logics as a result of institutional differences and constitute quite different forms of economic organisation, although there are also some variations within each economy. Ad van Iterson and René Olie apply a similar approach to the Netherlands with an interesting discussion of the continued importance of certain pre-industrial traditions. In Chapter 5 Peer Kristensen's account of successful small and medium-sized enterprises in Denmark provides a link between the debates over flexible specialisation and 'post-Fordist' modes of production and the institutionalist analysis of organisation. In contrast, the large, capital-intensive and oligopolistic forest sector firms in Finland are the subject of Chapter 6 by Kari Lilja, Keijo Räsänen and Risto Tainio. They see the successful growth of these firms as tied to particular features of the state, the banking system, the labour system and the dominant pattern of land ownership. Finally, Jane Marceau demonstrates the critical role of social institutions in structuring different forms of economic organisation by comparing the Anglo-Saxon economy of Australia with Denmark and Finland.

The four chapters in the third part of this book focus more on specific sectors and firms' behaviour. Bo Hellgren and Leif Melin discuss some of the major changes in the Swedish pulp and paper industry and suggest that these are linked to the growing internationalisation of that sector, which altered the prevailing 'industrial wisdom' in Sweden. In contrast, David Knights, Glenn Morgan and Fergus Murray show how particular features of the Italian political system and social structure have had major effects on the organisation of the financial services industry in Italy and continue to play an important role in current changes. Jacqueline O'Reilly also focuses on financial organisations in her comparison of British and French retail banking. This analysis of how differences in state policies and the education system have led to contrasting labour management strategies provides a useful contribution to the debates over labour flexibility and training by emphasising the institutional specificity of effective managerial practices. The last chapter in this section also highlights the crucial role of dominant institutions, together with strong cultural norms, in generating quite different patterns of firm growth and market relationships. Judith Nishida and Gordon Redding show how major differences in both the background and proximate institutions have produced distinctive firm–market relations in the Japanese and Hong Kong textile industries. While European cultures and institutions are not usually so homogenous and mutually distinctive, this chapter demonstrates how variations in economic cultures can generate distinctive forms of economic organisation in ways that might well recur in Eastern Europe, where trust relations are not highly institutionalised.

In the concluding chapter Richard Whitley discusses three important issues in the comparative analysis of business systems. First, whether these forms of economic and business organisation are primarily national, sectoral or cultural; second, the extent to which, and ways in which, business systems undergo substantial change once they have become established; and third, the consequences of the growing internationalisation of economic activity and whether the transfer of managerial practices by transnational corporations is likely to reduce the diversity of business system characteristics. Finally, the different ways in which the comparative analysis of European business systems could be carried out are considered. In sum, this volume shows how varied are European market economies as a result of major differences in key social institutions and also suggests how these variations can be analysed as part of the general study of economic structures and relations.

# THE COMPARATIVE ANALYSIS OF BUSINESS SYSTEMS

## 1
## Societies, Firms and Markets: the Social Structuring of Business Systems

### *Richard Whitley*

The recent economic success of the Korean conglomerate *chaebol* and the Chinese family businesses of Taiwan, Hong Kong and Southeast Asia have, together with the more widely recognised success of the post-war Japanese *kaisha*, emphasised two important points about market economies and effective forms of business organisation. First, there are a number of different ways of organising economic activities successfully in a market economy, and no single pattern is clearly superior to all the others. Second, these different patterns of economic organisation result from, and are effective within, particular institutional environments such that variations and changes in the latter generate differences in the former. This is especially marked in East Asia but is also apparent in Europe (cf. Hamilton and Biggart, 1988; Lane, 1989; Maurice et al., 1980; Redding, 1990; Whitley, 1990; 1991; 1992).

These points in turn suggest that the development and success of different kinds of managerial structures and practices in different contexts require explanation in terms of those contexts rather than being reduced to a single economic logic or it being assumed that market competition will, in some mysterious way, select the most efficient pattern of economic organisation. Equally, the search for some set of universal correlations between abstract contingencies and effective organisation structures across all market economies seems of limited value when it is realised that the effectiveness of particular forms of business organisation is institutionally relative, so that structures which are successful in one context may not be effective in others. Instead, I suggest that a key task in the analysis of market economies and organisations is to understand how distinctive patterns of economic organisation become established and effective in different societies and how they change in relation to their institutional contexts.

These patterns concern the nature of economic activities that are coordinated through managerial hierarchies and how these hierarchies organise their cooperative and competitive relations through markets. They can thus be summarised as configurations of hierarchy–market relations that become institutionalised in different market economies in different ways as the result of variations in dominant institutions. The systematic study of these configurations and how they become established is here termed the comparative analysis of business systems. In this chapter I present a framework for such an analysis, drawn largely from the comparison of East Asian economies (Whitley, 1992), which informs many of the studies in this book. Initially, I outline the major components of business systems as distinct ways of organising economic activities in market societies and identify their major characteristics which vary between institutional contexts. Next, the dominant institutions which help to explain these variations are discussed and some of the ways in which they impinge upon hierarchy–market relations are identified. Finally, I briefly consider the relations between business systems and national boundaries and the consequences of variations in their degree of integration and distinctiveness within and between nation states.

## The Nature of Business Systems and their Comparison

Business systems are particular arrangements of hierarchy–market relations which become institutionalised and relatively successful in particular contexts. They combine differences in the kinds of economic activities and skills which are authoritatively coordinated in firms, as opposed to being coordinated through market contracting, with variations in market organisation and differences in how activities are authoritatively directed. These differences can be seen as alternative responses to three fundamental issues in all market economies. First, how are economic activities and resources to be coordinated and controlled? Second, how are market connections between authoritatively coordinated economic activities in firms to be organised? Third, how are activities and skills within firms to be organised and directed through authority relations? The ways in which each of these issues is dealt with in different institutional contexts are, of course, interdependent and together constitute distinctive configurations of hierarchy–market relations in those contexts.

An important part of the comparative study of business systems therefore concerns the analysis of how 'firms' are constituted as relatively discrete collective entities which coordinate and control economic activities through authority relations in different market economies. While all market-based economic systems decentralise control over economic activities to property rights owners and their agents, the nature of the collective entities that exercise that control, and how they do so, vary considerably and so what a 'firm' is differs across institutional contexts. In particular, it is clearly misleading to rely on purely legal definitions of firms' boundaries and activities if we are concerned to explore their role as economic decision-making units. Not only are French industrial groups often much more important than their constituent firms in making strategic choices (Bauer and Cohen, 1981), but among the expatriate Chinese it is clear that the key decision unit is the family business rather than the, often numerous, legally defined 'firms' controlled by family heads (Tam, 1990; Wong, 1985). These differences are important features of distinctive business systems which are linked to the institutional environments in which they develop and emphasise the contextual nature of 'firms' as economic agents.

The variability of economic agents between societies, and the different roles of legally defined firms, mean that comparisons of business systems cannot rely on purely formal means of identifying key units of economic action. Similarly, the importance of business groups and networks of relationships between ostensibly independent firms in many countries, especially East Asian ones (Hamilton et al., 1990), raises questions about how economic agents are to be identified for comparative purposes. If business systems vary in how they constitute firms as units of economic action, in other words, how are we to compare and contrast them in a systematic way? The critical point here, it should be noted, is how we are to conceive of the critical economic agents in market societies so that we can compare them and explain their differences. This obviously depends on our view of how firms and markets function.

Firms are important economic agents in market societies because they, or their controllers, exercise considerable discretion over the acquisition, use and disposition of human and material resources. They function as economic actors by integrating, coordinating and controlling resources through an authority system, and it is this authoritative direction of economic activities which is their central characteristic. Authority relations provide the basis for continued and systematic coordination of activities and thus the integrated transformation of resources into productive services (Penrose, 1980:15–25; Whitley, 1987). It is through this system that firms 'add value' to resources and function as relatively separate units of economic decision-making. Although the degree of central direction of economic activities does, of course, vary, as does the primary basis of authority relations, it is this coordinated control of a varied set of resources which distinguishes firms as distinct economic agents from cooperative networks and *ad hoc* alliances.

As well as the nature of firms varying significantly across business systems, so too does the way in which they cooperate and compete through markets. As Richardson (1972), among others, has emphasised, markets vary in their degree and type of organisation, both across industries and across societies (cf. Imai and Itami, 1984). In particular, the longevity and reciprocity of linkages between particular firms differs considerably between those found in financial and commodity markets, on the one hand, and sub-contracting relations in Japanese business groups on the other hand (Dore, 1986; Orru et al., 1989). Together with the more widely studied differences between authority structures, these points suggest that business systems can be analysed in terms of three general components which vary significantly between institutional environments, as follows.

First, the nature of dominant economic agents controlling economic activities and resources. Important characteristics of this component include the ways in which decision-making discretion is allocated and exercised and patterns of firms' growth. Second, the structure of market relations, including the ways in which economic agents compete and cooperate with each other, both within and between industrial sectors. Third, the nature of authoritative coordination and control systems within firms, including prevalent patterns of employment and reward allocation. These three components of business systems can be further analysed in terms of a number of characteristics which form the basis for comparing them across institutional contexts. These are summarised in Table 1.1 and will now be discussed.

*1 The Nature of Firms as Economic Actors*
In considering the nature of firms in market economies, important variations concern the overall range and variety of economic activities coordinated through authority hierarchies, the ways in which control over economic agents is exercised and how controllers of firms deal with uncertainty. Thus, in any business system the extent to which large, privately owned firms dominate the economy, combine diverse resources and activities, are run by salaried managers with considerable autonomy from property rights owners, undergo discontinuous changes in their activities and resources and internalise risk, constitute key ways in which economic actors differ and can be compared.

Table 1.1  *Characteristics of business systems*

1 *The nature of the firm*
- The degree to which private managerial hierarchies coordinate economic activities
- The degree of managerial discretion from owners
- Specialisation of managerial capabilities and activities within authority hierarchies
- The degree to which growth is discontinuous and involves radical changes in skills and activities
- The extent to which risks are managed through mutual dependence with business partners and employees

2 *Market organisation*
- The extent of long-term cooperative relations between firms within and between sectors
- The significance of intermediaries in the coordination of market transactions
- Stability, integration and scope of business groups
- Dependence of cooperative relations on personal ties and trust

3 *Authoritative coordination and control systems*
- Integration and interdependence of economic activities
- Impersonality of authority and subordination relations
- Task, skill and role specialisation and individualisation
- Differentiation of authority roles and expertise
- Decentralisation of operational control and level of work group autonomy
- Distance and superiority of managers
- Extent of employer–employee commitment and organisation-based employment system

The degree of domination of market economies by large firms reflects the overall extent of reliance on authority hierarchies for coordinating economic activities which has, of course, grown considerably in most industrial economies over the past century. However, this expansion of the 'visible hand', celebrated by Chandler (1977), is by no means inevitable or universal, as recent discussions of flexible specialisation and business networks (e.g. Hamilton et al., 1990; Hirst and Zeitlin, 1991) have reminded us. The extent, then, of large firm dominance remains an important variable characteristic of business systems and one which is particularly affected by state structures and policies.

A related aspect of the overall decentralisation of control over economic resources in an economy is the degree of managerial discretion over resource acquisition, use and disposal from owners of property rights. Given that all market economies decentralise control of economic activities to private property holders to some degree, that is, to what extent, and in what way, do owners delegate that control to partners or managers? The way in which this query is answered reflects dominant mechanisms of establishing trust and accountability in a society, as the comparison of business systems in Japan, South Korea, Taiwan and Hong Kong clearly exemplifies (Redding, 1990: 66–72; Whitley, 1991). This characteristic also deals with the nature of ownership and relations between financial institutions and managerial elites in societies where financial intermediaries have developed an important role.

A third characteristic of firms as authoritative controllers of economic activities which varies between market economies – and, sometimes, between sectors within them – is the range and variety of activities and resources coordinated through authority hierarchies. The diversified US and UK corporation controls a much wider range of activities and functions than the post-war Japanese *kaisha*, let alone the typical Chinese family business (Clark, 1979: 221–2; Kagono et al., 1985). In Richardson's (1972) terminology, firms vary in the extent to which they specialise in particular capabilities for undertaking similar activities. Capabilities are here seen as distinctive combinations of knowledge, experience and skills which provide individual enterprises with some competitive advantage in carrying out economic activities. The more specialised are these, the more complementary activities – i.e. those representing different phases of production processes which have to be coordinated to produce commodities or services – are coordinated through various forms of market contracting. Firms incorporating a wide range of capabilities and activities, on the other hand, coordinate complementary and diverse skills and resources through various structures of authority relations. Thus, Japanese car manufacturers coordinate the production of most components by independent suppliers through long-term relational or obligational contracting (Dore, 1986: 72–85), while US ones rely much more on authoritative coordination of complementary activities within each firm (Cusumano, 1985: 186–93). Small firms in Taiwan and the industrial districts of North-East and Central Italy specialise even more and rely on reputationally controlled networks of suppliers in close proximity to carry out complementary activities (Amin, 1989; Greenhalgh, 1988; Orru, 1991).

The significance of owner-control and specialisation are clearly connected to a fourth important characteristic of firms: their preferred growth pattern and way of organising growing activities. The combination of family ownership and control with high levels of business specialisation and strongly personalistic relations between entrepreneurs in the Chinese family business, for example, results in expansion being typically achieved through opportunistic diversification and the creation of numerous separate companies controlled by family members or trusted partners (Hamilton and Kao, 1990; Redding, 1990: 219–24). In contrast, the managerially controlled but relatively specialised *kaisha* in Japan focuses on dominating its particular sector and tends to spin off fast-growing subsidiaries in other industries, not least because its managerial skills and knowledge are not readily generalisable to dealing with a wide variety of competences, resources and markets (Clark, 1979: 55–64). The diversified Anglo-Saxon corporation, in contrast, views its businesses more as a portfolio of resources which can be shuffled relatively easily and managed through formal financial and planning procedures. Growth is here discontinuous and 'lumpy' in terms of assets and capabilities (cf. Aoki, 1988: 204–8; Kagono et al., 1985: 64–87). Subsidiaries are usually wholly owned and integrated through authority hierarchies.

The final characteristic of firms to be considered here is also quite closely connected to owner control and specialisation, the prevalent pattern of risk management. In general terms, risks can either be 'internalised' within authority hierarchies, often through diversification into unrelated activities as in many US and UK conglomerates, or are externalised through reducing commitments and emphasising flexibility, as in the small Chinese family business in labour-intensive industries. Externalisation of risk may also, though, involve risk sharing with suppliers, customers, bankers and employees on a long-term basis of mutual trust and commitment, as in Japan. It may additionally involve risk sharing with state agencies, as in post-war France and South Korea. A simple way of contrasting patterns of risk management is in terms of the extent to which firms rely on relatively long-term relations of mutual dependence with key groups and exchange partners; this is highest in Japan, much more limited in Taiwan and Hong Kong, and lowest in the USA and UK.

## 2 Market Organisation

Turning to consider the second broad component of business systems, the level and type of market organisation, it is clear that this reflects certain characteristics of firms as economic actors. In particular, risk sharing between specialised enterprises implies a high level of inter-firm long-term obligations, so market trans-actions between large firms in Japan tend to be organised around networks of mutual dependence, information sharing and, some-times, ownership (Gerlach, 1987; Orru et al., 1989). Equally, where firms tend to internalise risk and coordinate a wide range of capabilities and activities through authority hierarchies, market relations are likely to be much more short-term, more specific to particular transactions and not be so restricted to particular business partners.

Market organisation, or inter-firm relations, can be broadly compared across economies in terms of the extent to which transactions are primarily organised around long-term relationships between particular exchange partners as distinct from being *ad hoc* and at arm's length. Generally, the more particularistic and long-term are connections between businesses, the more firms are committed to doing business with particular partners, the wider the range of transactions they engage in with those partners and the more reciprocal are relations between firms. In contrast, markets exhibiting low levels of organisation function more like spot markets in which standardised commodities are traded between anonymous buyers and sellers and price is the dominant, if not indeed the only, factor in undertaking transactions.

Cooperation between firms can occur either within particular sectors or between them, or of course both, as in Japan. Thus, vertical integration of activities within an industry can be accomplished either through common ownership and central direction implemented by authority relationships, or through networks of mutual obligation and long-term commitments between suppliers and customers, perhaps coordinated by a trading company such as the Japanese *sogo shosha* (Yoshino and Lifson, 1986: 38–56). Similarly, plans and investments can be coordinated across business sectors through extensive networks between firms, banks and, sometimes, state agencies. These networks may be largely informal and personal or may involve mutual shareholdings, joint ventures and overlapping personnel in top positions, as in the extensive analyses of overlapping directorships (cf. Mizruchi and Schwartz, 1987; Scott, 1986). Thus the extent and cohesion of inter-market groupings varies considerably between economies, as does the extent of central coordination carried out by key firms such as banks. As in the case of vertical connections, commitments can be more or less specific to particular partners, wide-ranging over a number of transactions and issues and varying in reciprocity (Goto, 1982).

The significance of intermediary organisations, such as trading companies and banks, in coordinating transactions between a number of different firms and sectors, is an important characteristic of market relations which varies considerably across economies. In the case of Japan, the coordinating role of these agencies has been particularly important in integrating economic activities and sharing risks between relatively specialised enterprises

(Yoshino and Lifson, 1986: 66–72). The general trading companies there have also helped to integrate small and medium-sized firms into the national financial system by channelling funds from the large 'city' banks to them on the basis of detailed knowledge of their activities and creditworthiness. While few economies have such strong intermediaries as the Japanese one, there are major differences between market economies in the extent to which banks and similar institutions act as coordinating agents in a quasi-contractual manner.

A further important aspect of market organisation in many economies is the existence of business groups (Hamilton et al., 1990). These are alliances of independent firms which have a variety of interconnections between them, sometimes including mutual shareholdings, and which exchange information, technology and personnel. While they vary in the closeness and stability of their interrelationships, and in the extent to which a wide range of activities are coordinated between member firms, business groups function as significant coordinating networks in many market economies, both vertically and horizontally (Encaoua and Jacquemin, 1982; Futatsugi, 1986; Gerlach, 1987). Although these groups are usually based on organisational alliances, in some societies they are more personal and depend on family-like trust relations between the owner-managers of each firm or set of firms. This is especially the case in Taiwan and other Chinese business communities (Hamilton and Kao, 1990; Numazaki, 1986; 1987). Thus, the dependence of close cooperative linkages between firms on personal ties and trust relations constitutes a further characteristic of market organisation.

### 3 Authoritative Coordination and Control Systems

There are a large number of ways in which formal organisations differ, both across sectors and across countries. Here, however, the primary emphasis is on the authoritative coordination and control of economic activities and so it is variations in the organisation and control of work, in the nature of managerial authority and how it is exercised, and in the ways that commitment to organisations is developed and maintained, that are of most interest. Considering first the extent of coordination and integration of activities and capabilities within managerial hierarchies, there are significant differences in the degree to which the work of varied departments, subsidiaries and divisions is systematically organised and drawn together between different societies. According to Granick (1972) and Horovitz (1980), for instance, many British companies control their operations through financial procedures and reporting systems and tend to treat each unit as a separate profit centre, while French and German firms practise a more centralised and integrated form of planning and direction. Similarly, many US corporations develop market-like relationships between their component parts while Japanese ones prefer much more unified and interdependent modes of organisation (Kagono et al., 1985: 102–6). This is reflected in the greater use of functional, or function-based, structures in many *kaisha* in contrast to the multi-divisional form common in the USA (Fligstein, 1985). This distinction refers to more than the simple centralisation of decision-making as measured in numerous studies of organisation structure; it focuses rather on the cohesion and integration of activities within the firm as opposed to enterprises being run largely as a portfolio of disparate and weakly connected businesses.

A related characteristic of authority systems for coordinating and controlling economic activities is their reliance on predominantly impersonal and formal procedures for managing them. As Kagono et al. (1985: 106–11) point out in their comparison of US and Japanese companies, while the former rely extensively on explicit and formally defined systems and procedures for coordinating the work of specialists, the latter are able to build on higher levels of shared values and commitments to ensure cooperation and collaboration in more informal and flexible ways (cf. Aoki, 1988: 11–20). Common experiences, multiple skills and shared areas of knowledge generated by long-term employment, extensive job rotation and information dissemination facilitate informal coordination within and between work groups in Japanese *kaisha*. In this comparison, high levels of skill and task specialisation in the USA, coupled with a strong tradition of contractual rules for governing exchanges and authority relations (d'Iribarne, 1989), are associated with high levels of formalisation of coordination and control procedures.

Such specialisation of tasks, skills and roles is a further important differentiating characteristic of work organisations, as has been emphasised by many writers (e.g. Lane, 1989: 138–56). The extent to which jobs and tasks are allocated to individuals with distinct skills varies considerably between East Asian countries and many Western countries, and Maurice et al. (1980; 1986) have shown how specialisation also differs significantly between French and German firms. The degree of formal specification of each individual's job is also related to how her or his performance is assessed. Generally, where tasks are more allocated towards groups, and they have substantial autonomy in managing task performance, as in Japan, the assessment of competence and allocation of rewards tend to be more group-based than tied to individual efforts and success (Lincoln and Kalleberg, 1990: 85–9). This specialisation of tasks and roles also extends to authority relations and responsibility for making decisions. In highly specialised authority structures, each manager's authority is quite specific, formally spelt out and demarcated from others'. Elsewhere, authority tends to be more diffuse and wide-ranging, covering a variety of areas of subordinates' concerns and activities (Kagono et al., 1985; Rohlen, 1974).

Another aspect of skill and authority specialisation is the extent to which technical skills are separated from operating tasks and form distinct departments in organisations. Such a separation of technical knowledge from the production system clearly increases coordination problems and also results in the relative devaluation of supervisors' authority and competences. As d'Iribarne (1989: 50–1) points out, the lack of clear technical superiority on the part of supervisors encourages considerable centralisation of personnel decisions and conflict resolution in French factories and also results in reduced supervisor discretion over work allocation and task performance (cf. Maurice et al., 1986). In contrast, the broader and publicly certified range of advanced skills characteristic of German supervisors both increases their legitimacy with their subordinates and provides the basis for decentralising considerable control over task performance to them.

Such decentralisation of operational control over how work is carried out is an additional important characteristic of authority systems which results from both worker and supervisor skill levels and plurality, as well as trust between employers and employees. It is partly reflected in the common distinction between 'direct' or managerial control over work and 'responsible autonomy' labour strategies (e.g. Friedman, 1977: 78), but it also encompasses the overall division of managerial and technical labour in enterprises, and often the level of long-term employer–employee commitment. High levels of work group autonomy are encouraged by 'dual' education and training systems (Maurice et al., 1986) which generate broad, polyvalent skills that are integrated into managerial positions as well as reflecting considerable trust between firms and their employees so that new technologies and work processes are quickly assimilated and accepted (Abegglen and Stalk, 1985: 130–2).

A further characteristic of authority and control systems to be considered here is the managerial role and differences in how it is conceived in different business systems. Two important aspects of managerial authority are, first, the extent to which managers are expected to play a major part in task performance and become involved in subordinates' activities, and, second, how much they can admit to limitations of knowledge and expertise without compromising their authority. The first aspect refers to the distance that superiors keep between themselves and subordinates. Typically, Chinese and Korean managers are much more aloof and remote from group activities than Japanese ones, for instance (Silin, 1976; Whitley, 1990). The second focuses on the need for superiors to display omniscience and omnicompetence as a crucial component of their authority. Where such managerial superiority is expected to be high, doubts and admissions of ignorance can threaten their status and so are rarely manifested. While many northern European and Japanese managers appear able to admit to limitations of knowledge without suffering loss of authority, this does not seem to be so true of southern Europeans, Chinese and Korean managers (Laurent, 1983; Redding, 1990). Overall, the managerial role in large Japanese *kaisha* seems to be more facilitative and concerned with improving group achievements and performance, such that the development of subordinates' skills is seen as a key part of the manager's role, whereas Chinese and Korean managers are expected to be more directive, patriarchal and are threatened by displays of subordinates' prowess (Liebenberg, 1982; Rohlen, 1974; Silin, 1976; Whitley, 1991).

These characteristics of authority relations and the organisation of work are connected to employment and personnel practices such as the level of employer–employee commitment, recruitment, reward and promotion procedures, training policies and top management selection methods. Broadly, two basic approaches can be distinguished to employment policies. Either employers rely primarily on market relationships and standards for recruiting and retaining employees or they establish long-term connections with their core workforce and develop distinctive patterns of skill and job organisation. The first, market-based, employment system is approximated by the British pattern of employer–employee relations while the second, organisation-based, one is most similar to the Japanese (Dore, 1973; Clark, 1979). General characteristics of the first are: (1) short-term and specific employer–employee commitments; (2) low levels of firm-based training and limited development of firm-specific skills; (3) considerable mobility between firms but limited flexibility and movement within them; (4) standardised payment norms for standard skills set by labour markets; (5) segmentation of jobs and skills by publicly certified competences and, sometimes, by craft unions. The second, on the other hand, is characterised by: (1) long-term and diffuse employer–employee commitments resulting in high levels of mutual dependence; (2) segmentation of the labour force by employers between 'core', 'temporary' and, in some societies, female workers with different levels of commitment and training for each segment; (3) extensive on-the-job training and development of firm-specific polyvalent skills; (4) seniority-based reward and promotion systems, at least up to middle management levels, and the institutionalisation of organisational 'careers' for manual as well as non-manual workers, thus leading to idiosyncratic and distinctive payment levels and systems between employers. Finally, in the Japanese case, of course, unions are predominantly enterprise-based rather than being founded around skills or industrial sectors.

This broad distinction between types of employment systems has clear implications for top management selection, although other characteristics of business systems such as the significance of owner control are also critical. Long-term commitments to core employees implies a policy of internal promotions for managerial posts, and hence organisation-based employment systems generate top management teams with quite firm-specific skills and experiences. In contrast, market-based employment systems are more likely to recruit top managers externally and thus to have dominant coalitions with a wider range of expertise. Depending on the degree of business specialisation and type of internal organisation typical of economic actors in particular market economies, this difference may result in top management teams with considerable depth of expertise and knowledge about one industry or much more diversified ones. Thus, the post-war Japanese *kaisha* is usually managed by internally promoted managers with industry-specific skills and knowledge, typically from production and/or sales activities with extensive 'work site' experience (Kagono et al., 1985: 186). Consequently, radical changes in direction and activities coordinated through the authority system are not frequent. In contrast, large US and UK firms recruit senior and top managers externally more often and so tend to have a more varied range of experience and expertise at the top. Additionally, of course, since they tend to be more diversified than Japanese firms, internally promoted managers collectively have experience of a wider range of industries and so are less likely to view their firms as belonging to particular industrial sectors.

These 16 characteristics of business systems together constitute the major dimensions on which hierarchy–market configurations vary and form distinctive business systems. Clearly, some dimensions are closely interconnected such that, for example, strong owner control of firms will usually be associated with a low degree of formalisation of coordination and control procedures and high levels of centralisation. Equally, it will typically imply highly personalistic connections between firms. These sorts of interconnection restrict the number of distinct configurations that become established as successful forms of business organisation and enable us to construct a smaller set of combined dimensions which bring together characteristics of firms and markets. Thus, high levels of owner control are usually combined with a preference for personal ties between firms and personal, centralised authority relations within them. Reliance on purely formal coordination and control procedures seems improbable in such businesses.

A second combination brings together considerable diversity of economic activities with a reliance on formal coordination and control procedures for integrating and controlling different components of firms. This relatively high level of 'internalisation' of distinct capabilities and risks also implies limited risk sharing with business partners and employees, and hence low levels of market organisation. Relatedly, where risks are shared on a relatively long-term basis between firms, we would expect high levels of market organisation with extensive reliance on intermediaries to coordinate transactions and the emergence of stable business groups. In the post-war Japanese *kaisha* these characteristics are combined with high levels of employer–employee commitment, but this seems to be more a contingent relation which will not always occur. Finally, high levels of task and skill specialisation imply a considerable division of labour which will typically be associated with extensive reliance on formal control procedures together with relatively formalised employment and personnel procedures to deal with recruitment and reward issues.

These interconnections between characteristics of business systems constrain, but do not determine, the development of distinct hierarchy–market configurations. For example, while managerial specialisation of activities implies considerable interdependence of firms in a business system, it does not directly determine how those interdependencies will be managed, as the contrast between the Japanese *kaisha* and the Chinese family business illustrates. Both of these kinds of enterprise are relatively specialised when compared to the Korean *chaebol* and the large US corporation, and so need to develop linkages with other businesses. However, the ways in which risks are managed and inter-firm linkages organised are quite different between Japan, Taiwan and Hong Kong because of major variations in the political and agricultural systems of pre-industrial Japan and China and in patterns of industrialisation in Japan, Taiwan and Hong Kong (Redding, 1990; Whitley, 1992). Certain combinations of firm type, market organisation and authority systems are, then, more probable than others; but which particular configuration becomes established in each institutional environment depends on the specific combination of dominant institutions in that environment. The critical institutions which affect the development of business systems will now be discussed.

## The Institutional Contexts of Business Systems

In considering the key social institutions that influence the sorts of business systems that become established in different market economies and the ways in which they vary, it is useful to distinguish between those that structure general patterns of trust, cooperation, identity and subordination in a society and those that are more directly involved in the economic system and constitute the more immediate business environment. The former, background, social institutions underpin the organisation of all economic systems and form the background to industrialisation and the development of modern market economies. Typically, they are reproduced through the family, religious organisations and the education system, and often manifest considerable continuity from pre-industrial societies, especially where industrialisation has been relatively recent and fast.

The latter, proximate, social institutions are more often a product of the industrialisation process itself and frequently develop with the formation of the modern state. As well as reflecting particular features of pre-industrial political and economic organisation, these proximate social institutions are also the result of more recent events such as war, occupation and large-scale political changes. Thus, the power and centralised nature of the South Korean state reflect certain features of the pre-industrial patrimonial political system of Korea, but are also the product of Japanese colonialism and the disruption generated by the Korean war (Henderson, 1968; Jacobs, 1985). We will now turn to the major features of background and proximate institutions and their consequences for business systems.

### Background Social Institutions

All market economies institutionalise particular ways of ensuring trust between exchange partners, coordinating economic activities between firms and organising work within them. These reflect more general and underlying principles of cooperation, identity and subordination which have become institutionalised in different societies and, which are usually derived from: (a) the pre-industrial political system and its legitimation principles; (b) traditional elite attitudes towards privately controlled concentrations of wealth; and (c) the organisation and control of agricultural activities. Key background institutions for explaining differences in business systems thus include those dealing with trust relations, those organising collective loyalties and ensuring cooperation between individuals and families and those governing relations of subordination and obedience. At least six separate background institutional features which affect the development of distinctive hierarchy–market relations can be identified and are listed below.

1 Degree and basis of trust between non-kin.
2 Commitment and loyalty to collectivities beyond the family.
3 Importance of individual identities, rights and commitments.
4 Depersonalisation and formalisation of authority relations.
5 Differentiation of authority roles.
6 Reciprocity, distance and scope of authority relations.

Trust is a key component of any market economy because of transactional uncertainties and the considerable temporal and geographical range over which exchanges occur between more or less mutually anonymous agents. Without minimal levels of trust and confidence that commitments will be honoured, markets cannot function (North, 1990: 34–5). Some system for establishing and maintaining trust between economic agents is thus essential for any market economy and its efficacy and type have strong consequences for the organisation and control of economic activities. Zucker (1986), for example, has suggested that the rapid urbanisation of, and high rate of immigration to, the USA at the end of the nineteenth century led to the breakdown of reputational, ascriptive and personal means of ensuring trust and encouraged the rapid development of more formal procedures based on the legal system. These procedures in turn facilitated the growth of the national market and large-scale managerial bureaucracies controlling economic activities on a national scale. Equally, the lack of institutional trust mechanisms in traditional Chinese and Korean societies has resulted in a very high reliance on personal contacts and networks for business transactions and a strong preference for personal introductions and testimonials about a person's reliability and probity before considering business propositions (Redding, 1990; Ward, 1972).

Trust is also a crucial factor in delegating control over economic resources to agents and employees. Where it is low, and formal means of monitoring outputs are not regarded as reliable, direct personal control of activities by owners and their families is likely, so that the discretion and autonomy of non-family managers is quite limited. To a considerable extent, the close control exercised by owners of firms in Chinese and Korean communities is a result of low trust levels between non-family members and the difficulty of ensuring high levels of managerial loyalty. These features in turn stem from the considerable political insecurity of merchants and the lack of intermediate institutions between families and the state in pre-industrial Korea and China coupled with severe disruption during industrialisation, together with the overweening power of the state in South Korea and Taiwan (Whitley, 1991). Similarly, 'responsible autonomy' labour management strategies (Friedman, 1977: 78–9) and high levels of work group autonomy presume considerable trust between employers and employees within authority hierarchies as well as effective means of monitoring outputs. Such trust is obviously less likely to develop where employment relations are dominated by short-term formal contracts and the level of employer–employee commitment has traditionally been low.

The extent to which, and ways in which, loyalties and commitments can be mobilised to collective entities beyond the immediate family and cooperation between relative strangers ensured are crucial to the development of large managerial hierarchies coordinating a range of economic activities. In Japan, for example, the cohesive and highly integrated village communities in the pre-industrial Tokugawa period were characterised by considerable cooperation between families and strong dependence on the village as a whole (Smith, 1959). This background facilitated the development of collective loyalties to large employers and cooperation between individuals and groups within firms. In contrast, Southern Chinese villages were characterised by low levels of inter-family cooperation and considerable competition for access to land. Few resources were collectively owned and local officials more often seen as agents of the central state or landlords than as representatives of peasant interests. Thus, villages as collective entities generated little loyalty or cohesion (Fukutake, 1967; Moore, 1966: 206–11; 169–80). As a result, family loyalties and identities tend to override broader collective commitments in Taiwan and Hong Kong and cooperation between organisational units is less reliable and easy to obtain than in Japanese firms (Silin, 1976). Generally, in societies where collective loyalties beyond the family can be mobilised relatively easily, and cooperation between groups is not difficult to obtain, we would expect the degree of close supervision and reliance on formal rules to coordinate and control work to be low. Employers are here more likely to exhibit high levels of commitment to, and trust in, employees than where these features do not obtain.

A closely related feature of the institutional context is the overall level of individualism as distinct from 'communitarianism' in Lodge's (1987) terms. While individualism has been extensively discussed as a political philosophy and as a set of values and norms, often in connection with utilitarianism and atomism (e.g. MacPherson, 1962; Parsons, 1968: 51–74), it refers here to the importance of the individual as the central social actor and focus of rights and duties, as contrasted with the family or other collective entity, and the extent to which individuals are seen as separate social units with distinct capacities, skills and desires that are naturally equal and not subservient to the claims of collectivities. In its strong form, individualism as an ideology asserts the illegitimacy of collective claims and the reducibility of collective institutions to individual self-interest. Typically, it is associated with an emphasis on private property rights, reliance on formal contracts to coordinate exchanges and activities, and reductionist political philosophies and theories of knowledge. Thus, highly individualistic societies, such as the USA and to a lesser extent the UK, tend to have 'regulatory' rather than 'developmental' states (Johnson, C., 1982: 18–22), a preference for formal, contractual regulation of social relationships and market-based employment and skill development systems (Dore, 1973).

Cooperation and the pursuit of collective interests in such societies are achieved primarily through the contractual, limited and specific organisation of the self-interests of sovereign individuals. Since firms, states and families are nothing more than temporary alliances and utilitarian partnerships between discrete, utility-maximising individuals in these ideologies, cooperation and coordination cannot rely on common loyalties and identities but have to be formally contracted and specified. The anonymous market composed of atomistic, self-seeking individuals is the dominant metaphor of social organisation in such societies. Organisations are therefore more likely to rely on formal specification of specialised roles and tasks in allocating and controlling work in highly individualistic societies than where the legitimacy of collective claims and goals is more widely institutionalised.

Authority relationships vary in their formalisation and depersonalisation, which affects the development of large, diversified managerial hierarchies since highly personal forms of authority limit the effective use of formal rules and procedures to coordinate economic activities on a large scale. Thus, Chinese family businesses, in which formal position in the managerial hierarchy is often less important than personal closeness to the owner, tend to be smaller than and not so successful in capital-intensive industry as Japanese *kaisha* (Silin, 1976). The pervasive personalism of Chinese social relationships restricts the establishment of large, formally coordinated enterprises (Redding, 1990). Partly as a result, Taiwanese economic growth has followed a different path to that in South Korea over the past 30 years (Levy, 1988). Highly personal authority relations also result in centralised decision-making and a preference for direct personal coordination of different activities. Thus, diversified Chinese businesses in Taiwan are integrated through family ownership and family management rather than by formal rules and procedures. Similarly, business groups tend to be constituted more by networks of personal alliances and partnerships than by formally linked businesses which engage in long-term joint activities (Hamilton and Kao, 1990; Hamilton et al., 1990).

The extent to which authority rests upon formal rules and procedures does, of course, vary considerably between Western societies as well as East Asian ones. The widespread reliance on formal contracts is a well-known feature of US society which is linked to the strong commitment to individualism there (Lodge, 1987). As a result, authority relations within firms are more specific and formally bounded in the USA than elsewhere and activities are more coordinated through formal plans and procedures. This means, of course, that cooperation beyond contractual obligations is not easy to obtain in such a society, and conflict over the interpretation of rules and formal agreements can have major consequences (d'Iribarne, 1989: 140–160). The preference for formal specification of rights and duties both reinforces and facilitates this standardisation of jobs and roles within hierarchies and the standardisation of skills through the educational training system. The growth of credentialisation of expertise in the USA has been encouraged by, and in turn has reinforced, the standardisation of organisational roles and extensive reliance on their coordination and control through formal procedures. In turn, these have facilitated the decomposition of large firms into constituent profit centres and their management through largely formal techniques and market-like relationships. The diversity of economic activities which can be coordinated through authority hierarchies is thus considerable in the USA by comparison with other countries (cf. Kagono et al., 1985).

As well as the formalisation and depersonalisation of authority being important features of firms' institutional environments, the extent to which power and authority positions are differentiated, and those in positions of authority are seen as remote and distant from the bulk of the population, also vary significantly between societies. Additionally, the degree of reciprocity between superiors and subordinates in authority systems differs considerably. Traditional Chinese and Korean Confucian ideologies, for example, distinguished between rulers and the ruled in terms of the superior moral worth of the former as revealed by success in literary examinations. This legitimation of power institutionalised a strong barrier between the patrimonial elite and the peasantry and reduced the need for that elite to perform useful services in exchange for subordinates' loyalty and defence. As a corollary of superior moral status, power needed no further justification or demonstration of competence. This conception of legitimacy also meant that any criticism of decisions or policies automatically implied an attack on the moral worth of those who made them and so became highly personal; as a result, discussion of the merits of alternative policies became dangerous and threatening (Jacobs, 1985; Pye, 1985; 1988).

In contrast, Japanese feudalism institutionalised the distinction between reigning and ruling and the competitive pursuit of power through mobilising troops for military campaigns. Power in Japan was thus not a static attribute of morally superior people but rather the outcome of competitive struggles in which clan leaders had to maintain order and personal loyalty. Partly as a result, when the Tokugawa Shogunate established peace at the beginning of the seventeenth century it did so through a hierarchy of personal loyalties and obligations which integrated village communities with castle towns and the central state. Authority relations were thus local and stable compared to those in Korea and China; village headmen were local leaders rather than agents of a distant and rapacious state and sometimes sided with villagers rather than the overlord. Furthermore, leadership within the Tokugawa village was consensual and group-based so that the headmen led from behind rather than imposing their views upon village elders (Fukutake, 1967; Jacobs, 1958; Johnson, E.H. 1967; Smith, 1959; 1988). These broad differences in pre-industrial East Asian political systems were echoed by, and continue to be reproduced in, family authority patterns, as Pye (1985: 61–72) has emphasised.

In Western societies, of course, power tends to be more instrumental and authority linked to expertise and formally prescribed positions. However, there are significant differences between European and North American societies in terms of what

Hofstede (1980) terms 'power distance' between political leaders and their followers, as well as in the extent to which leaders are seen as generally powerful and responsible for a wide range of economic and political outcomes. Broadly, political authority tends to be seen as more limited and bounded in many northern European societies than in Mediterranean ones and leaders less remote from the bulk of the population. Relatedly, there are significant differences between nation states regarding the importance of reciprocity in authority relationships and the acceptance of bargaining and compromise between interest groups as an essential component of policy-making. What may be seen as strong and effective government in one country may be considered near-dictatorship in another. Responsibilities of leaders may similarly vary in scope, as the varied role of the state in providing welfare and other public services across Europe illustrates.

The implications of these six broad background institutions for certain characteristics of business systems are summarised in Table 1.2. In most cases, one end of the institutional variable has been emphasised because the consequences for business system characteristics are much clearer and easier to demonstrate. While low levels of institutionalised trust, for example, are likely to limit managerial discretion and encourage centralisation, it does not follow that societies with high levels of institutionalised trust always encourage considerable managerial discretion and low centralisation. As can be seen, not all the characteristics listed in Table 1.1 are connected to these institutions directly, and, of course, many are related to a number of them. In practice, most business systems characteristics develop from combinations of features of social institutions and cannot be analysed as separate, discrete features stemming from single institutions. They are also affected strongly by more proximate institutions which developed during and after industrialisation took place and which frequently vary significantly between nation states.

*Proximate Social Institutions*
In considering the major proximate social institutions which affect forms of business organisation – and which in turn become influenced by long-established and successful business systems – those dealing with the availability of, and conditions governing access to, financial resources and different kinds of labour power are clearly crucial, as is, of course, the overall political and legal system which institutionalises property rights, provides security and stability and varies in its degree and type of support for private business activities. The critical features of these institutions which

Table 1.2  *Background institutions and business system characteristics*

| Background institutions | Managerial discretion | Long-term risk sharing | Market organis- ation | Personal inter-firm links | Centralis- ation of authority | Reliance on formal procedures and rules | Role specialis- ation | Employee commit- ment | Distant, omnicom- petent managerial role |
|---|---|---|---|---|---|---|---|---|---|
| Low levels of institutionalised trust | − | − | − | + | + | − | | − | |
| Low levels of inter-family cooperation and collective loyalty | − | − | − | + | + | | | | |
| High level of individualism | | − | − | | | + | + | − | |
| Low formalisation and depersonalisation of authority | − | | | + | + | − | − | | + |
| Low differentiation of power | − | | | + | + | − | | | + |
| Aloof, non-reciprocal and omniscient conceptions of authority | | | | | + | | | − | + |

impinge directly on business systems are summarised in Table 1.3 and clearly reflect general patterns of institutional development. In particular, the role of the state during industrialisation and its ability to implement developmentalist policies are crucial to both the way business–government relations develop and to patterns of risk management and strategic decision-making. Equally, the strength of skill-based unions and of professional identities results from long-established ways of organising and controlling skill development and its certification together with the support, or acquiescence, of the state for these patterns. I shall first discuss some key features of the state and then consider the financial system, the education and training system, and the structure and control of labour markets.

Table 1.3 *Critical features of proximate social institutions*

- Business dependence on strong, cohesive state
- State commitment to industrial development and risk sharing
- Capital market or credit-based financial system
- Unitary or dual education and training systems
- Strength of skill-based trade unions
- Significance of publicly certified skills and professional expertise

The importance of the state in processes of economic development is widely acknowledged and variations in its structure and policies are closely related to differences in business system characteristics, as the comparison of East Asian business systems illustrates (Greenhalgh, 1988; Haggard and Cheng, 1987; Wade, 1990; Whitley, 1991). Two key features of the state are its ability to develop and implement coherent policies for economic growth and its dependence – or more exactly, that of dominant groups in its central components – upon such growth for continued legitimacy and retention of power and thus its willingness to pursue growth policies at the expense of other objectives.

The first feature has been characterised as the extent to which states can function as 'hard' states where the executive can enforce its economic policies and ensure that leading economic actors follow its commands (Jones and Sakong, 1980: 132–4). It focuses on the cohesion and integration of major state components, especially the political executive and the bureaucracy, and their relative autonomy from pressure groups and established elites. In the cases of South Korea and Taiwan in the 1960s, 1970s and 1980s, the military-backed regimes were clearly able to ensure compliance with their policies and dominated the bureaucracy

(Amsden, 1989; Gold, 1986; Winckler, 1988). In contrast, where state powers are separated between the legislature, the executive and the bureaucracy, and no single component dominates the others, it is obviously much more difficult to ensure that coherent industrial policies are followed. Equally, societies in which political, bureaucratic and industrial elites come from different backgrounds and do not share common objectives or overlapping career paths are less likely to have 'developmental' states than those in which elites are highly selected through common educational institutions and economic development ministries dominate the state system, as in Japan (Johnson, C. 1982). An important aspect of this integration of components of the state is the extent of decentralisation of economic powers to provincial and local governments. Where this is considerable, as in the United States, coherent central plans and coordination of economic activity are not likely to be particularly effective and may also, under appropriate circumstances, encourage the success of small and medium-sized enterprises as in Denmark and, perhaps, Italy (Kristensen, 1989; Nanetti, 1988; Weiss, 1984; 1988).

The autonomy of the state and its ability to carry through policies against opposition reflects the balance of power between the executive and the legislature in democratic societies, as well as the overall level of institutional differentiation and separation of elites' spheres of action. Where the legislature is relatively independent and has distinct powers of its own, as in the USA, it is clearly more of a constraint on executive action than where it is subservient to political party organisations in an electoral system that generates considerable majorities, as in the UK. Equally, the state is less likely to be able to act consistently and effectively where major activities and institutions are controlled by separate bodies such as professional institutions and independent public corporations, as tends to be the case in Anglo-Saxon societies in contrast to many continental European ones (cf. Dyson, 1980). Indeed, the whole identity of the state as distinct from the government of the day tends to be weaker in the former kinds of society and so its ability to pursue coherent economic policies over an extended period of time is much less.

The degree of state commitment to, and dependence on, economic development and growth reflect the conditions surrounding the establishment of the central state in a country, together with the need for the political elite to legitimise its position through industrial growth. Where the dominant institutions of the central state pre-dated industrialisation, as in Britain, political elites are less likely to see their position depending on their successful management of economic development. In contrast, where the modern nation state became established after the first industrial revolution and was linked to national economic development, as in many nineteenth-century European states, political and bureaucratic elites are much more likely to identify their interests with industrial growth and commit state resources to it. Such commitment does, of course, also depend on the availability of other sources of economic wealth and growth and the strength of groups based on them, such as mercantile, financial and agricultural elites.

The greater the level of state commitment to industrial development, the more likely state agencies will be willing to share risks and information with major firms, as well as ensuring that macroeconomic policies do not inhibit or constrain such development. Obviously this does not mean that they will necessarily become as directly involved in the steering of firms' strategic choices as the Korean state does, but political and bureaucratic elites will probably underwrite major investment decisions and provide considerable infrastructural support for new developments so that firms can plan ahead with some confidence and assume continued economic and political stability. Depending on the overall level of state integration and autonomy, this may result in considerable business dependence on the state and a strong need for firms to coordinate their strategies with state policies. At the very least, such state commitment is likely to mean that major firms will maintain close links with members of the bureaucratic and political elites and be more willing to undertake risky projects than where it is absent. Clear and strong public support for industrial development is also likely to enhance the prestige of industrial management and so increase its attractiveness for the educated children of elite groups. In turn, this is likely to encourage further elite integration between industry and the state.

Overall, high levels of state support for industrial development and risk sharing will encourage firms to develop long-term commitments with business partners and employees by reducing the risks associated with such commitments, or at least the absence of such state support is likely to inhibit them. The lack of state risk sharing will also encourage firms to 'internalise' risk management by diversifying their activities within authority hierarchies. Additionally, where state commitment to economic growth is high and leads to strong central steering of firms' strategic choices, as in South Korea, business dependence on the state is likely to lead to centralised control and decision-making together with limited inter-firm cooperation since firms are more concerned with 'vertical' linkages and uncertainties.

A second crucial component of the business environment, the financial system, affects both the ability of the state to support and guide industrial development and the nature of firms' strategic choices and risk management (Zysman, 1983). Where the financial system is largely capital-market-based, as in Britain and the USA, the state is limited to a predominantly regulatory role and cannot readily intervene in firms' decisions or channel funds towards particular sectors. Credit-based financial systems, on the other hand, enable state agencies to play a major role in the allocation of resources and thus direct firms' choices, especially where the banking system is dominated by the state, as in France, so that it can determine the cost of investment funds and ensure high levels of demand for them, which in turn means that their supply becomes an administrative matter. As a result, firms are often more dependent on the state where financial systems are credit-based than when they are capital-market-based. Equally, they are more directly linked to state priorities and coordination plans where the state participates as an actor in the banking system than where the banks are more autonomous, as in Germany (Zysman, 1983: 55–80). As Cox (1986) points out, the nature of financial systems can change, as in the case of Japan in the post-war period, but nonetheless in any one period it does severely condition the ability of the state to implement industrial policies.

It also affects relations between banks and industrial firms and the latters' financial policies. Basically, capital-market-based financial systems have relatively specialised financial institutions competing for capital and assets through market transactions and the prices of financial assets are largely set by competition. Here, firms raise capital in a variety of ways depending on relative costs and terms. Thus, their relationships with banks tend to be impersonal, short-term and specific to particular transactions. Bank and other financial institutions, on the other hand, concentrate on allocating funds on a portfolio basis to a range of activities and borrowers. As a result, they are less concerned with the long-term development of any single customer than with the relative attractiveness of competing projects from a variety of borrowers at any one time. Consequently, firms depend more on their rating in impersonal financial markets, as measured by standardised financial accounting measures, when seeking to raise investment funds than on their close relations with particular banks. They therefore invest considerable resources in preparing financial accounts for the capital markets, and grant more autonomy and influence to the finance function than do firms operating in credit-based financial systems. An additional consequence of operating in a capital-market-based financial system is that long-term risk sharing between financial and industrial companies is low and so firms are encouraged to 'internalise' risks within their boundaries, which in turn affects their strategic choices by increasing the risks of business specialisation. Since risk sharing between businesses is not encouraged by capital-market-based financial systems, firms are more likely to diversify their capabilities and develop formal control procedures for co-ordinating different kinds of economic activities.

In credit-based financial systems capital markets are weaker and most investment credit is provided by banks, which sometimes, as in Germany (Dyson, 1986), own significant proportions of their corporate customers' shares. Financial institutions are here more dependent on the growth and success of particular borrowers since they cannot easily trade standardised financial assets on liquid secondary markets. They therefore invest more resources in acquiring detailed knowledge of firms and industries to evaluate risks and ensure they are kept fully informed about their customers' activities and performance. This in turn encourages risk sharing, since banks have an interest in providing a wide range of financial services and larger loans for growing businesses, as well of course as acquiring more information about firms' strategies and abilities to manage risky projects. Equally, firms become more dependent on particular banks, especially in high growth periods or when large sums are required for capital investment, since banks will only invest in firms that they already know quite well and have confidence in. As a result, public financial reporting is less important in credit-based financial systems and the banks take on some of the functions carried out by financial managers within firms in capital market financial systems. Firms thus give up some autonomy and independence in exchange for some risk sharing and stability in their relations with financial institutions.

The third important proximate institution which varies significantly between nation states and affects employment practices and patterns of work organisation is the education and training system. Although similarities do occur across nation states, such as those influenced by the Germanic system in the nineteenth-century, there are major differences between many countries in the organisation and structure of formal educational institutions, and in their links to labour markets. These differences have important consequences for firms' recruitment, promotion and training policies, as well as their organisation and control of the division of labour, as Maurice et al. (1980; 1986) and others have demonstrated (e.g. Lane, 1988; and Chapter 3 in this volume). Perhaps the most important difference concerns the extent to which the educational system is dominated by formal academic standards and measures of competence as opposed to incorporating systematic training in practical skills. In unitary systems, such as the French and Japanese, academic success is the crucial criterion of selection for elite institutions and practical training is relatively poorly funded and low in prestige. Essentially, the educational system functions as a series of filters designed to select the most academically competent, who are then guaranteed access to elite positions in the state and private industry. As a result, employers are excluded from the formal system and have to provide practical training themselves, which often tends to be task- and firm-specific. Practical skills are therefore not very standardised or generalisable across work organisations and industries. Firms' internal work organisation and control patterns are here quite idiosyncratic and not constrained by standard specialist skills.

Dual educational systems on the other hand, of which the best example is perhaps the German one (Lane, 1989: 64–8; Maurice et al., 1980), separate technical and practical training from academic competences at quite an early stage and produce a wide range of practical skills in collaboration with employers, as well as filtering the academically gifted. These practical skills have higher social prestige than similar ones in unitary systems and are quite sought after by young workers. They combine formal knowledge with practical competences and are formally taught and assessed so that skills are broader and more standardised than in unitary systems. Because employers are involved in their determination and standard setting, they rely on them in making recruitment and promotion decisions and therefore are more constrained by publicly certified skills than are their equivalents in unitary systems. Furthermore, because practical skills here are not particularly task-specific, they tend to encourage greater flexibility and accommodation to technical change than those tied to specific tasks. The greater prestige of such skills in these systems encourages supervisors and managers to obtain them so that the authority hierarchy is often also a hierarchy of certified expertise. This, in turn, facilitates managerial control and the delegation of operational decision-making and work allocation to supervisors. This integration of technical and supervisory authority also leads to a continuity of expertise up the managerial hierarchy and so limits the distance between managers and skilled workers.

These differences between education and training systems are clearly connected to the fourth major institutional arena that differs significantly between Western nation states: the structure of labour organisations and labour markets. The overall strength of labour organisations obviously affects firms' management practices and ways of structuring employee relations, as we have seen in East Asia, as does their incorporation into political movements and state bodies. The numerical weakness of French trade unions, for example, is exacerbated by their division along political lines and has tended to encourage them to seek redress through the state rather than by direct confrontation with private employers, who can often afford to ignore union demands. In contrast, the strength of the Swedish and Austrian trade union movement is both symbolised and reinforced by its incorporation into the state policy-making machinery and the correspondingly centralised systems of wage bargaining (Katzenstein, 1985: 115–33). Firms in these countries have to adapt to central agreements and maintain close links with their central coordinating body. Many employment and personnel practices are accordingly much more homogenous and standardised across firms than in countries where unions are weaker and unable to influence state policies.

The ways in which labour organisations are constituted are important influences on work organisation and control when union strength is high. In particular, their organisation around separate craft skills and control over the definition and certification of such skills clearly restricts employers' ability to establish idiosyncratic and highly flexible systems of work organisation. Tasks and skills in this situation are more standardised across firms and less firm-specific than where unions are weak and/or structured around industries or in 'general' unions. Loyalties tend to be more focused on occupational identities than on particular firms and mobility between employers correspondingly easier. In Denmark the high degree of craft consciousness and union control of skill development and definition has meant that large firms are structured around groups of craft workers who have considerable autonomy and control over the workflow, according to Kristensen (1989; 1990; and Chapter 5 in this volume). Attempts to 'rationalise' and increase direct managerial control over task definition and organisation have not been particularly successful because the competitiveness of many firms depended on the high level of craft expertise of the workforce. In contrast, the strength of the British craft unions and their concentration in maintenance functions has encouraged both the separation of maintenance activities from operations in many industries and the restriction of many operatives' skill levels, so that the coordination of production with maintenance has been a major managerial problem in British firms (Dubois, 1981). Thus, the extent to which, and the ways in which, unions control skill definition and allocation have important consequences for patterns of work organisation and control in different countries.

More generally, the extent to which labour markets are structured around publicly certified skills, and occupational identities are firmly attached to specialised certified skills, affect employee mobility and identification with distinct expertise. As Dore (1973: 264–79) emphasised in his contrast of organisation and market-based reward systems, British managers and workers were highly conscious of their professional and craft competences and aware of their market value. Typically, loyalties and commitments to these identities were greater than those to individual employers, and wages and other rewards were more tied to such generalised, certified skills than to seniority in, and loyalty to, particular firms. Prestige and social standing in such market-oriented employment systems are more dependent on the general worth of particular specialist expertise than on the success and size of the particular employer of the moment. Identities and status are more dependent on the skill 'owned' by the individual, and its value on the labour market, than on the collective organisation to which the individual temporarily belongs. In Anglo-Saxon societies this emphasis on specialist skills is additionally reinforced by the prestige of professional identities which fragment managerial labour markets and roles and thus increase coordination costs (cf. Child et al., 1983).

High levels of skill standardisation and certification by practitioners additionally limit employers' ability to organise tasks and responsibilities idiosyncratically and change these unilaterally. They also facilitate considerable inter-firm mobility and thus increase the risks of skilled employees leaving. Investment in long-term commitments to employees is therefore not encouraged in market-based employment systems, and the high level of skills differentiation limits the development of common attitudes and loyalties. As a result, coordination and control processes are more likely to be formal and mimic market relations in societies where labour markets are organised around publicly standardised and certified skills, especially where managers do not share skills and experiences with skilled workers and cannot rely on their superior expertise to elicit respect and support.

The major implications of these six features of proximate social institutions for business system characteristics are summarised in Table 1.4. As mentioned above, the connections between social institutions and business system characteristics are not necessarily reversible. Thus the implication that low levels of state risk sharing encourages a low degree of market organisation does not mean that

Table 1.4  *Proximate institutions and business system characteristics*

| | Institutional features | | | | | |
|---|---|---|---|---|---|---|
| | Low state risk sharing | High business dependence on strong state | Capital-market-based financial system | Dual education and training system | Strong skill-based unions | Strong occupational identities |
| *Business system characteristics* | | | | | | |
| Diversified firms exhibiting discontinuous growth | + | | + | | | |
| Low levels of long-term risk sharing between firms | + | + | + | | | |
| Low levels of market organisation | + | + | + | | | |
| Reliance on formal procedures | | | + | | | |
| Delegation of task performance | | − | | + | + | + |
| Role standardisation and specialisation | | | | + | + | + |
| Integration of technical and formal authority | | | | + | + | |
| Remote and omnicompetent managerial role | | + | | − | − | |
| Market-based wage system | | | | | + | + |

where the state does support industrial development, inter-firm relations are more collaborative, long-term and involve reciprocal commitments. As the example of South Korea clearly shows, that depends on the way the state supports industry and, in particular, the extent to which the political executive dominates the market economy and directly intervenes in firms' decisions (Amsden, 1989: 84–92). In general, particular characteristics of business systems, and the ways in which they are interconnected to constitute distinct hierarchy–market configurations, are the result of combinations of institutional features rather than the direct outcome of individual ones. In accounting for the differences between the post-war Japanese *kaisha*, the Korean conglomerate *chaebol* and the Chinese family business, for example, it is the combination of pre-industrial institutions and industrialisation patterns which help us to make sense of them (Redding, 1990; Whitley, 1992). Similarly in Europe and North America, few distinctive characteristics of business systems can be explained solely in terms of a single contextual feature. This leads us to consider how this general framework can be applied to the overlapping and heterogenous forms of business organisation that have become established in different Western societies and, in particular, the implications of business systems' variable cohesion and distinctiveness within and between national boundaries.

### The National Specificity of Business Systems

So far I have assumed that business systems are relatively stable and cohesive configurations of hierarchy–market relations that have developed, and remain effective, in particular and separate institutional contexts, typically within the boundaries of the nation state. However, the extent to which national economies are characterised by homogenous and distinctive business systems clearly varies, as the contributions to this volume show, and so too does the national specificity of particular institutions. Thus, while authority relations and structures vary significantly between Japan, South Korea, Taiwan and Hong Kong, those in most Western firms are typically derived from, and share a common reliance on, legal-rational norms and bases of legitimacy. Similarly, the capital-market-based financial system and reliance on 'professional' modes of skill development and organisation which are shared by most 'Anglo-Saxon' societies, especially the USA and UK, ensure that business systems in these societies have certain characteristics in common, such as a strong finance function and preference for internalising risk in the absence of close bank–firm connections, which are less apparent in many continental European business systems (Granick, 1972; Horovitz, 1980; Lane, Chapter 3 in this volume; Lawrence, 1980).

Such variations in the national homogeneity and distinctiveness of business systems and dominant institutions emphasise the contingent nature of national hierarchy–market configurations. It is only when both the background and the proximate social institutions are distinctive and cohesive within the boundaries of the nation state that separate national business systems become established. Thus, the degree to which they are nationally distinctive reflects the national distinctiveness of cultural systems, socialisation patterns, state institutions and financial systems. Where, as in Europe, many states exhibit greater institutional pluralism than in East Asia and some share similar institutions, radically different business systems between nation states have not become established. Instead, some countries, such as Italy, have a variety of distinct business systems as a result of strong regional variations in processes of industrialisation and considerable local political and financial autonomy (Amin, 1989; Bamford, 1987; Lazerson, 1988), while others, such as Germany and the Netherlands, have business systems with some common characteristics as a result of similar institutional features, such as the organisation of vocational training. Business systems, then, are not necessarily homogenous within nation states nor sharply different between them. However, because the nation state is the dominant collectivity for organising so many of the social institutions which impinge directly on economic activities, such as the legal, education and financial systems, as well as itself constituting one of the major influences on firm structure and behaviour, it is the obvious starting point for any comparative analysis of business systems.

In comparing hierarchy–market configurations between countries, it is the dominant pattern of organising economic activities which is the central focus. Thus, where the small-firm sector is largely subservient to, and governed by the operations of, large enterprises, it cannot be said to constitute a distinctive business system. In contrast, the ability of firms in the industrial districts of north-east and central Italy collectively to organise production and distribution through to final consumers indicates a separate business system from the large-firm sector which dominates northwestern Italy. Similarly, the SME sector in Denmark seems to constitute a distinct way of organising production and distribution which impinges upon the operation of large firms to the extent of affecting their labour management practices and systems of work organisation. Or, at least, the same institutional factors that support the SME sector also constrain and structure the internal organisation of large firms (Kristensen, 1989; 1990; and Chapter 5 in this volume).

The national specificity of business systems is also affected by the growth of international firms and markets which has modified the significance of purely national institutions. Nationally distinctive forms of economic organisation and ways of doing business are increasingly open to external influences and models. However, the impact of such internationalisation clearly varies between societies and sectors according to the national specificity and cohesion of dominant institutions. States which exercise strong control over foreign direct investment, and where there are strong legal constraints on firms' actions, are less susceptible to outside influences than those with more differentiated and divergent institutions and where the state is primarily 'regulatory' rather than 'developmental'.

Additionally, it is important to note that international markets and firms reflect the characteristics of the dominant business system in different sectors and therefore the influence of national institutions. Thus, where firms from one particular country establish the rules of the game and play the dominant role in international markets, and any international regulatory institutions that are established reflect the norms current in that society, effective patterns of firm behaviour are likely to follow the logics established in that business system. An example of this is the structure of the international securities markets, which are dominated by Anglo-Saxon – especially US – modes of operating rather than, say, German or Japanese ones. Global markets are structured, then, by competition between firms from particular business systems which follow varied logics of action as a result of different institutional pressures. They thus reflect the continuing conflict between contrasting configurations of hierarchy–market relations which derive from differences in institutional contexts. In a sense, the structure and organising principles of oligopolistic worldwide industries are the outcomes of competition between different ways of organising economic activities in different business systems.

This competition between firms from different institutional contexts for domination of international markets implies that economies with business system characteristics which do not follow the dominant rules of the game effectively will fail to play a leading role in those markets. Institutional contexts which are not, for example, supportive of large-scale managerial bureaucracies that can effectively integrate interdependent activities on a long-term basis are unlikely to generate leading firms in sectors where such competences are crucial for international success. Thus, it could be argued that the UK business environment is not as conducive to the development of effective forms of business organisation in high-technology industries as is the German one, and therefore Britain will have fewer large firms in such areas (cf. Dunning and Pearce, 1985). This does not rule out, of course, the possibility that such societies may, over time, develop alternative ways of coordinating economic activities which could prove more effective in those sectors, just as previously peripheral firms often succeed in dominating particular markets by transforming the 'rules of the game' so that their distinctive capability becomes a crucial asset (cf. Prahalad and Hamel, 1990; Richardson, 1972).

In sum, the degree of cohesion and distinctiveness of business systems within nation states varies according to the strength, integration and uniformity of dominant institutions across sectors. The more homogenous and cohesive are national institutions, and the faster and more centrally directed was industrialisation, the more likely is a society to produce one distinctive way of organising economic activities which dominates that economy. Where the state, broadly conceived, the financial system, and the education and training system and labour markets are quite differentiated as institutional arenas, and also vary in their dominant pattern or organisation between parts of the economy, no single hierarchy-market configuration is likely to dominate, although certain characteristics, such as the role of financial controls and the degree of diversification against risk, may well be common to all sectors.

This variability of business system cohesion, distinctiveness and boundaries does, of course, mean that where major institutions in different countries have certain features in common, then dominant ways of organising economic activities will also share some characteristics. The similar legal and financial systems of the Anglo-Saxon economies, together with their general tendency to develop 'regulatory' rather than 'developmental' states (Johnson, C., 1982: 18–22), have resulted in a particular kind of economic agent, i.e. the legally and financially distinct corporation, becoming the dominant unit of authoritative coordination of economic activities in most of them. Typically, this agent 'internalises' risks and has developed a strong finance department. These commonalities mean that some managerial practices and procedures, such as financial control techniques, are more readily transferred between firms in these countries than they are to firms in countries with different institutional contexts.

Similarly, the common emphasis on 'professional' conceptions of expertise, and ways of organising and certifying it, has encouraged comparable levels of skill specialisation and concern with professional identities and personal ownership of skills across many of the Anglo-Saxon economies, especially when contrasted with many continental European ones. However, even here there are substantial differences in the organisation of education systems, in the strength and structure of trade unions and professional associations, and in the overall cohesion and priorities of the state which limit the transferability of managerial structures and practices, as is demonstrated by the different ways in which divisionalisation developed in the UK relative to the USA (Hill and Pickering, 1986) and the different approaches to the MBA degree and its use in Britain (Whitley et al., 1981). While, then, many nation states may share some institutional features which result in certain characteristics of business systems being common across national boundaries, there are also significant differences between many nationally specific institutions which limit the extent to which hierarchy–market configurations as a whole become multinational. Not the least of these, of course, is the organisation and direction of the political system. Consequently, the development of fully 'transnational' corporations and market relationships which transcend national institutions seems unlikely as long as educational, financial, legal, labour market and political systems remain nationally distinct.

In this connection, the move towards economic and political union in Europe provides an interesting occasion for studying the relationships between changing national institutions and the organisation of economic activities. Since the UK has a number of distinctive institutional features which are not shared by most of its continental neighbours, it seems likely that these may well change over the next decade and so alter the context in which British firms and markets operate. In turn, these changes are likely to affect their organisation and behaviour. No doubt other countries' institutions will also change, but the British state, legal, financial and credentialling systems are more distinctively different than those of most EC countries, and so should undergo the most far-reaching transformations. If, of course, full economic and political union is achieved then we could expect a distinctly 'European' business system to develop but differences in labour market structures and traditions, patterns of family organisation and other institutions are likely to persist and limit the extent of such a development.

## Conclusions

The comparative analysis of business systems assumes not only that markets, firms and economic outcomes are socially structured and embedded phenomena, but also that they are significantly affected by variations in social institutions and structures so that paths to competitive effectiveness and economic success differ across institutional contexts. Thus, economic rationalities reflect differences in social institutions and there are a variety of distinct ways of organising economic activities which are effective in different contexts. These contrasting patterns of economic organisation contribute different ways of dealing with the basic issues of any market economy: which activities and capabilities should be coordinated through authority hierarchies and which through market exchanges, how should such exchanges be organised and how should activities within firms be structured, directed and controlled? Each business system represents a particular configuration of hierarchy–market relationships that responds to these issues in a distinctive manner as a result of the institutional context in which it developed.

Consequently, the approach to organisational analysis that is being proposed here seeks to identify the social processes by which different kinds of business system became established in different institutional environments and which enable them to continue to operate effectively. It therefore takes seriously the socially constructed nature of imperfect markets and focuses on the comparative understanding of how societies, markets and firms are mutually constituted and changed. In this chapter, I have outlined a framework for the comparative analysis of business systems which is intended to contribute to that understanding and encourage further research in that direction.

## References

Abegglen, James C. and Stalk, George (1985) *Kaisha, the Japanese Corporation*. New York: Basic Books.

Amin, A. (1989) 'A Model of the Small Firm in Italy', in E. Goodman and J. Bamford (eds), *Small Firms and Industrial Districts in Italy*. London: Routledge. pp. 111–120.

Amsden, A.H. (1989) *Asia's Next Giant*. Oxford: Oxford University Press.

Aoki, M. (1988) *Information, Incentives, and Bargaining in the Japanese Economy*. Cambridge: Cambridge University Press.

Bamford, J. (1987) 'The Development of Small Firms, the Traditional Family and Agrarian Families in Italy', in R. Goffee and R. Scase (eds), *Entrepreneurship in Europe*. London: Croom Helm.

Bauer, M. and Cohen, E. (1981) *Qui gouverne les groupes industriels?*. Paris: Seuil.

Chandler, A.D. (1977) *The Visible Hand*. Cambridge, MA: Harvard University Press.

Child, J., Fores, M., Glover, I. and Lawrence, P. (1983) 'A Price to Pay? Professionalism in Work Organisation in Britain and West Germany', *Sociology*. 17: 63–78.

Chung, K.H., Lee, H.C. and Okumura, A. (1988) 'The Managerial Practices of Korean, American and Japanese Firms', *Journal of East and West Studies*. 17: 45–74.

Clark, R. (1979) *The Japanese Company*. New Haven: Yale University Press.

Cox, A. (1986) 'State, Finance and Industry in Comparative Perspective', in A. Cox (ed.), *State, Finance and Industry*. Brighton: Wheatsheaf. pp. 1–59.

Cusumano, M.A. (1985) *The Japanese Automobile Industry: Technology and Management at Nissan and Toyota*. Cambridge, MA: Harvard University Press.

Dore, R.P. (1973) *British Factory – Japanese Factory*. London: Allen & Unwin.

Dore, R.P. (1986) *Flexible Rigidities*. Stanford: Stanford University Press.

Dubois, P. (1981) 'Workers' Control Over the Organisation of Work: French and English Maintenance Workers in Mass Production Industry', *Organisation Studies*. 2: 347–60.

Dunning, J.H. and Pearce, R.D. (1985) *The World's Largest Industrial Enterprises 1962–83*. Aldershot: Gower.

Dyson, K. (1980) *The State Tradition in Western Europe*. Oxford: Oxford University Press.

Dyson, K. (1986) 'The State, Banks and Industry: the West German Case', in A. Cox (ed.), pp. 118–141 *The State, Finance and Industry*. Brighton: Wheatsheaf, pp. 118–41.

Encaoua, D. and Jacquemin, A. (1982) 'Organisational Efficiency and Monopoly Power: the case of French industrial groups', *European Economic Review*. 19: 25–51.

Fligstein, N. (1985) 'The Spread of the Multidivisional Form', *American Sociological Review*. 50: 377–91.

Friedman, A.L. (1977) *Industry and Labour*. London: Macmillan.

Fukutake, T. (1967) 'Chinese Village and Japanese Village', in T. Fukutake, *Asian Rural Society*. Tokyo: University of Tokyo Press.

Futatsugi, Y. (1986) *Japanese Enterprise Groups*. Kobe: School of Business Administration, Kobe University.

Gerlach, M. (1987) 'Business Alliances and the Strategy of the Japanese Firm', *California Management Review*. (Fall): 126–42.

Gold, T.B. (1986) *State and Society in the Taiwan Miracle*. Armonk, NY: M.E. Sharpe.

Goto, A. (1982) 'Business Groups in a Market Economy', *European Economic Review*. 19: 53–70.

Granick, D. (1972) *Managerial Comparisons of Four Developed Countries*. Cambridge, MA: MIT Press.

Greenhalgh, S. (1988) 'Families and Networks in Taiwan's Economic Development', in E.A. Winckler and S. Greenhalgh (eds), *Contending Approaches to the Political Economy of Taiwan*. Armonk, NY: M.E. Sharpe.

Haggard, S. and Cheng, T-J. (1987) 'State and Foreign Capital in the East Asian NICs', in F. Deyo (ed.), *The Political Economy of East Asian Industrialism*. Ithaca, NY: Cornell University Press. pp. 84–135.

Hamilton, G. and Biggart, N.W. (1988) 'Market, Culture and Authority: a Comparative Analysis of Management and Organisation in the Far East',

*American Journal of Sociology*. 94, Supplement, 552–94.

Hamilton, G. and Kao, C.S. (1990) 'The Institutional Foundation of Chinese Business: the Family Firm in Taiwan', *Comparative Social Research*. 12: 95–112.

Hamilton, G., Zeile W. and Kim, W.J. (1990) 'The Network Structures of East Asian Economies', in S. Clegg and G. Redding (eds), *Capitalism in Contrasting Cultures*. Berlin: de Gruyter. 105–29.

Henderson, G. (1968) *Korea: the Politics of the Vortex*. Cambridge, MA: Harvard University Press.

Hill, C.W.L. and Pickering, J.F. (1986) 'Divisionalisation, Decentralisation and Performance of Large UK Companies', *Journal of Management Studies*. 23: 26–50.

Hirst, P. and Zeitlin, J. (1991) 'Flexible Specialisation vs. Post-Fordism: Theory, Evidence and Policy Implications', *Economy and Society*. 20: 1–56.

Hofstede, G. (1980) *Culture's Consequences*. London/Beverly Hills, CA: Sage.

Horovitz, J.H. (1980) *Top Management Control in Europe*. London: Macmillan.

Imai, K. and Itami, H. (1984) 'Interpretation of Organisation and Market. Japan's Firm and Market in Comparison with the U.S.', *International Journal of Industrial Organisation*. 2: 285–310.

d'Iribarne, P. (1989) *La Logique de l'honneur*. Paris: Seuil.

Jacobs, N. (1958) *The Origin of Modern Capitalism and Eastern Asia*. Hong Kong: Hong Kong University Press.

Jacobs, N. (1985) *The Korean Road to Modernisation and Development*. Urbana: University of Illinois Press.

Johnson, C. (1982) *MITI and the Japanese Miracle*. Stanford: Stanford University Press.

Johnson, E.H. (1967) 'Status Changes in Hamlet Structure Accompanying Modernisation', in R.P. Dore (ed), *Aspects of Social Change in Modern Japan*. Princeton, NJ: Princeton University Press.

Jones, L. and Sakong, I. (1980) *Government, Business and Entrepreneurship in Economic Development: the Korean Case*. Cambridge, MA: Harvard University Press.

Kagono, T., Alonaka, I., Sakakibara, K. and Okumara, A. (1985) *Strategic vs. Evolutionary Management*. Amsterdam: North Holland.

Katzenstein, P.J. (1985) *Small States in World Markets*. Ithaca, NY: Cornell University Press.

Kristensen, P.H. (1989) 'Denmark: an Experimental Laboratory for New Industrial Models', *Entrepreneurship and Regional Development*. 1: 245–55.

Kristensen, P.H. (1990) 'Denmark's Concealed Production Culture, its Socio-Historical Construction and Dynamics at Work', in F. Borum and P.H. Kristensen (eds), *Technological Innovation and Organisational Change*. Copenhagen: New Social Science Monographs.

Lane, C. (1988), 'Industrial Change in Europe: the Pursuit of Flexible Specialisation in Britain and West Germany', *Work, Employment and Society*. 2: 141–68.

Lane, C. (1989) *Management and Labour in Europe. The Industrial Enterprise in Germany, Britain and France*. Aldershot: Edward Elgar.

Laurent, A. (1983) 'The Cultural Diversity of Western Conceptions of Management', *International Studies of Management and Organisation*. 13: 75–96.

Lawrence, P. (1980) *Managers and Management in West Germany*. London: Croom Helm.

Lazerson, M.H. (1988) 'Organisational Growth of Small Firms: an Outcome of

Markets and Hierarchies', *American Sociological Review*. 53: 330–42.

Levy, B. (1988) 'Korean and Taiwanese Firms as International Competitors: the Challenges Ahead', *Columbia Journal of World Business*. (Spring): 43–51.

Liebenberg, R.D. (1982) 'Japan Incorporated' and 'The Korean Troops': a Comparative Analysis of Korean Business Organisations. Unpublished MA thesis, Dept of Asian Studies, University of Hawaii.

Lincoln, J.R. and Kalleberg, A.L. (1990) *Culture, Control and Commitment*. Cambridge: Cambridge University Press.

Lodge, G.C. (1987) 'Introduction: Ideology and Country Analysis', in G.C. Lodge and E.F. Vogel (eds), *Ideology and National Competitiveness*. Cambridge, MA: Harvard Business School Press.

MacPherson, C.B. (1962) *The Political Theory of Possessive Individualism*. Oxford: Oxford University Press.

Maurice M., Sorge, A. and Warner, M. (1980) 'Societal Differences in Organising Manufacturing Units', *Organization Studies*. 1: 59–86.

Maurice, M., Sellier, F. and Silvestre, J.J. (1986) *The Social Foundations of Industrial Power*. Cambridge, MA: MIT Press.

Mizruchi, M.S. and Schwartz, M. (1987) 'The Structural Analysis of Business', in M.S. Mizruchi and M. Schwartz (eds), *Intercorporate Relations*. Cambridge: Cambridge University Press. pp. 3–21.

Moore, B. (1966) *The Social Origins of Dictatorship and Democracy*. Boston: Beacon Press.

Nanetti, R. (1988) *Growth and Territorial Policies: the Italian Model of Social Capitalism*. London: Frances Pinter.

North, D.C. (1990) *Institutions, Institutional Change and Economic Performance*. Cambridge: Cambridge University Press.

Numazaki, I. (1986) 'Networks of Taiwanese Big Business', *Modern China*. 12: 487–534.

Numazaki, I. (1987) 'Enterprise Groups in Taiwan', *Shoken Keisai*. (December): 162: 15–23.

Orru, M. (1991) 'Business Organisations in a Comparative Perspective: Small Firms in Taiwan and Italy', *Studies in Comparative International Development*. 26.

Orru, M., Hamilton, G. and Suzuki, M. (1989) 'Patterns of Inter-Firm Control in Japanese Business', *Organization Studies*. 10: 549–74.

Parsons, T. (1968) *The Structure of Social Action*. New York: Free Press.

Penrose, E. (1980) *The Theory of the Growth of the Firm*. Oxford: Blackwell. [First published 1959.]

Prahalad, C.K. and Hamel, G. (1990) 'The Core Competence of the Corporation', *Harvard Business Review*. (May–June): 79–91.

Pye, L.W. (1985) *Asian Power and Politics: the Cultural Dimensions of Authority*. Cambridge, MA: Harvard University Press.

Pye, L.W. (1988) 'The New Asian Capitalism: a Political Portrait', in P.L. Berger and H-H.M. Hsiao (eds), *In Search of an East Asian Development Model*. New Brunswick, NJ: Transaction Books. pp. 81–98.

Redding, S.G. (1990) *The Spirit of Chinese Capitalism*. Berlin: de Gruyter.

Richardson, G. (1972) 'The Organisation of Industry', *Economic Journal*. 82: 883–96.

Rohlen, T.P. (1974) *For Harmony and Strength: Japanese White-Collar Organisation in Anthropological Perspective*. Berkeley, CA: University of California Press.

Sayer, A. (1984) *Method in Social Science*. London: Hutchinson.

Scott, J. (1986) *Capitalist Property and Financial Power*. Brighton: Wheatsheaf.

Silin, R.H. (1976) *Leadership and Values. The Organisation of Large Scale Taiwanese Enterprises*. Cambridge, MA: Harvard University Press.

Smith, T.C. (1959) *The Agrarian Origins of Modern Japan*. Stanford: Stanford University Press.

Smith, T.C. (1988) *Native Sources of Japanese Industrialisation, 1750–1920*. Berkeley, CA: University of California Press.

Tam, S. (1990) 'Centrifugal versus Centripetal Growth Processes: Contrasting Ideal Types for Conceptualising the Developmental Patterns of Chinese and Japanese Firms', in S. Clegg and G. Redding (eds), *Capitalism in Contrasting Cultures*. Berlin: de Gruyter. pp. 153–83.

Wade, R. (1990) *Governing the Market*. Princeton, NJ: Princeton University Press.

Ward, B.E. (1972) 'A Small Factory in Hong Kong: Some Aspects of its Internal Organisation', in W.E. Willmott (ed.), *Economic Organisation in Chinese Society*. Stanford: Stanford University Press.

Weiss, L. (1984) 'The Italian State and Small Business', *European Journal of Sociology*. 25: 214–41.

Weiss, L. (1988) *Creating Capitalism. The State and Small Business Since 1945*. Oxford: Blackwell.

Whitley, R.D. (1987) 'Taking Firms Seriously as Economic Actors: Towards a Sociology of Firm Behaviour', *Organisation Studies*. 8: 125–47.

Whitley, R.D. (1990) 'Eastern Asian Enterprise Structures and the Comparative Analysis of Forms of Business Organisation', *Organization Studies*. 11(1): 47–54.

Whitley, R.D. (1991) 'The Social Construction of Business Systems in East Asia', *Organization Studies*. 12(1): 1–28.

Whitley, R.D. (1992) *Business Systems in East Asia: Firms, Markets and Societies*. London: Sage.

Whitley, R.D., Thomas, A.B. and Marceau, J. (1981) *Masters of Business? Business Schools and Business Graduates in Britain and France*. London: Tavistock.

Winckler, E.A. (1988) 'Elite Political Struggle, 1945-1985', in E.A. Winckler and S. Greenhalgh (eds), *Contending Approaches to the Political Economy of Taiwan*. Armonk, NY: M.E. Sharpe.

Wong, S-L. (1985) 'The Chinese Family Firm: a Model', *British Journal of Sociology*. 36: 58–72.

Yoshino, M.Y. and Lifson, T.B. (1986) *The Invisible Link: Japan's Sogo Shosha and the Organisation of Trade*. Cambridge, MA: MIT Press.

Zucker, L. (1986) 'Production of Trust: Institutional Sources of Economic Structure, 1840-1920', *Research in Organisational Behaviour*. 8: 53–111.

Zysman, John (1983) *Governments, Markets and Growth: Financial Systems and the Politics of Industrial Change*. Ithaca, NY: Cornell University Press.

# 2
# National Business Recipes:
# A Sector Perspective

*Keijo Räsänen and Richard Whipp*

The chapters in this volume describe and explain the logics of organising business enterprises and their competitive and cooperative relations in different national contexts. In their approach to these tasks, all the authors acknowledge the need for perspectives which go beyond the extreme positions of cultural relativism and economic determinism. They all aim to pay attention to the social and institutional determinants of business organisation. They also seek to reconsider what is the proper object of comparisons across varying institutional contexts.

Richard Whitley (Chapter 1 in this volume) has developed a conceptual framework for redefining the object of comparative research through the role of national social institutions. His work is helpful in locating the issues which need further attention and development. Some of the authors in this volume have already taken Whitley's framework as their starting point for the description of their own case (Iterson and Olie; Lane; Marceau; Nishida and Redding), while others have used somewhat different perspectives (Hellgren and Melin; Kristensen; Lilja, Räsänen and Tainio; Knights, Morgan and Murray; O'Reilly). The purpose of the present chapter is to discuss some of the basic issues which are relevant to the comparative work started in this volume.

Challenging problems appear in two areas: first, in the units and levels of analysis; and second, in the way national business systems can be discovered through empirical research. Whitley's approach basically assumes that 'business systems are relatively stable and cohesive configurations of hierarchy–market relations that have developed, and remain effective, in particular and separate institutional contexts, typically within the boundaries of the nation state' (Whitley, Chapter 1 in this volume: 36). The nation state is considered the obvious starting point for any analysis of comparative business systems, because it 'is the dominant collectivity for organizing so many social institutions which impinge directly on economic activities, such as legal, education and financial systems. . .' (ibid.: 37). However, existing comparative research leads us to doubt that the nation state could serve alone as the primary unit of analysis and that macro-level generalisations would uncover distinctive national patterns in business organisation. In contrast, it may be necessary to pay careful attention to a host of meso-level and even micro-level units around which collective action can be organised within a country, and sometimes across national borders. These alternative emergent or 'natural' units of collective action include: industries, sectors; districts, regions; production systems; crafts, professions, elites; corporations; kin networks; cultures, religions; parties, ideologies.

Paying attention to the meso-and micro-levels of analysis, and to the diversity of collectives found there, leads us to see how problematic it is to assume that there exists one dominant and stable business recipe within a nation state. This point can be developed by an examination of one of these units, namely the sector. Without pretending that this particular perspective is the key to all societies, its elaboration may help us to see the relevance of such frameworks for comparative research.

## An Institutional and Historical Sector Perspective

National and international economies can be seen as combinations of various sectors. In some European countries national economies include several strong sectors, but there are also countries like Finland where one sector more or less dominates the economy (see Lilja et al., Chapter 6 in this volume). The sector perspective outlined here aims to conceptualise how these sectors emerge and become constituted in certain ways, how they are reproduced and developed, and how their dynamics influence individual businesses and corporations. To the extent that sectors form a significant base for organising an economy, this perspective may also bear on the issues of how national business systems are generated and sustained, and of how national social institutions are created, reproduced and modified.

### Redefining the Sector Concept

By the term sector we refer to an historical formation of complementary, interlinked and co-evolving business activities. It is often, though not uniformly, linked to certain geographic locations (e.g. a region or a country) and it appears in a certain period of time. A sector contains organisations which provide similar goods or services, together with those who regularly transact with them in supplying, servicing, regulatory or customer roles (cf. Child, 1988; Whipp and Clark, 1986). In a mature sector, the individual organisations form a social network through formal and informal connections and there exist actors who think in terms of the whole sector. Their capacity to coordinate the whole, may, though, be limited and sectors cannot be taken as governance structures in a strong sense. Rather, they are arenas of cooperation and competition.

It is a common habit in comparative studies to use the terms 'industry' and 'sector' interchangeably (see e.g. Whitley, Chapter 1 in this volume; Sorge, 1991). In this usage, both terms refer to economic and technical units understood in the same way as in economics. Here we propose to redefine the sector concept to take distance from the industry concept of the economists. Because a sector is a cluster of industries, the traditional economic industry concept cannot capture even its economic and technical dynamics. Because it is a community of diverse actors, any economic concept is too limited to capture the social processes involved.

An example of a well-developed sector is provided by the Finnish forest sector (see Lilja et al., Chapter 6 in this volume). This industrial complex of various businesses has emerged over about 130 years. This sector is well-connected to the forest sectors in other competitor countries (especially Sweden, Canada, and the USA) and to markets all over the world, Europe in particular. The Finnish forest sector can, however, be distinguished from the global forest sector by its social networks, ownership and control relationships and vertical logistical links. It is clearly of a 'national' character.

Forestry and the forest industry have certain technical and economic features (e.g. vertical integration, capital intensity, economies of scale, low and cyclically varying returns) which precondition the potential forms of business organisation in the sector. The actual form of organisation developed in this industry cannot, however, be derived from these features. This community of diverse actors and its individual participants are organised in ways which are influenced also by social, political and psychological processes. It is the interplay between these various mechanisms and perspectives that lies at the core of the sector perspective. Therefore it clearly deviates from the economic industry concept towards more 'sociological' understandings.

In our conception of the sector, one crucial element is the idea that a sector is an accomplishment of many actors, working in several periods and with diverse logics of action. It is in this sense never a completed and coherent project, but a contradictory whole, the nature of which is under constant contest. It involves simultaneously multiple principles of constitution and multiple material realities. In other words, there are all the time various alternative interpretations and applications of the 'sectoral business recipe' (defined as the way in which the various logics are to be hybridised or detached); or there may even be several contesting recipes advocated simultaneously by some factions of the sectoral network.

For instance, in the case of the Finnish forest sector, one issue of debate has frequently been whether the fate of the sector as a whole should be controlled and planned by some kind of quasi-boards or other arrangements (cf. Korhonen, 1991). Sectors should not be taken as organisations with a strong government structure. The mechanisms of coordination and mutual adjustment can be of various types, and are likely to be only partial, not total. It is sensible, though, to expect that at least during certain critical periods, logics of action and frameworks of legitimation exist which emphasise the unity of the sector. In the Finnish case, this was observed clearly during the performance crisis of the forest industry in the late 1970s and early 1980s, when the slogan 'Finland lives on its forests' was widely advocated and accepted within the sector. Behind this unity, however, there were differing views on how to get out of the crisis.

Thus we suggest that sectors are historically evolving wholes of interrelated economic and political relationships. Sector-specific business recipes are the logics by which the conflicting rationalities of the various actors are fused on the basis of the changing relations of power within the sector. Nation states contain particular configurations of sectors, each of them trying to develop their own business recipe within the national business system. In so doing they utilise and modify existing national institutions in their favour. Instead of assuming that there is one dominant business system and recipe in a country, this perspective suggests that there is an evolving set of multiple, competing and internally contested sector-specific recipes. These processes of contestation between and inside the sectors constitute the dynamics through which the national business systems evolve.

This perspective of multiple realities and recipes is inherently dynamic. Its main implication is that comparative analyses should be centred on the way in which different and contradictory logics of action are fused in the countries under examination. The emergent business recipe of the 'Forest Sector Finland', as described by Lilja et al. (Chapter 6 in this volume), generates the idea that the recipes could be interpreted as particular historical compromises which make the business system (sector) work. Through these compromises and related modifications resources are secured for the business system. The point is to understand how these kind of compromises, or other solutions to the coexistence of conflicting interests and rationalities, are made in different countries.

## How, When and Where Do Sectors Emerge?

In terms of the dimensions introduced above (cf. Whipp and Räsänen, 1991; Räsänen, and Whipp, 1991: 4-8), we can say that a sector exists in a strong sense when:

1 There is an extensive cluster of complementary and co-evolving economic activities in regular transaction relationships;
2 A social network which connects the various parts of these clusters and its sub-communities;
3 Such a cultural unity exists between the parts that the interaction needed for cooperation is possible and accepted (i.e. there is some general unifying identity among the actors); and
4 the whole is somehow politically represented in relation to societal regulators such as the state (and international power centres such as the EC).

Sectors cannot be taken as given institutions in market economies. They have emerged only under particular historical conditions. The precise nature of these conditions is largely unknown, given the lack of relevant research, but it is possible to present some tentative ideas about this problem.

As to the emergence and evolution of sectors, Shearman and Burrell (1987) present a helpful 'social model' of an industry. Their analysis of an industry can be seen to discuss an embryonic sector. A single industry can contain the main social elements of a sector, although the processes are more complicated in a more developed case of several connected industries. Shearman and Burrell (1987: 328) suggest that '[i]t is only with an understanding of the social networks through and within which managers develop and modify their ideas that one can fully appreciate the dynamics of industrial development.' They focus on the contextualisation of the dynamics of cooperative and competitive interaction in these networks over time. They contextualise technological and economic relationships in terms of social relationships, that is, in terms of power, status, trust, loyalty, identity and negotiated order. They suggest four ideal-typical stages for industry evolution: (1) the community; (2) the informal network; (3) the formal network; (4) the club. In this cycle, industries are first born within local communities where shared world-views and mutual trust enable the adoption of significant technological innovations. Then they evolve into more structured and self-aware, but still informally connected, networks of specialised actors and firms. In the third stage these networks are formalised and the system comes to be coordinated by a core elite. Finally, an exclusive club-like structure is often used to defend a declining industry.

This model implies that sectors may be formed in conditions where a sufficiently large but geographically proximate community provides the basic social unity for industrial innovators and entrepreneurs (e.g. the 'high-tech' sector of Silicon Valley, California, or the UK engineering sector which emerged in the West Midlands, South Wales, central Scotland and the trans-Pennine region). There must also be an external source of infrastructure for the related industries. This source is typically a nation state. There must also be available a new basic technology around which the related industries can be formed. This technology must, however, be of such a nature that its development can be carried out by local organisations and not only by the original external (foreign) sources. Moreover, the emergence of an awareness of a common identity is more likely when there is a political counterpart which necessitates increased levels of internal organisation. The state with its resources can be this external catalyst of political activity within related industries. All these factors point towards the fact that small homogeneous nation states might be more conducive contexts for sector formation than large, heterogeneous countries with distant state apparatuses. In a small state, nationalistic ideas can be the value basis for cooperation and ambitious targets of development. The formation of an extended sector takes a long time, and therefore the political stability of the nation state is important, and the core industries have to be successful over a sufficient period of time (often decades) to allow for the development of various adjacent supplier and service businesses. The basic technology also has to be usable for a long time and the customer needs have to remain relatively stable (e.g. chemicals, aerospace). The original comparative advantages of the area in terms of natural resources may, of course, influence the type of economic activity around which such a sector can be built.

An essential condition for the formation of a sector is that any alternative organisational solutions are historically deemed inferior to it. In particular, the execution and coordination of the distinct businesses cannot be done either solely within corporate hierarchies or geographically more limited industrial districts. In analysing these struggles between alternative and complementary institutional structures, the economic and technical 'imperatives' have to be taken into account, since they are used by the contesting agents as bases of argumentation and power.

## Issues in Comparative Research

How does Whitley's framework stand against the sector perspective and other similar 'meso-level' perspectives? What are the potential issues of debate? The foregoing sketch of a sector perspective leads us to raise the following questions:

1 Should one assume that each nation state has one dominant business system or multiple contesting business recipes? What if the sectors (or sub-economies defined in some other way) have their own distinct and competing recipes?
2 Should one assume that the business recipes are stable over time (after industrialisation), or should we study the dynamics of their evolution?
3 Should we assume that the pre-existing national social institutions causally influence the formation of the national business systems, or should we study how these two mutually interact and condition the creation and development of each other?
4 Should we apply the same conceptual business system framework in all countries to describe and analyse them or should we primarily produce country-specific descriptions based on different substantive theorisations and various kinds of empirical designs?

A full discussion of all these issues is beyond the scope of this chapter, especially since most are embedded in the following chapters. Some clarifying comments on the core issue, question 1, are, however, necessary.

### *One System or Multiple Recipes?*

Whitley (Chapter 1 in this volume: 36–9) presents important qualifications to the basic assumptions that national economies have externally distinctive and internally homogenous business systems. He notes that countries which share similar institutions cannot have radically different business systems (e.g. Germany and the Netherlands). In the same way, he emphasises the role of national institutions in accounting for the possible internal incoherence of business systems. He maintains that a country may either have no dominant business system or a variety of systems, if it exhibits institutional pluralism (e.g. the regional variation in Italy). In this way he plays down all the sources of diversity within a country other than the general national institutions. As to the differences across 'industries or sectors', Whitley admits that in some respects, and 'for economic factors or some other reasons', industries may be different in countries where institutions are highly differentiated (e.g. market organisation in Anglo-Saxon countries and in Japan). But, Whitley argues, even in these cases the industries do not differ significantly enough along the other dimensions to form industry-specific business systems.

It seems to be an essential assumption for the national business systems approach that 'institutional contexts generate particular kinds of business systems [organisational forms] which compete effectively in certain industries rather than the [technological and market imperatives of the] industry determining the appropriate organisational form' (Whitley, Chapter 1 in this volume). This institutional and sociological approach is, however, not necessarily abandoned if it is accepted that there are other important influences on the nature of business organisation than the nation-wide institutions.

The other sources of diversity can be not only the economic and technical imperatives of an industry, but also its local social and institutional mechanisms. This is exactly what the redefined sector concept suggests: there may be essential local differences across sectors in the nature of their social networks, cultures and political strategies towards the state. These patterns may be 'institutionalised' in the same basic sense as the nation-wide patterns of practice are. There may be good reasons to criticise the economic approach to industries – this criticism is shared with the sector approach (Whipp and Räsänen, 1991) – but this criticism is misplaced if it is used to defend a macro-level approach against perspectives which emphasise local, micro-level and meso-level diversity within a country. We would prefer an approach which tries to bridge these levels of analysis.

Another important point concerning local diversity within a country is that the general, nation-wide institutions can be used locally in different ways and for different purposes. For instance, the financial system can operate differently or the role of owning families and kinship networks may be different across sectors, depending on the endogenous logic of development within the sectors and on the strategies of their actors. The sectors and other units of collective activity should not be taken only as passive objects of institutional influences. They also use the institutions for particular, local purposes.

This highlights the point that, if we assume the existence of multiple, competing business recipes within a nation state, then we necessarily have to adopt a dynamic approach. Business systems and recipes evolve through the contestation of the dominant recipes by alternatives. National institutions are created and modified in response to specific problems in economic stability (or development) and social order. Within this dynamic perspective, there still remains a role to be played by general nation-specific institutions, but this role is now a different one. In the dynamic process of contestation and hybridisation, national social institutions provide generalised solutions for the problems of managing conflict and imbalances. Sorge (1991: 184) presents this idea in the following way:

> Wider societal arrangements have an important function, within this framework. Through providing relatively problem-unspecific institutions in the widest sense (Berger and Luckmann 1971), 'normal' practices and implicit mental definitions, they allow actors to combine seemingly contradictory or conflicting elements. They make them work out effective compromises between distinct and opposed elements . . . Successful patterns are those which make the combination or speedy adaptation of countervailing strategies feasible.

National institutions do not determine the form of the business organisation. They have an impact on the nature of the process through which the historical compromises called business recipes and systems are negotiated and build up in different national settings.

In this view, the performance problems of the British economy, for instance, could be partly accounted for by social institutions which favour the detachment of different logics of actions and actors having different specialised skills. In contrast, Finnish firms have been able to solve severe resource and developmental problems with the help of a generalised practice of collaborative self-help: existing formal structures and divisions of labour have not prevented the formation of new task forces with the necessary combination of specialists and skills. One extreme illustration for this practice can be found in the events during and after the Second World War in which the engineering corporation Valmet was able to generate totally new product lines during its conversion first from military production to war indemnities production, and then again to peacetime production (Björklund, 1991; Rissanen, 1966; Jokinen, 1988; Räsänen and Kivisaari, 1989). This difference between the UK and Finland in the ease with which different skills are fused under joint projects will, of course, need further elaboration. Is it real, why does it exist, and how long will it exist?

### One Conceptual Framework or Multiple Perspectives?
Methodologically, Whitley's analysis is done in the spirit of comparative statistics, that is, the properties of 'national business systems' and 'national social institutions' are described and compared as outcomes of historical processes without any serious

attempt to study and conceptualise these processes. Or to be more precise in interpretation, Whitley actually suggests that the impact of national social institutions on the national business system has taken place in the process of industrialisation. This indicates that the approach could be applied in a dynamic way, but it would lead to empirical studies of the industrialisation process in each of the countries under research.

For example, Whitley (Chapter 1 in this volume) argues that firms in Taiwan and South Korea concentrate on particular, different export industries because 'differences in their patterns of industrialisation and the experience of Japanese colonialism produced quite different forms of business organisation' in these countries (ibid). Wouldn't this argument lead to empirical research in the patterns of industrialisation in Taiwan and South Korea? How and why did it actually happen that certain industries were 'selected' and concentrated on? How did the social institutions influence this development, and how did other factors influence it? How can we isolate the 'national institution-effect' from the other effects? Or should we study how it interacts with the other influences (cf. Mäki (1991) on the method of 'isolation' and its alternatives)?

But how should we study current businesses or their more recent history in order to advance our understanding of the specificity of national business systems? If we believe that there are multiple recipes in a country and that these are carried by some meso-level (or micro-level) units like sectors, how should we then proceed in empirical research? The macro-level framework, assuming general-ised practices throughout the country, would not do as a frame of reference. What is required is an open attitude with different substantive frameworks and sensitivity to the research object. This problem can be illustrated by reference to an analogy which compares a country with a hologram.

A hologram looks different from each of its sides. One can see all the parts inside the hologram from each of the sides, but they and their gestalt look different from the different sides. These sides can be equated with the different perspectives on the meso-level units of social organisations. A country looks different in a sector perspective than in a corporate perspective. But it may well be that one of these perspectives can reach a better understanding of the core relationships in this particular society. Understanding one principle of collective organisation may be more important in one country than another and capturing it may lead to sensitive insights on the dynamics by which business is run and developed in that country, and on the way the institutions are joined together.

This analogy has clear implications for the way in which comparative projects should be carried out and for the nature of the potential results of these projects. It implies that each country should be studied from several (partial) perspectives with various research designs. The resulting account of a particular country should include (synthesise) all the relevant concepts and perspectives, but in a way which is sensitive to the research object. It should not be decided *a priori* what is the most essential principle and unit of collective action, but the actual combination of principles should be generated from the case itself. Kristensen (Chapter 5 in this volume) may be right in emphasising the role of craft-based skill, networks and identities as the heart of the Danish economy, but in Finland the forest sector (as defined by the corporations) may be the most important mobilising collective project, and in Italy it may be the regions that matter most. Such countries as the UK may be nowadays fragmented mixtures of various collective units and logics of action. Major developmental steps requiring unified action may be drastic and violent, if not impossible.

Working through these partial analyses requires, in addition to careful empirical research, substantive theorisation within and across the partial perspectives. Developing the sector perspective is one of these tasks. It is among the most urgent ones for us because its substantive theorisations are relatively undeveloped in comparison to some other concepts,[1] and because it is important to an understanding of Finland (strong forest sector) and possibly also the UK (weak sectoral formations, fragmented economy) – these two opposing extreme cases. We believe that building this concept (see Whipp and Räsänen, 1991) and linking with it the other concepts such as that of the corporation (Räsänen, 1991) will be able to provide for more informed opportunities to characterise the countries under comparison.

The national business recipe approach assumes, on the basis of previous studies, that there are various effective and successful ways of organising business enterprise. In a research design this assumption can be taken into account explicitly by focusing on such cases in which international competitive success (or failure) has already been achieved. The question is how can we account for the success or failure of particular businesses originating from a certain country. The sector perspective is able to add important elements to an adequate answer. The sectoral home base has been observed to be a very important source of resources and skills, even in the multinational corporations.

Porter (1990) among others, has, argued for the importance of the existence of clusters of businesses for the development of national competitive advantages. His study provides support for arguments that there are multiple bases of competition and competitive advantage: firm, sector and economy (Whipp et al., 1989). Even in large corporations, the sustained development of businesses also requires linkages to sectoral mechanisms which provide for and upgrade resources (Räsänen, 1991). This insight will lead us to the analysis of corporate resourcing practices: how corporations get and combine national resources and upgrade or deplete them, and how resources circulate between small and large firms, and between the private organisations and public organisations (e.g. companies and universities). Technological innovations, for example, are usually outcomes of interaction between firms operating in different but related industries (Pavitt, 1984). This is evident in the Finnish forest sector case, where machinery producers and paper producers are linked in many ways and supported by specialised educational, research and development organisations (Lilja et al., Chapter 6 in this volume; Räsänen and Kivisaari, 1989).

In Finland, nation state policies and agencies have been much influenced by the needs of the leading forest sector. The existence of educational and research support for the forest sector is not an accident. The forest industrialists have been actively promoting policies which secure competent workers and the availability of modern technology (e.g. Aho, 1910, on Antti Ahlströms statesman career). The commercial banks were also founded by the industrialists to help capital-intensive industry. We can conclude that at least in Finland the formation of various (proximate) social institutions (Whitley, Chapter 1 in this volume) was influenced by the needs and actual demands of the key sector. Even if the influence is not that strong in other European countries, it might still be important to study how the sectors and national social institutions have co-evolved in these countries, instead of assuming that the national institutions were there first and remained intact.

### Conclusions

In comparative studies the researcher has to decide how she or he is going to reach understandings of distinctive national dynamics. In this chapter, we have presented some constructive comments on the business system approach in order to specify issues which it is important to discuss and study. We have done this exercise from a particular perspective, namely a sector perspective. This perspective was taken as representing a whole variety of frameworks conceptualising meso-level processes and units of collective organisation in market societies. Some of these concepts share the same emphasis in the need to locate the practices of some 'natural' (emergent) social unit in time and space. They present alternative centres and principles around which collective action can be organised. Indeed, it is an empirical question how these units of analysis are interrelated in a particular country, and through which one the configuration as a whole is mobilised and understandable. Nevertheless, it is an important exercise to try to organise conceptually these various elements from certain perspectives, such as the sector perspective. The nature of the national hologram can be understood only by looking at it carefully from many angles. The level of analysis where multiple angles are especially needed is between the national macro-level and the micro-level of individual business actors.

It is possible to gain a sensitive understanding of the distinctive features of national business recipes only by careful empirical analyses which use multiple conceptual perspectives and work on a number of levels. Such deep insights as, for instance, Kristensen (Chapter 5 in this volume) has provided on Denmark cannot be reached by mechanical applications of fixed, macro-level frameworks, but require continuous development of substantive theory through different empirical designs. Because these studies have to be carefully carried out at the micro-level of individual firms and businesses, it is necessary to have a framework which links the particular micro-findings to nation state level patterns. The sector concept can be one of these mediators.

Comparative research needs the nation state as a level and unit of analysis. This approach deserves serious study and careful application. The problem discussed in this commentary centres on how the nation state level framework may be related to frameworks operating on other levels of analysis. Major challenges within the research programme represented by this volume include the task of identifying actual configurations of recipe and institutional dimensions and the relationships between them in different countries. This task, we believe, will be complicated by the fact that the institutions in a country may not form an harmonious whole, but a contradictory and tension-laden set inherited from various periods. These sets can give grounds for diverse development paths in terms of business recipes. The expressions of these kind of complications are indeed non-trivial.

# Note

1 The same research object has been labelled in various ways in parallel streams of research, but the concept still remains undeveloped. These labels include, for example, 'organisational fields' (Knoke and Rogers, 1979) 'organisational communities' composed of various populations (Astley and Fombrun, 1987; Barley et al., 1991) 'inter-sectoral linkages' (Pavitt, 1984), 'industrial complexes' (Anderssen et al., 1981; Kosonen, 1987), 'industrial (and service) networks' (Håkansson, 1989), 'development networks' and 'network economies' (Lovio, 1989); and 'development blocks' (Dahmen, 1988). Porter's (1990: 156) 'industry cluster' notion can also be seen as an attempt to specify the same object. See Whipp and Räsänen (1991) and Räsänen and Whipp (1991: 4–8) for tentative attempts to present the major components which define a sector (i.e. economic characteristics, social bases of technology and knowledge, cultures, political representation) and to apply this concept to the cases of Finland and the UK.

# References

Aho, J. (1910) *Antti Ahlströmin elämäntyö*. Helsinki: Helsingin uusi kirjapaino Osakeyhtiö.

Anderssen, E.S. Dalum, B. and Villumsen, G. (1981) *International Specialization and the Home Market: an Empirical Analysis*. Industrial Development Research Series No. 19, Research Report. Aalborg: Aalborg University Press.

Astley, W.G. and Fombrun, C.J. (1987) 'Organizational Communities: an Ecological Perspective', in S. Barbarach and N. Di Tomaso (eds) *Research in the Sociology of Organizations*. Greenwich, CT: JAI Press, 163–85.

Barley, S.R., Freeman, J. and Hybels, R.C. (1991) *Strategic Alliances in Commercial Biotechnology*. Paper presented to the 10th EGOS Colloquium, Vienna, 15–18 July 1991.

Berger, P. and Luckmann, T. (1971) *The Social Construction of Reality*. Harmondsworth: Penguin.

Björklund, N.G. (1991) *Valmet – asetehtaista kansainväliseksi suuryritykseksi*. Jyväskylä: Gummerus.

Child, J. (1988) 'On Organizations in their Sectors', *Organization Studies*. 9 (1): 13–19.

Dahmen, E. (1988) 'Development Blocks in Industrial Economics', *Scandinavian Economic History Review*. 34 (1): 3–14.

Håkansson, H. (1989) *Corporate Technological Behavior: Co-operation and Networks*. London: Routledge.

Jokinen, J. (1988) *From Field-Gun to Paper Machine*. Jyväskylä: Gummerus.

Knoke, D. and Rogers, D.L. (1979) 'A Block Model Analysis of Interorganizational Networks', *Sociology and Social Research*. 64: 28–52.

Korhonen, M. (1991) *Emergence and Transformation of a Sectoral Quasiboard: the Case of the Finnish Forest Sector*. Paper presented to the 10th EGOS Colloquium, Vienna, 15–18 July 1991.

Kosonen, P. (1987) *Hyvinvointivaltion haasteet ja pohjoismaiset mallit*. Tampere: Vastapaino.

Lovio, R. (1989) *Suomalainen menestystarina?* Tampere: Hanki ja Jää.

Mäki, U. (1991) 'On the Method of Isolation in Economics', *Poznan Studies in the Philosophy of the Sciences and the Humanities*. 25: 319–54.

Melin, L. (1985) 'Strategies in Managing Turnaround', *Long Range Planning*. 18 (1): 80–6.

Pavitt, K. (1984) 'Sectoral Patterns of Technical Change', *Research Policy*. 13: 343–73.

Porter, M.E. (1990) *The Competitive Advantage of Nations*. New York: Free Press.

Räsänen, K. (1991) *Paths of Corporate Change and the Metaphor of 'Sectoral Roots'*. Helsinki School of Economics, Working Paper F-274.

Räsänen, K. and Kivisaari, S. (1989) 'Managerial Work in Corporate Innovation: Fields of Work and Frontiers of Control', *International Journal of Sociology and Social Policy*. 9 (5/6): 57–87.

Räsänen, K. and Whipp, R. (1991) *Challenges of Comparative Research in National Business Recipes*. Paper presented in the workshop 'Changing Europe and Comparative Research', Lammi, Finland, 15–16 November 1991.

Rissanen, R. (1966) 'Valtion lentokonetehdas, sen kehitys ja osuus teknillisen tutkimuksen edistämiseen', *Teknillinen aikakauslehti*. (March). pp. 135–70.

Shearman, C. and Burrell, G. (1987) 'The Structures of Industrial Development'. *Journal of Management Studies*. 24 (4), 325–45.

Sorge, A. (1991) 'Strategic Fit and the Societal Effect: Interpreting Cross-national Comparisons of Technology, Organization and Human Resources', *Organization Studies*. 12 (2), 161–90.

Whipp, R. and Clark, P. (1986) *Innovation and the Auto Industry: Product, Process and Work Organisation*. London: Frances Pinter.

Whipp, R. and Räsänen, K. (1991) *Corporations and Sectors: an International Exploration of Business Recipes*. Paper presented to the 10th EGOS Colloquium, Vienna, 15–18 July 1991.

Whipp, R., Rosenfeld, R. and Pettigrew, A. (1989) 'Cultures and Competitiveness: Evidence from Mature UK Industries', *Journal of Management Studies*. 26 (6), 561–86.

Whitley, R. (1987) 'Taking Firms Seriously as Economic Actors: Towards a Sociology of Firm Behaviour', *Organization Studies*. 8 (2), 125–47.

# NATIONAL BUSINESS SYSTEMS IN EUROPE

## Introduction

### Richard Whitley

The importance of the state and closely related institutions, such as the education and training system, for the development of distinctive patterns of economic organisation, together with significant differences between states in Europe, make the nation state an appropriate unit of analysis for comparing European business systems. The chapters in this part analyse relations between key national institutions and distinctive characteristics of the business systems that have developed in different European countries. While these configurations of hierarchy–market relations are not as nationally specific or homogenous as those in East Asia, they do constitute distinct and mutually reinforcing ways of organising economic activities that reflect the national institutional contexts in which they became established.

The national distinctiveness of European business systems is particularly emphasised in the first two chapters, by Lane and by van Iterson and Olie. Here, the main characteristics of the British, German and Dutch ways of organising economic activities are outlined and their links to particular national institutions analysed. Christel Lane highlights the significant differences that exist between dominant patterns of firm and market organisation in Britain and Germany, despite some variations between industrial sectors, and shows how these stem from major contrasts in the structure and operation of the state, the financial system and the labour system in these two countries. In particular, the much denser institutional environment of German firms is seen by Lane as facilitating – and also being reproduced by – higher levels of inter-firm cooperation and risk sharing with business partners and employees in Germany than in Britain.

The Dutch business system analysed by van Iterson and Olie is an interesting contrast to the British and German ones because it contains some characteristics of both. As in Britain, the financial and distributive services sectors are strong and there are relatively few medium-sized enterprises, but, on the other hand, the dual board structure and the legal framework provides senior management in large firms with considerable autonomy from owners and encourages them to pursue the common interests of all the major stakeholders in the firm, not just the shareholders. Although the Dutch banks have not developed such close links with large firms as their counterparts have done in Germany, and the shares of leading companies are quite widely held, there is only a very limited market for corporate control in the Netherlands. This is partly because institutional shareholders are legally limited in their ownership of equities and partly because they do not compete aggressively for funds to manage. Finally, compared to both Britain and Germany, authority relations in large Dutch firms are collegial and cooperative, according to van Iterson and Olie. They suggest that these characteristics are derived from key features of pre-industrial Dutch society, especially the long tradition of compromise and consensus in the political system and the anti-elitist cultural norm.

The next two chapters focus on the organisation of particular sectors in two northern European societies, Denmark and Finland, but see these as reflecting general characteristics of the overall business system dominant in these countries which stem from certain distinctive features of their national institutional contexts. Peer Kristensen focuses on the food processing, metal and machinery industrial sectors in discussing the surprising strength of the small and medium-sized enterprise sector in Denmark, despite continuing attempts at 'rationalisation' of the economic system along Taylorist and Chandlerian lines. This strength, and the related success of this sector in international markets, is linked to what Kristensen terms the 'craft-educational complex' in Denmark, whereby the powerful craft unions maintain control over skill development and the introduction of new technologies through their influence on training schools and technical colleges. This control, and the associated strength of local and regional centres of economic activity, is partly a result of the historically powerful yeoman farmers and the decentralised system of agricultural production and land ownership in Denmark. Thus, here the combination of particular features of the political system, the labour system and the education system have enabled a distinctive form of economic organisation to develop and remain effective in the face of corporate rationalisers.

In contrast, the industrialisation of Finland was characterised by the emergence of large, oligopolistic firms in the forest sector whose distinctive 'business recipe' remains the dominant principle of economic organisation there. The combination of continuous technological improvement, diversification in technologically and market-related areas of economic activity, closely coordinated marketing and sales operations and long-term commitments to key members of the workforce was strongly encouraged by a supportive state and financial institutions, together with the politically powerful small landowners. Initially protected from international competition by Russian tariffs and other trade barriers, the Finnish paper, pulp and board industry developed a highly successful 'recipe' for international success in partnership with the state, banks and small proprietors. As Lilja et al. show, the dominant position of the forest sector as a whole in Finland remains strong despite efforts to develop newer industries such as electronics, and the major characteristics of this sector as a particular form of economic organisation can reasonably be seen as those of the Finnish business system overall.

The final chapter in this section contrasts these two distinctive business systems with another 'small state' where the primary sector has played a major part in economic development and the political system: Australia. This contrast is particularly interesting because of the strong influence of English institutions and cultural conventions there, which have inhibited the development of an internationally competitive capital-intensive manufacturing sector. A further contrast is manifested by the strong trade union movement, which has pursued quite different goals and used different methods from the Danish unions and, historically, has shown relatively little interest in developing new skills and encouraging technical change. Strong interdependence with the British, and later US, economies has led to high levels of foreign ownership, as Marceau shows, and has substantially limited the development of integrated downstream industries on the basis of primary sector outputs in the Finnish manner. Anglo-Saxon financial markets and English-dominated ideals in the education and training system additionally restricted the development of heavy industry in Australia. Thus, the combination of different features of the political, financial and labour systems of Denmark, Finland and Australia led to different kinds of business systems becoming established in these countries in the twentieth century.

# 3
# European Business Systems:
# Britain and Germany Compared

## Christel Lane

Business systems (Whitley, 1991) are understood as the sum of general practices and value orientations which characterise both the internal organisation of business units and their relations with their external environment. They are regarded as constituted by the social-institutional environment in which they are embedded. It is now widely accepted that the impact of such social-institutional factors is so significant that they can almost be regarded as additional factors of production which become the basis of competitive advantage or disadvantage (Elbaum and Lazonick, 1987; Maurice et al., 1980; Sorge and Warner, 1986; Streeck, 1990). Such business systems should neither be viewed as 'iron cages', which prevent managerial strategic choice and policy innovation from below (from the labour movement) or above (government reform), nor as generalisable 'business recipe', freely transferable from one national context to another. Business systems do not prevent change at the level of the individual business unit. Incremental adaptation in response to challenges from the global economic system can occur within the parameters of the business system and be absorbed in nationally specific ways. But radical change against the grain of the wider institutional fabric will be difficult to sustain in the long run. Institutional transformation at sectoral or societal level can be successfully achieved, provided that the inter-relatedness of given institutional complexes is taken into consideration.

The adoption of the term 'system' does not imply a functionalist equation of system durability with effectiveness or success, as will become evident from the evaluation of the British system. Lastly, it should be noted that influence does not flow unidirectionally from social institutions to business systems, but that there occurs reciprocal conditioning of business organisations and institutional complexes.

Business systems receive their distinctive character at a very early stage of the industrialisation process, but develop and adapt over time in response to broader economic and technological challenges as well as social and political pressures. Britain and Germany have undergone the industrialisation process at very different times and under highly divergent circumstances, as well as experiencing the discrepant political and economic consequences of being winners and losers respectively in two world wars. Britain's early start on the road to industrialism and its experience of incremental social change since that time have made for an exceptional degree of continuity in deeply implanted social-institutional patterns. Germany's experience of political and social upheaval has brought some ruptures in these patterns. But even in Germany there has been striking institutional inertia within radical political change (in the financial and training systems), and the post-war period has demonstrated the exceptional stability of the new structures, such as the system of industrial relations.

The business systems of these two societies have, therefore, developed along fundamentally different lines and, given their common European heritage and similar size and industrial structure, provide the material for a very instructive comparison. In both cases it is possible to identify nationally bounded, homogenous systems which override regional/industrial differences and to delimit them, in the case of Germany, from those of neighbouring countries or, in the case of Britain, from countries shaped by the Anglo-Saxon tradition (the USA and Australia). These countries share some of the crucial institutional factors, though not the whole bundle of interacting institutional complexes. These contrasting systems will be analysed only in relation to manufacturing industry.

This chapter is structured in the following way. The first section contains brief descriptions and comparisons of institutional complexes in the two societies, commonly seen as having an impact on business systems either singly or in combination. The state, the financial system and the system of education and training are accorded the strongest and most pervasive impact. A lesser, though by no means insignificant, influence is attributed to the network of business associations and to the system of industrial relations. The second section discusses the impact of the above complexes on the following four aspects of British and German business systems: the nature of firms and their patterns of growth; market organisation; coordination and control systems; and employment and personnel practices. An attempt is made to systematise these institutional influences in tabular form and to record their differential strength. Such representation inevitably oversimplifies relations and ignores both interrelations *between* institutions and the way business practices strengthen and sustain institutional arrangements. The conclusion summarises the argument and relates the evolving business systems to a brief outline of current and projected national business performance.

## The Social-Institutional Environment of Business Systems

### The State

The institution of the state is seen to be particularly influential in moulding business systems as it exerts both a direct influence and an indirect one through its shaping of the other institutional complexes under discussion. In Germany, there has occurred a significant disjuncture between pre- and post-war forms of state. Although there was significant variation in this respect during the period 1871–1945, one can nevertheless talk of a centralised and interventionist state throughout this time, and the legacy of this period has left a considerable impact on the business system. Since the Second World War, a democratic political system has become firmly implanted. The state has assumed a federal structure which grants local states (*Länder*) significant economic resources and competences and thus makes it more likely that state-sponsored support for industry is attuned to local needs, particularly those of the small firm (Allen, 1987: 88 ff.). The Länder governments develop regional growth plans, promote exports and innovation and plan and finance vocational education, corresponding to local need.

The system of proportional representation for political parties has resulted in frequent coalition governments. It has ensured that governments enjoy majority support and political legitimacy and that policy initiatives have not usually been overturned after government changes. The resultant high degree of political stability has strongly contributed to a stable framework for industrial decision-making. Legitimacy and stability have also been boosted by the well-established procedures for consultation and cooperation with the representatives of both capital and labour.

The political philosophy of the social Market Economy, dominant since the Second World War, emphasises competition in the free market and eschews detailed intervention in industry but compensates labour for the social costs which the working of the market inevitably imposes. This philosophy respects and perpetuates the long-established German tradition of industrial self-regulation and self-help, based both on the banking system and on the dense network of trade associations and Chambers of Industry and Commerce. Individual businesses cannot rely on the state to share business risks nor expect to be bailed out in times of trouble. The non-interventionist stance of the state, however, does not mean that the state remains aloof from industrial concerns. Together with the federal bank, it provides a stable economic environment as well as uniform regulatory frameworks, resulting in considerable national homogeneity of structural arrangements. In recent decades, the state has adopted a more proactive role, particularly in the area of technological innovation, where financial support for specific innovation projects has been aimed at the establishment of inter-industrial cooperative networks and at the intensification of existing ties between firms and research institutions (Sorge and Maurice, 1990: 162 on the engineering industry). Local states have been more interventionist than the central state, but such intervention is rarely direct and is exercised through the medium of, and in consultation with, regional trade associations.

In Britain, the structure of the state and the philosophy of state–industry relations have provided a very different institutional/ ideological framework. The state has long been very centralised and during the 1980s has striven to undermine remaining structures of local power. The structure of the British state, particularly the dominance of the independent Bank of England over fiscal/financial policy and the preeminence of the Treasury, have had a very negative impact on industrial policy (Hall, 1987: 282). The absence of constitutionally regulated representation of regional economic interests has made elected representatives very vulnerable to local pressures and has resulted in an unstable and haphazard representation of regional and other specialist economic interests. Regional policy has concentrated on transferring funds to depressed areas but has neglected to tie them to restructuring (ibid.: 274). The electoral system, which has recently given rise to an executive, based on the support of only a minority of voters, undermines the legitimacy of government policy and makes it vulnerable to reversal by a change in the party of government (Gamble, 1985: 209). The systematic exclusion of the unions from consultative forums during the Thatcher years has further diminished the legitimacy of many policies. Together, these factors have resulted in an unstable economic framework and, in some areas, perpetually changing institutional structures and procedures, as, for example, in the case of the training system and the agency dealing with technology policy.

Local political bodies did adopt a more interventionist stance during the 1980s in an effort to revive the economic strength of their locality. But their limited budgets and the absence of intermediate institutions, facilitating liaison with most of the firms in the area or industry, have endowed their efforts with only limited success.

In the area of industrial policy, the philosophy of *laissez-faire* has been dominant during most of the post-war period (with the exception of the late 1960s/early 1970s) and reached its apex during the 1980s in the idea of the minimalist state. Frequent economic crises have, however, forced governments to abandon this non-interventionist stance. Consequently, industrial policy – if, indeed, it deserves this title – has been haphazard and ineffective in instituting any long-term and sustained industrial change, and in several instances (Concorde, shipbuilding, the nuclear reactor programme) badly misdirected. Although the financial resources made available during recent decades have been roughly comparable to those in other advanced European societies they have mainly been used 'as inducements and not for sanctioning purposes' (Hall, 1987: 275) and thus rarely effected restructuring. State reluctance to intervene has been mirrored by industry's insistence on a hands-off policy. Comprehensive regulatory frameworks on aspects of industrial organisation were never developed although, paradoxically, beginnings were made during the 1980s in the areas of industrial relations and vocational training. But the principle of voluntarism is still being upheld and makes for considerable diversity and complexity in the institutional structures bearing on business systems.

*The Financial System*

Large British firms have traditionally raised their capital mainly by issuing shares on the stock market, and the financial institutions have never tied the provision of capital to demands for, and involvement in, the restructuring of individual firms or whole sectors. At the present time, the bulk of new investment, as in the case of Germany, comes from internally generated funds (Edwards and Fischer, 1991: 17). Among outside sources of finance, institutional investors predominate, and the banks are only one group of players among several. The banking system is highly centralised, and bank lending tends to be short-term and has not entailed the establishment of close industry–bank relations. The British financial system has imposed constraints on industrial managements of high, short-term returns on capital, without offering any support or monitoring functions. The ease of takeover has lent additional urgency to the achievement of short-term returns on capital and high dividend payouts (*Bank of England Quarterly Bulletin*, August 1991: 364). In addition, it has encouraged the search for economic gain from purely financial transactions to the detriment of concentration on manufacturing concerns (Williams et al., 1990).

The legitimacy of the takeover option has also militated against enterprise growth from small to medium size (Hughes, 1990) and has thus contributed to the creation of a polarized industrial structure. Thus, to sum up, the essence of the British relation between the financial and the industrial sector lies not so much in a shortage of investment capital but more in the conditions under which it is made available (Best and Humphries, 1987).

The German financial system is mainly based on bank credit, and the stock market remains underdeveloped. The large universal banks form the centre of the financial system, and they maintain very close links with industry. Banks own substantial amounts of industrial equity, as well as acting as proxies for small investors. Long-term relationships are built up between given banks and firms, and this relationship is not only expressed in mutual board membership but is also accompanied by consultancy and supervision, though not usually by interference in management (Edwards and Fischer, 1991). The high degree of concentration of corporate control (in terms of bank ownership and/or voting rights), together with legal safeguards, written into company statutes, make hostile takeover rare. Groups of banks have acted as 'crisis cartels' to assist in the restructuring of traditional industries or to rescue ailing giants.

The high degree of bank concentration at national level (the Big Three) is counterbalanced by decentralisation at the level of local states. Smaller firms tend to obtain credit from the many regional cooperative and municipal banks. The close relation of the former with local industry is evidenced by the fact that their boards are typically composed of local industrialists (Sabel et al., 1987: 36). This provides not only a close connection between industry and banking but also forges horizontal links between SMEs in a region. This more assured financial support enables SMEs to grow more easily into medium-sized firms than is the case for their British counterparts.

*The System of Education and Training*

Industry depends not only on money capital but also on human capital, in the form of skills, professional expertise and scientific/ technological knowledge. This section will focus on the system of vocational education and training (VET); on management education; and on the generation and transfer of scientific knowledge.

Germany is known for its highly developed system of VET, sustained by the long survival of the craft sector, but now diffused throughout industry. It is a dual system, i.e. both college- and industry-based, and provides nationally standardised courses for both manual and lower non-manual occupations from the apprenticeship level upwards to that of the master craftsman and/or engineer. It thus offers career ladders and ensures homogeneity of competence and orientation at various hierarchical levels. Examination and certification by Chambers of Craft and Industry safeguard standards and ensure vocational education a relatively high prestige, as well as tying promotion to increase in qualification. Financing is a joint effort by employers and the state (two-thirds and one-third respectively), and the coverage of both theoretical and practical aspects of VET results in broadly based skills and competences. Unions are involved in course design in a consultative manner but have never had the strong influence of their British counterparts. During the 1970s and 1980s, partly as a result of union and more general public pressure, training was significantly stepped up, increasing the proportion of apprentices in the labour force from 4.5 per cent in 1964 to 6 per cent in 1986 (Marsden and Ryan, 1991: 259, table 11.2). The increase in provision, together with the high market value of vocational qualifications, has resulted in a high participation rate – 65 per cent of the eligible group in the 1980s – and in a broadening of appeal also to those already in possession of academic qualifications. The 1980s also witnessed a substantial increase in advanced (certified) and further training (internal) (Janoski, 1990).

In Britain VET has always been of secondary importance and has never attained the same social prestige as German VET nor the same wide social diffusion. The weaknesses of the British system are now widely recognised, and a fundamental overhaul of the whole system is in train, but current business recipes have been only marginally affected by new practices. The two main components of British VET are the traditional apprenticeship system and the Youth Training Schemes (YTS). The former trains mainly craftsmen to high standards of practical competence and traditionally provided a springboard to the higher levels of technician and engineer. The shortcomings of the traditional apprenticeship have come to be seen as insufficient external monitoring of standards, the union-determined rigidity of acquired skills and the low and declining level of its take-up/provision from 3 per cent of the industrial labour force in 1964 to a mere 1.2 per cent in 1986 (Marsden and Ryan, 1991: 259, table 11.2).

The YTS schemes have overcome the problems of demarcation and low diffusion, but are fundamentally flawed by their low standards of attainment and their lack of legitimacy among both trainees and employers (ibid.). The greater formalisation and professionalisation of technician and engineering training in recent years have destroyed the former ease of progression to higher levels of the career ladder. The biggest discrepancy with the German system exists at the supervisory level, where a total absence of training schemes has resulted in foremen of low technical competence, unsuited to execute a training function (Prais and Wagner, 1988).

Management education is an important focus of study not only for its obvious impact on levels and nature of technical competence but also for its influence on managerial identity and value orientations. The latter become reinforced by the connection between social origin and educational route adopted. Management education has become increasingly 'professionalised' in both Britain and Germany, but professionalisation has proceeded to different degrees and in different directions. Comparative data from the 1970s and 1980s, collected by NEDO (1987: 2, table 1), show the German proportion of graduate managers to be significantly higher at 62 per cent, as compared with the British 24 per cent. When we examine the content of management education, we find the following contrast: among German managers those with an engineering education dominate (although business economics is becoming more prevalent among younger managers), whereas a more general educational preparation in arts, social sciences and management studies is acceptable in Britain. But high flyers frequently possess a more specialised accountancy qualification, and engineers are sought after in certain industries and staff functions. The second important difference between the countries is the British emphasis, from the 1960s onwards, on a postgraduate general management education on the American model. In Germany, in contrast, this generalist approach has received no institutionalised recognition, and additional qualifications highly rewarded are either a doctorate in science or engineering or, alternatively, an apprenticeship (NEDO, 1987: 2; *Manager Magazin*, 1986: 11, 343).

The third kind of expertise needed by manufacturing firms in many sectors lies in the area of Research and Development (R & D). The problem is not merely one of producing the scientific/technological knowledge but also one of transfer between knowledge producers and users. The relation between industry and research departments in institutes of higher eduction is said to be closer in Germany than in Britain (van Tulder and Junne, 1988; Mowery, 1987). In Germany, this close tie between scientists and industry was forged at the beginning of the industrialisation process (Trebilcock, 1981: 63) and is ascribed to two developments in higher and further education. The first is the founding of technical universities and their early (1899) attainment of equality of status with traditional universities, which created and legitimated a more applied tradition (Sorge and Maurice, 1990: 147). The second is the founding of the vocationally oriented *Fachhochschulen* (polytechnics) at the end of the nineteenth century, which are both very practice- and locality-orientated and a valuable resource particularly for SMEs (Sabel et al., 1987; van Tulder and Junne, 1988: 171). Lastly, research institutes are also based in industry and are organised on a sectoral or transsectoral basis. They were first founded in 1911 and receive support both from central and state governments, as well as from trade associations and individual firms (Best, 1990: 99). They constitute a valuable collective resource, close to industry's needs, which is particularly beneficial to SMEs.

In Britain, the importance of R & D was recognised much later than in Germany. Up to the First World War, there was still 'a wide-spread abjuration of science in industry' (Levine, 1967: 70), and even in later periods it never acquired the centrality it had in German industry, despite an excellent science base in universities (Mowery, 1987). The broad development of a vocational tradition in higher education occurred only in the 1960s with the introduction of polytechnics and technological universities. The latter have not attained the same status as their more traditional counterparts, nor have they managed to sustain an undiluted vocational/applied focus. Also industry has been less forthcoming in sponsoring university research and, with the exception of the government-funded research associations between the world wars (Mowery, 1987: 205 ff.), has not benefited from the provision of research-based knowledge on a collective basis. Although government funding and direction of R & D has increased in more recent decades, it is generally considered remarkably unsuccessful (Mowery, 1987).

*Trade Associations and Chambers*
Although the collective organisation of firms on an industry and geographical basis is common in both societies, there are important differences between them in the support given to such associations and in the breadth of functions and services provided by them. In Germany, the surviving craft tradition is still embodied and defended by the Chambers of Industry, Commerce and Craft which are prominently involved in training. As statutory bodies, the Chambers can impose a compulsory levy on firms. They are thus well endowed and provide a variety of producer services,

particularly for the SMEs (Streeck, 1986). The trade associations, formed on the nationally uniform principles of both industry and territory, enjoy high levels of membership participation and exercise a wide range of functions, ranging from the provision of services such as research facilities, via tasks of self-administration of the industrial community (industrial restructuring or arbitration between buyer and supplier firms), to political presentation and negotiation with state agencies – as, for example, participation in the formulation of technology policy. Separate regional and national associations represent employer interests vis-à-vis the unions. (For details see Simon, 1976; Streeck, 1986.) Lastly, employer associations act jointly with unions in self-administration bodies in such areas as labour market policy and social insurance provision (Janoski, 1990).

In Britain, Chambers of Commerce do not enjoy statutory status and are thus much more marginal to industry. Trade associations are not subject to uniform regulation and have grown historically in a more haphazard manner, often leading to wasteful overlap and competition for membership. The resulting lower membership, less secure financial basis and voluntarist constitution curtail the width and depth of functions they are able to perform and leave British firms more institutionally isolated. The latter affects SMEs more severely than large firms, which are more able to buy in consultancy services or keep up political pressures. (For a British–German comparison, see Grant, 1986). Many of the self-administration functions, noted in the German context, do not exist at all in British associations but are handled by the state. This lack of cohesion and consequent inaction is particularly damaging in the area of sectoral restructuring, given that neither banks nor the state have taken an active role. Thus, the contrast between British and German associations can be summed up in the following way: British associations act defensively to protect members against public policies or global competition; German associations, in contrast, also take a proactive and strategic role in shaping their sector (Allen, 1987: 96).

*The System of Industrial Relations*
The system of industrial relations (IR) influences business organisation both through its structural features and through the tenor of its underlying class relations. In both respects the British and German systems are polar opposites. The German system is highly juridified and nationally homogenous. The representation and defence of the interests of labour are served by a dual structure: industry-based trade unions, authorised to engage in collective

bargaining and to call strikes in defence of their claims; and enterprise-based organs of codetermination and consultation, functioning firstly through elected employee representation at board level and secondly, and more importantly, through works councils. This orderly structure, with clear lines of differentiation according to area of competence and lines of support and enforcement, has made for effective conflict resolution and methods of interest representation. The underlying ideological goals of social partnership and industrial harmony have, during the post-war period, achieved a large measure of acceptance and have become expressed in what has been called a cooperative style of IR. Union organisation on an industry basis, together with a strong central organisation, results in solidaristic rather than sectional demands and facilitates the formulation of social demands, going beyond shopfloor concerns. The degree of unionisation is moderately high – 40 per cent – and unions are well organised to pursue their claims. Employer organisations also have a high degree of cohesiveness and strength, but on the whole share the unions' commitment to the current structure and style of IR.

The British system of industrial relations has grown incrementally over a long historical period, and until the 1980s was regulated only by tradition and custom. Multi-unionism has entailed different modes of bargaining, but during the post-war period decentralised plant bargaining has become very common. Unions have been relatively strong, particularly in large firms, and have resisted the introduction of parallel bodies of representation. Bargaining has usually been about issues close to the shop floor, and work stoppages and other forms of conflictual behaviour have been readily practised to lend force to claims. Widely adopted practices of job demarcation have introduced a high level of rigidity into work organisation which was, in any case, strongly influenced by unions. An adversarial style of industrial relations and a high level, by European standards, of conflict were tolerated by relatively weakly organised employers. The 1980s saw extensive change in many of these aspects, but it is too early to judge how permanent they are. Although union membership dropped considerably during the 1980s, the degree of organisation – at 50 per cent – is still considerable, and shop-floor organisation has remained intact. At the national level, however, union influence is now weak.

To conclude this section on the institutional environment of business organisations in the two societies, a systematic overview of the effects of institutional differences is given in Table 3.1. These contrasting effects can be further summarised by pointing to

Table 3.1  *Effects of institutional differences in Britain and Germany*

|  | Britain | Germany |
|---|---|---|
| *The state* | | |
| Decentralization of economic policy-making | Low | High |
| Reliance on intermediate organisations and self-regulation of industry | Low | High |
| Stability of economic framework | Low | High |
| Legitimacy of policy-making | Medium | High |
| Degree of state involvement: | | |
|    risk sharing | Low | Low |
|    regulatory | Low | Medium |
| | | |
| *The financial system* | | |
| Degree of pressure for high short-term return on capital | High | Low |
| Participation in rationalisation of firms/industries | Low | High |
| Ease of takeover | High | Low |
| Impact on industrial concentration | High | High |
| Attention to 'small firm' needs | Low | Medium |
| | | |
| *The system of education and training* | | |
| (a) *Vocational education and training* | | |
|    Prestige of VET | Low | High |
|    Availability of highly skilled, flexibly deployable human resources | Low | High |
|    Homogeneity of competences/orientations within firm | Low | High |
| (b) *Management education* | | |
|    Availability of managers with high level of technical competence | Low | High |
|    Availability of managers with high level of 'generalist' training | Medium | Low |
| (c) *Scientific research* | | |
|    Degree of industry–university cooperation | Low | High |
|    Degree of industrial self-organisation of R & D | Low | High |
| | | |
| *Trade associations and chambers* | | |
| Degree of industrial self-administration | Low | High |
| Degree of formalisation of inter-firm relations | Low | High |
| | | |
| *The system of industrial relations* | | |
| Effectiveness of conflict resolution | Low | High |
| Degree of flexibility in labour deployment | Low | High |
| Union recognition of 'the right to manage' | Medium | High |
| National homogeneity of negotiated bargains | Low | High |

the resulting degree of either isolation or social embeddedness in which business organisations find themselves. Whereas German business organisations are connected by a multiplicity of ties both to a very dense socio-institutional framework and to each other, their British counterparts tend to be more institutionally isolated. These structural features are reflected in, and reinforced by, different business philosophies. Whereas British firms jealously guard their independence and espouse voluntarism and arm's-length relationships, German firms lean more towards a limited communitarianism and a willing acceptance of some regulatory frameworks.

## The Impact on Business Organisation

### The Structure and Development of Firms

In both Britain and Germany the large managerial enterprise is now the dominant type of firm. But this superficial similarity hides important differences in the timing of the transition from the personal to the managerial enterprise and in both developmental paths and current organisational structures.

In Germany, extensive state involvement and long-term bank lending at the beginning of industrialisation led to the early establishment of large firms in key industries of the time, such as coal, steel and electrical (Kocka, 1975a: 89). Vertical integration and diversification (in related products/processes) emerged relatively early, due to a number of reasons: the underdevelopment and lack of transparency of markets and the absence of merchant middlemen; the availability of organisational models and management techniques for large complex units provided by the highly developed and positively perceived public bureaucracies which predated industrialisation; the early dominance of joint stock companies – in both 1887 and 1907 four-fifths of the 100 largest manufacturing firms were joint stock companies (Kocka and Siegrist, 1979: 82); and from the dominance of investment banks, sufficiently strong to finance such growth patterns and to insist on rationalisation of merged units (Best, 1990: 102; Kocka, 1975b; Kocka and Siegrist, 1979: 82).

Early diversification was not only associated with under-developed and uncertain markets but also with the intention to utilise capital-intensive plant and know-how more effectively (Siegrist, 1980: 81). Thus, of the 100 largest manufacturing firms in 1907, two-thirds had integrated both backward and forward, as well as being diversified, and by 1927 this trend had proceeded even further (Kocka and Siegrist, 1979; Siegrist, 1980). (This pattern was very close to that established in the USA at this time and much more advanced than that found in Britain (ibid.: 82, 87).) But in contrast to both the US and the British pattern of diversification, German efforts rarely resulted in conglomerates: firms stayed in commercially or, more frequently, technically related areas (Dyas and Thanheiser, 1976: 89, 96; Kocka and Siegrist, 1979; Siegrist, 1980). Management educational background in engineering is bound to have influenced this diversification strategy.

Although the early reasons for vertical integration, connected with economic backwardness, lost their force as economic development proceeded, these growth patterns survived their origins. Consequently, persistent structures and habits were available when new impetuses for integration arose at later times. The cartel movement, particularly its development of sales syndicates (see below, on market organisation), which achieved a peak during the 1920s, provided one such impetus (Dascher, 1974; Dyas and Thanheiser, 1976: 52), and various tax measures during the post-Second World War period provided another (Dyas and Thanheiser, 1976: 54).

Family ownership of substantial share holdings and/or control of large companies was common in the decades around the turn of the century (Kocka and Siegrist, 1979) and has remained relatively significant even in later decades. But it has proved much less of an obstacle to the development of modern organisational and management forms than in Britain. Thus concentration increased steadily, joint stock companies proliferated and diversification was vigorously promoted. By 1907, personal enterprises (both top and middle management functions are executed by owners) had been replaced by entrepreneurial ones (only top management functions remain in the hands of owners), and by 1927 increasingly by managerial enterprises (managers have replaced owners at both levels) (Siegrist, 1980). Two likely reasons for this reconciliation of family control and modern business organisation come to mind: expansion financed by bank credit was less likely to lead to loss of family influence; and the bureaucratic management tradition, associated with a high level of education, integrity and a sense of duty and accountability, checked fraudulent activity and thus lessened the fear of passing control to non-family middle managers, as well as requiring family managers to acquire an adequate level of education.

Expansion of firms occurred both by internal and external growth. Merger movements occurred around the turn of the century, in the mid-1920s – the creation of the two giants IG Farben and Vereinigte Stahlwerke – and again in the late

1960s/early 1970s, but they were less common than in Britain. Merger waves were also clearly distinguished from their British equivalents by two facts: first, they were followed by thorough rationalisation of capacity and organisation, and, indeed, were often undertaken with the explicit goal of rationalisation in mind (Best, 1990; Dascher, 1974: 130). This crucial difference was undoubtedly due to the fact that German banks undertook the rationalisation of sectors, rather than just of firms. Secondly, mergers were predominantly horizontal and aimed to eliminate competition rather than create conglomerates (Dyas and Thanheiser, 1976: 50 ff.).

By 1927, large German companies were mostly associations of legally independent companies, organised under a mother company, and they assumed the forms of a holding company or of a trust (*Konzern*) (Siegrist, 1980: 86). Some of the giants, like IG Farben and Siemens, deliberately accompanied growing size by decentralisation measures (Dascher, 1974: 131), but generally centralisation was more pronounced than in comparable British firms. Centralisation received a further impulse during the Nazi period, particularly during the war years, when political direction became very strong. Divisionalisation came only from the 1960s onwards. It made less progress than in the UK and has experienced a partial reversal during the 1980s (Cable and Dirrheimer, 1983: 46). This difference is said to be due to two facts: first, incompatibility with pre-existing structures, such as functional specialisation and collegiate management (Dyas and Thanheiser, 1976); and second, better pre-existing owner control by banks and families, obviating the necessity for improved control through divisionalisation (Cable and Dirrheimer, 1983: 49).

The close relation between industry and banking received its organisational expression in the two-tier board structure (a supervisory and a management board) in 1870 (Dyson, 1986), affording banks a supervisory and advisory role. The latter has endured even after the decline of bank lending as an important source of new capital and an attendant reduction in bank influence over individual firms. (In the 1971–85 period, internally generated funds formed by far the largest part of investment capital for joint stock companies (AG) in manufacturing, although bank loans were of greater importance for other manufacturing firms (Edwards and Fischer, 1991: 19–22).) Although the supervisory board is potentially influential – it can reject management strategic decisions and block reappointment of incompetent managers – it does not have the legal power to force the adoption of alternative strategies. In general, management does not feel unduly constrained by the board (see Lane, 1989: ch. 2).

Most of the features of large German firms, crystallised during the first 50-odd years of industrial development, have endured up to the present time. The American intervention during the early post-war years brought some partial, though temporary, reversal of concentration and a more effective curtailment of cartellisation (Berghahn, 1986). Thus, at the present time, large German firms remain highly concentrated, diversified (but not conglomerates), centralised (Child and Kieser, 1979) and vertically integrated. The fragmentation strategies of the 1980s, discussed for Anglo-Saxon countries, such as splitting-off or spinning-off divisions or departments into independent units, are said to have found no parallel among large German companies, with the exception of Siemens and Loewe Opta (Weimer, 1990: 129). Greater rationalisation of acquired firms is still indicated by the much lower number of establishments per company than in Britain (Prais, 1981). Family ownership and control has, of course, greatly receded, and the managerial firm has long since been the norm, but family control of large firms has nevertheless remained more significant than in Britain (Scott, 1985: 128).

State protection of the artisan sector in engineering and more traditional industries ensured the survival of SMEs and the early establishment of business ties and attitudinal cross-fertilisation with the large-firm sector. The greater survival in Germany of small and medium-sized family-owned and -managed enterprises presents one of the most striking differences from the British pattern (Doran, 1984). Historically, the family has been regarded as a business resource – in terms of capital, labour and patterns of organisation – which is combined with a more calculative orientation towards its external environment (Kocka, 1975a: 93). But a third important reason for its superior survival capacity is no doubt the German financial system and the greater protection from hostile takeover afforded by it.

Due to the absence of either state or bank involvement, British firms grew only slowly up to 1880. The first merger wave during the 1880–1918 period affected mainly firms in traditional industries such as textiles and brewing, and due to the adoption of a loosely federated holding company structure did not lead to actual capital concentration, permitting economies of scale (Hannah, 1976a; Levine, 1967: 43 ff.). In 1919, according to Chandler (Chandler and Daems, 1980: 28), 'there were few middle and almost no top salaried, non-owning career managers working in British enterprises'.

The creation of large publicly-quoted multiple-site companies in a cross-section of industries came only at the end of the 1920s

(Hannah, 1976a). The new ease of raising capital on the stock market at that time led to a rapid expansion of the corporate sector and to the development of the then modern industries. Hannah (1980) dates the emergence of the modern company to the early 1930s whereas Chandler (Chandler and Daems, 1980) is inclined to postpone it to the post-war period, pointing to the underdevelopment of many features commonly associated with modern status.

The lack of involvement of financial institutions in industry meant that both individual firms and industries were seldom forced to restructure and modernise. Not only did the family-dominated large enterprise persist much longer than in Germany but it also proved less able to reconcile family control with modernisation of organisation structures and modes of management (Pollard, 1965: 23). Among the 200 largest firms, family directors were a clear majority of board members well into the post-war period (Hannah, 1980: 53), and family vested interest often inhibited desirable change (Hannah, 1976b: 12).

Although British historical data on business structure for the early (pre-Second World War) period are patchy (Hannah, 1980: 82) some generalisations can nevertheless be made. Large companies, in the majority of cases, remained very loose federations of family firms under a holding company structure. Vertical integration and diversification remained relatively low, and the absence of a management hierarchy, together with low levels of managerial competence, prevented organisational and technological innovation on the scale experienced in Germany. Although individual companies, such as ICI, began to develop a sizeable R & D facility during the 1920s, most companies lagged behind their continental competitors in this respect too.

The main structural and managerial transformations in British large companies came about in the 1960s. A further important merger wave led to a level of capital concentration which gave Britain the most highly concentrated large-firm sector in the world. Mergers were now more frequently followed by structural modernisation, but even in the 1960s the loose holding-company structure persisted in many of the large companies (Hannah, 1976b: 199). The remnants of family capitalism were finally superseded by managerial capitalism. This period also saw the widespread adoption of divisionalisation, adapted from the American pattern to British organisational forms. Diverging evaluations of the effects of this implantation make an unambiguous comparative assessment impossible. (See, for example, Hannah, 1980; Cable and Dirrheimer, 1983; Best, 1990: 102.) Although traditional, technologically sluggish firms still have an undue weight in the British economy, there are now a significant number of technologically advanced and innovative firms. One final feature of British large firms is that they have always been, and still are, much more international in character than their German counterparts, with both outward and inward direct investment on a significantly higher level.

The large modern British corporation thus developed significantly later than its German counterpart, and development involved more drastic change, stimulated particularly by the American example. Growth by merger and acquisition, without the intervention of either banks or the state, was more predominant than in Germany. The resultant current organisational pattern still preserves some distinctively British features. The level of concentration is higher and that of family influence lower than in German firms. Vertical integration, internal rationalisation and centralisation are still less pronounced, and diversification is more often of the conglomerate type. Despite a high incidence of share ownership by financial institutions, there has occurred no institutionalisation of this tie at board level, and their active participation in, and control over, strategic decision-making remains rare.

Due to lack of state involvement in this industrial transformation, the British small-firm sector was left exposed to market forces. The consolidation of large corporations in a cross-section of industries led to the rapid decline, from the late 1930s onwards, of small manufacturing firms which was only halted in the early 1970s and reversed in the 1980s. (The decline in both numbers and employment share of small – < 200 employees – and very small – < 50 employees – establishments began in the 1935–48 period and continued until 1973, when it reached its lowest point (Hughes, 1990: 10, table 8). This exceptionally rapid decline, due to both competitive pressure from large firms and the higher incidence of acquisition and takeover, has given Britain a somewhat unbalanced industrial structure and composition. Particularly notable in comparison with Germany is the low incidence of family-managed craft enterprises (Doran, 1984) and of medium-sized companies (Hughes, 1990). These features have crucial effects on market organisation.

*Market Organisation*
The current dominance, in both societies, of large, impersonally owned corporations has led to the prevalence of a relatively low degree of market organisation in each, but there are nevertheless some important differences between them. These relate chiefly to the manner in which market relationships are organised. These

different patterns have been significantly shaped by the timing and especially the speed of the industrialisation process in the two countries.

In Germany one needs to distinguish between a large-firm and a small-firm pattern of market organisation. The large German corporation is said to have a significantly higher degree of vertical integration than its British counterpart, retaining both up-stream supply functions and down-stream distribution functions under its own control. Kocka (1975a: 82) traces the origins of this back to Germany's very rapid industrialisation process which gave no scope for the development of a market tradition and resulted in mistrust of merchants and suppliers. Other external influences, detailed in the second half of this chapter, have perpetuated this feature since that formative period. Recent comparative data on manufacturing depth (calculated in terms of the relation between number of employees and turnover in *Wirtschaftswoche*, 1989, 38: 146 ff.) show that this remains much greater in all of Germany's major industries than in its competitor countries. The more recent claim (Altmann and Sauer 1989; Sabel et al., 1987) that substantial vertical disintegration has occurred in both large and smaller firms, evidenced in the contracting out of more manufacturing and design tasks has, as yet, not received substantiation by large-scale cross-sectoral surveys (Weimer, 1990: 127–8).

The relatively high degree of vertical integration has led one commentator (Herrigel, 1989) to speak of the 'autarkous' large German firm. But such a characterisation neglects the many ways in which even large German firms have always maintained links with other firms and the many institutional supports for such links. The prime historical example of extensive market organisation is given by the far-reaching cartelisation of German industry which started in the 1890s and reached a peak in 1929–30 (Best, 1990: 96 ff.; Dyas and Thanheiser, 1976: 52). Cartels and syndicates (cartels with joint marketing arrangements), although particularly strong in the heavy industry sector, affected the majority of large firms in all sectors and, by 1938, provided 50 per cent of industrial output (Kocka, 1980). They regulated competition not primarily by price control but by sectoral rationalisation. The latter aimed, firstly, at the universal application of scientific methods and techniques, and secondly, at cooperative effort in all phases of the industrial process (ibid.). Cartelisation was made illegal, through American intervention, in the aftermath of the Second World War (Berghahn, 1986), and today it is of limited importance.

Historical dominance of horizontal combination has exerted a strong formative influence on large German firms, and many forms of cooperation have remained prevalent up to the present day. The pattern of financial interlocks, expressed in interlocking directorships, has remained very prevalent and dense (Scott, 1985: 130). Close links with customers and suppliers are maintained in the same way. Connections with firms in the same industry are cultivated through the strong and active trade and employers' associations (Grant, 1986; Wilks and Wright, 1987), which have a well-known record for organising collective activities in such diverse areas as R & D, export diplomacy and wage setting respectively.

Such horizontal links between both competitors and suppliers are much more pronounced among SMEs and have recently been commented upon in the discussion of German industrial districts, such as those of Baden-Württemberg (Sabel et al., 1987; Herrigel, 1989). Cooperative ties are said to be particularly developed among craft enterprises, and Weimer (1990: 103) claims that 'the economic success of the craft sector could even be attributed to the fact that firms in the sector succeeded at an early stage in setting up powerful self-help and interest groups', albeit with considerable state support. It is, however, notable that, in contrast to other industrial societies (e.g. Italy or the Southeast Asian countries), inter-firm networks do not rest on direct, personal and familial ties but on an institutionalised form of market organisation through Chambers and business associations. This renders market organisation very stable and effective but may lack the flexibility of networks built on personal contacts.

The existence of such mediated horizontal cooperation is well documented for the state of Baden-Württemberg by the work of Sabel et al. (1987) and is shown to pre-date the more recent emergence of industrial districts in countries like Italy. This capacity to cooperate, they point out, is premised on a market strategy of specialisation in complementary products which in turn depends on the regulation of competition by intermediate bodies, such as sectoral trade associations. Cooperation has been practised in such activities as advertising and selling in foreign markets, research and training (ibid.: 22 ff.). There is, as yet, little systematic research on such horizontal links between SMEs in other German regions. But it should be noted that the preconditions for such cooperation – sectoral agglomerations of small and medium-sized craft enterprises, active trade associations and an abundance of skilled labour – can also be found in other German states. In the craft sector more generally, the following collective practices are common: collective purchasing in the food sector; the provision of joint pension funds to improve the attractiveness of small firms to scarce skilled labour; and the formation of cooperatives of small building firms in order to gain and carry out larger contracts (Weimer, 1990: 106). One striking instance of cooperation of SMEs, reported in the *Economist* (4 November 1989: 112), speaks of the formation of a consortium with a predominance of '*Mittelstand*' firms to get the licence to build and run Germany's first mobile telephone service.

Britain, in contrast, has traditionally accorded the market more emphasis in the coordination of economic activities. But it has been associated with a pattern of market organisation where inter-firm relations are purely contractual, restricted in scope, short-term and conducted at arm's length or even in an adversarial style (Hirst and Zeitlin, 1989). The historically high geographic concentration of industry and the more drawn-out British process of industrialisation meant that, in the past, large firms could rely on a 'highly developed and efficient system of markets' with a developed network of marketing middlemen (Hannah, 1980: 63, 64). While these could be regarded as equalling hierarchies in efficiency up to a certain stage of industrial development, market relationships proved inadequate to the tasks of industrial restructuring and technological modernisation.

A more recent emphasis on the importance of market organisation to competitive strategy has focused on the peculiar quality of British market organisation, which is seen to militate against the evolution of trust relationships. Relations between firms are no longer mediated by family networks, and their regulation through trade associations is fragmented and underdeveloped. Although there exists a large variety of such industry-based associations, they are much less effective than their German counterparts and tend to provide more individual than collective goods. Their relatively weak influence over firms in a given sector precludes them from adopting regulatory functions, such as in the area of competition, and thus leaves smaller firms unprotected (see, for example, the account of Whitson (1989) on the foundry industry). Large firms are also said to be very insular and to disdain contact with small, innovative firms, except as acquisitions (Saxenian, 1989: 464). Hence it is significant that the recent small-firm revival has not led to any horizontal cooperation in the face of ever-increasing demands on small-firm capability by large buyers. Industrial districts, although a feature of British industrial life in the past (Sabel and Zeitlin, 1985), are notably absent at the present time.

*Coordination and Control Systems*

Turning to the organisational structure within establishments, the studies of the French Aix Group and of their British and German associates have revealed that British and German patterns are also divergent at this level. This work, together with the many excellent studies by the National Institute of Economic and Social Research, have now convincingly related these organisational divergencies to the differing approaches to both vocational training and management education. Whereas British production units tend to be highly compartmentalised both vertically and horizontally, German ones are characterised by more permeable boundaries in both respects. Thus in Britain task differentiation is strong between production and maintenance workers, between technical and supervisory workers and between management and technical staff. This is said to create operational rigidity, as well as problems of communication and of dual authority. In Germany, in contrast, due to the higher level of technical expertise at all levels, roles are defined in a more fluid manner and facilitate not only task integration and a high degree of flexibility but also a lower level of overall staffing (see, for example, the findings of Finlay, 1981).

A much greater German emphasis on the utilisation of shop-floor expertise makes production and associated functions the organisational hub of establishments, whereas the British preoccupation with financial matters gives much greater emphasis to relevant managerial positions. A particularly pronounced difference between the two national organisational configurations exists at the supervisory level, where the German *Meister*'s technical, managerial and pedagogical expertise makes him/her a pivotal figure at various organisational interfaces in a way which has no parallel in the role of the largely untrained British foreman (Prais and Wagner, 1988).

The lesser emphasis on production tasks and the disassociation of technical and supervisory authority in British manufacturing firms also result in a different conception of managerial identity and claim to authority, which are shaped by both social origin and education. British managers are much more likely to see themselves as generalists than technical specialists and, due to their frequently very low level of formal education, claim positional rather than expert authority (Lawrence, 1980), particularly at lower levels. At top level, authority is also often derived from the social capital of upper-class background, giving rise to claims of natural leadership skills. Positional or class-based authority is, of course, more fragile and open to challenge as credentialism is becoming ever more widely accepted. Where authority is knowledge-based, it is usually financially oriented.

In Germany, in contrast, legitimacy of managerial authority is almost invariably based on certified skill, and the latter ranges from the craft-based type – witness the many managers with a completed apprenticeship – to the research-based variety, as evidenced in the significant proportion of managers with doctorates in science subjects (Lane, 1989: 92–3). These organisational differences have become expressed in, and reinforced by, profoundly different business orientations. Whereas the productivist ethos of the German firm suffuses all hierarchical layers and acts as an integrating mechanism, the British predominantly financial orientation fails to provide such a common focus.

These different bases of authority in the two societies have some influence on the way authority is exercised, although other factors also affect managerial style. Such influences are patterns of primary socialisation in the family, types of ownership and enterprise size, the political culture of the wider society, the industrial relations system and the social/educational distance between managers and managed. As argued elsewhere (Lane, 1989: ch. 4), the common stereotypes of authoritarian German versus democratic British managerial style no longer capture the complex reality, particularly where German managers are concerned. During the post-war period, far-reaching democratisation of political and industrial relations, as well as of parent–child and teacher–pupil interaction, has notably undermined the authoritarian tendency so evident in Germany's earlier history. Autocratic management style is also curbed by the collegiate form of top management. The trend towards a more democratic management has, however, been more pronounced in the large corporations than in the small and medium-sized family-managed firms where paternalistic and authoritarian styles have remained more prevalent (Kotthoff 1981). In both large and smaller firms the craft ethos, with its emphasis on worker autonomy, imposes democratic norms on shop-floor management–employee relations (Lawrence, 1980; Maurice et al., 1980). In the administrative sphere, in contrast, management control in most aspects remains much more centralised than in British firms (Child and Kieser, 1979; Horovitz, 1980; Weimer, 1990: 130). Power distance, defined as the difference between the extent to which managers can influence the behaviour of employees and vice-versa, was found to be of the same magnitude in both societies (Hofstede, 1980).

In British society, there has been relatively little change in the institutional structures impinging on management style until the

1980s. The democratic or constitutional management style is said to have predominated in most operational spheres (Gallie, 1978; Maitland, 1983), although it is by no means certain to what extent loose control had a normative basis and to what extent it resulted from management weakness and/or incompetence (Maitland 1983). Management style can also be seen as shaped by enterprise growth through undigested acquisitions, which made a decentralised form of management 'more natural' (Hannah, 1976a: 97). During the 1980s, high unemployment, the weakening of the unions and government moral support for management led to a widespread reassertion of the right to manage, but not to a fundamental change in management style (Edwards, 1987). Although paternalism is also more common in British smaller firms, the difference between large firms and SMEs is not as marked as in Germany, due to the much looser connection in contemporary Britain between family and business.

### Employment System and Personnel Procedures

In both countries the employment system is heavily influenced by the system of VET and, to a lesser degree, by industrial relations practices. In both societies the apprenticeship system, providing workers with certified skills which possess validity on a national labour market, has historically accorded occupational labour markets an important place in employment systems (Marsden and Ryan, 1991: 256 ff.). Standardised payment norms for standardised skills have been enforced by union influence. But in recent decades, internal labour markets have gained more importance in both Britain and Germany, albeit for different reasons and with different structural outcomes, and the employment system of both countries is now characterised by a mixture of partially overlapping principles. This blending of internal and occupational structures is said to have been accomplished more successfully in Germany (ibid.).

In Germany's large corporations internal labour markets have become very developed, and employment security has been high by European standards. Such firms train large numbers of apprentices and retain most of them after the completion of their training course (Casey, 1986). Although such training is not firm-specific, its broad and flexible nature nevertheless makes it a valuable resource which large firms are anxious to retain. Further flexibility is acquired by more informal and firm-specific upgrading of training (*Weiterbildung*), which greatly increased in volume during the 1980s, and by works councils' support for the flexible utilisation of core labour (Bosch, 1988: 180). Employment stability as a function of employer investment in training is reinforced by employee pressure through codetermination structures (works councils and representation on supervisory boards) (Streeck, 1984). The attraction of external labour markets is reduced by the following circumstances: first, wage determination at regional/industry level entails relatively low wage differentials between large firms; and second, promotion into technical, supervisory and often managerial positions, although dependent on further formally certified training, is rendered more likely by loyalty to a given firm and thus best pursued in internal labour markets. The much-discussed drive towards numerical flexibility during the 1980s appears to have had only a minimal impact on large manufacturing firms (Lane, 1989).

Although initial recruitment of managers now occurs predominantly on external labour markets, promotion is still dependent on long, loyal service and thus mainly internal. Thus top management teams have considerable depth of expertise and knowledge about one industry which is consistent with their predominantly 'productivist' orientation but may impede the development of broader strategic visions. In smaller firms management is usually not divorced from ownership and tends to come from a craft background. Such firms also train a large number of apprentices but, in contrast, are unable to retain more than a few on completion of training.

The newly trained surplus workers have to move via external labour markets to larger firms; but, given that their training is frequently in outmoded or irrelevant trades, are forced to enter large firms initially as semi-skilled workers. Their background is, however, not totally irrelevant. Managerial practices of work organisation have to take some cognisance of their skills, attitudes and expectations, and have increasingly been influenced to extend the 'responsible autonomy' approach downwards in the manual hierarchy (Kern and Schumann, 1984; Schumann et al., 1990). In several industries formerly dominated by semi-skilled workers, such as the chemical and steel industries, a policy of formal upgrading to skilled status was adopted in the 1980s (ibid.).

Employment/personnel policy in Germany is thus internally very consistent. Training, employment, promotion, pay and work organisation practices are logically connected and reinforce each other. They are designed to stimulate the acquisition of formal qualifications and to create and retain the long-term commitment of workers. Although the latter are equipped to obtain employment on external labour markets, both push (recession) and pull (reward of qualification plus loyalty by promotion) factors have inclined large-firm workers increasingly towards internal markets. The ideology of the works community has been an additional contributory factor. The latter originated in the 1889 writings of the influential reformist economist Gustav Schmoller (Homburg, 1991), and has frequently been reinterpreted since then in line with the dominant political ideology (Plumpe, 1991). During the post-war period it has again become an accepted integrating mechanism. The active involvement in, and assumption of co-responsibility for, business administration by the works council (Lane, 1989: 232 ff.) and the predominantly cooperative style of industrial relations are related factors which increase worker commitment to the firm.

In Britain the development of internal labour markets is combined with different employment and personnel practices, and consistency between the various elements is much lower. The increasing importance of internal labour markets from the late 1950s onwards can be attributed to several factors: the shift in the locus of pay bargaining from the industry level to that of the firm (Sisson, 1987: 90 ff.); the decline of industries with a high concentration of skilled workers, such as shipbuilding and engineering; and the steep overall decline over the last 25 years of apprenticeship training and skilled workers (Marsden and Ryan, 1991: 257 ff.). Large employers have not only moved to company- or plant-level pay bargaining but have also favoured internal promotion, company training schemes and flexibility agreements (ibid.). But the establishment of internal markets has affected different types of worker unevenly, and employment security was significantly reduced during the 1980s – although this affected industry much less than the service sector (Lane, 1989: 282 ff.). Furthermore, security of employment has never figured as prominently on union agendas as it has in Germany. A comparison of employment stability in the mid-1980s shows this to be significantly lower in Britain than in Germany – 30 per cent of British, as compared with 46 per cent of German, workers had been with the same employer for more than ten years (*Arbeitsmarktchronik*, 1986, 24: 1, Wissenschaftszentrum Berlin).

Hence the development of internal structures in British firms has remained uneven and incomplete (Marsden and Ryan, 1991: 257), and management attachment to an ideology of worker involvement and commitment is very recent and still fragile. The long tradition of a 'minimum involvement' philosophy and of a purely contractual approach, espoused by both sides of industry, cannot be easily superseded. Thus work organisation strategies have only very partially moved towards the 'high skill–high autonomy' principles of flexible specialisation (Hirst and Zeitlin, 1990; Wood, 1989), and training and skill upgrading have been uneven and patchy. Marsden and Ryan (1991: 257) point out that internal upgrading is mainly confined to new and foreign-owned plants and that flexibility agreements have almost totally bypassed the semi-skilled. This is partly attributable to existing union structures and practices. The continued segregation of semi-skilled workers from skilled craftsmen in separate unions makes it difficult to overcome demarcation practices. The numerical dominance of the unions of the semi- and unskilled has led to very low wage differentials compared with skilled workers, and the union-controlled apprenticeship system prevents adult workers from gaining access to traditional craft training. Informal upgrading from craft worker to technician, engineer or managerial status, while relatively common in some industries up to the early 1980s, has been made more difficult by the greater formalisation of technical training on the one side and the trend towards management recruitment from graduates on the other. But even in the early 1980s, Sorge et al. (1983) found the continuity from worker to technician jobs to be significantly greater in Germany than in Britain.

Management promotion in Britain is more often gained by movement between firms. The generalist education and/or predominantly financial orientation among top managers and the more diversified nature of British firms makes movement between firms and even industries relatively easy, and more frequent movement between firms gives British managers a wider industrial perspective. At the same time, however, it is bound to lower identification with, and commitment to, the employing firms. The lack of provision of structural supports for worker loyalty and commitment by the employing firm, the greater managerial turnover and the traditional union rejection of responsibility for enterprise competitiveness make it unlikely that the hoped for increases in employee involvement will materialise in the near future.

Table 3.2 provides a summary, in systematic form, of the impact of the institutional environment on the development and current structure of British and German business organisations.

**Conclusions**

The above analyses have shown that the British and German business systems possess sufficient stability and distinctiveness to merit the application of this concept. But there is a much greater looseness of fit between the elements of the British system which, as Knights et al. (Chapter 9 in this volume) point out, leaves it much more vulnerable to 'becoming unlocked'. The tight integration of

Table 3.2 *Impact on business organisation*

|  | Britain | Germany |
|---|---|---|
| *Development and structure of firms* |  |  |
| Transition to managerial enterprise | Late | Early |
| Development of modern industries | Late | Early |
| Degree of vertical integration | Medium | High |
| Degree of structural rationalisation | Low to medium | High |
| Degree of centralisation | Low | High |
| Owner control | Low | LEs: low |
|  |  | SMEs: High |
| Emphasis on technological innovation | Low to medium | High |
| Incidence of conglomerates | High | Low |
| *Market organisation* |  |  |
| Degree of polarisation between large and SMEs | High | Low |
| Degree of horizontal inter-firm cooperation | Low | LEs: medium |
|  |  | SMEs: High |
| Reliance on personal networks | Low | Low |
| Reliance on institutionalised networks | Low | High |
| *Coordination and control systems* |  |  |
| Compartmentalisation of business units | High | Low |
| Delegation to middle management | High | Low |
| Granting of shop-floor work autonomy | Medium | High |
| Managerial style: |  |  |
| large firms | Facilitative | Facilitative |
| SMEs | – | paternalist/ autocratic |
| *Employment system and personnel procedures* |  |  |
| Development of internal labour markets | Medium | Medium |
| Development of employee competences | Low | High |
| Degree of employment stability | Medium | High |
| Degree of employee commitment/ involvement: |  |  |
| workers | Low | High |
| managers | Medium | High |

elements in the German case, conversely, make the system much more stable and able to withstand the potential dislocating effects of changes in markets and technology, as demonstrated by Sorge (1991: 181) for the mechanical engineering industry.

The identification of such national business systems has been undertaken by focusing on constituent structures at a high level of generality and does, therefore, not preclude the existence of diversity within these systems. In the German case, the dual structure of large vertically integrated corporations on the one side and owner-managed SMEs on the other was seen as characterised by more common than divergent features and thus deemed to be part of the same system. In both Germany and Britain there exists also considerable diversity along sectoral and regional lines. This is more pronounced in the British case, due to the absence of homogenising national regulatory frameworks. The national business system should be seen as a dominant pattern (Sorge, 1991: 183) which accommodates a measure of sectoral/regional variety. It is impossible to understand the success/failure of a region (see Saxenian's (1989) analysis of the Cambridge high-tech industry) or sector (Sorge and Maurice, 1990) without consideration of the overarching national business system.

The two business systems have been portrayed as polar opposites in all their fundamental components. German firms have been described as being embedded in an institutional framework, which provides them with multiple support structures and gives them access to capital, human resources and technical know-how on very favourable terms, as well as encouraging them to combine these resources in a highly productive way. British firms, in contrast, have been described as institutionally isolated and hence more reliant on internal resources which are often lacking in both quantitative and qualitative terms. Structural isolation of British firms has long been recognised as a resource-depleting influence on the business system. A long history of reform projects to remedy this situation exists, but only very partial institutional change has been achieved to date.

It will be obvious from this evaluation that the sometimes asserted functional equivalence of different business systems (Maurice et al., 1980), i.e. the claim that these systems merely constitute different ways of reaching the same final goals, is rejected by this analysis. The analysis offered by Porter (1990) and Whitley (1991), that institutional environments, shaping business systems, give different nations a competitive advantage in different industries, is more persuasive. Thus the combination and flexible utilisation of highly skilled workers/advanced technology and engineering skill/high R & D intensity is said to give German firms an edge in the machine tool and car industries, whereas British firms, according to Porter (1990), fare better where mass production of standardised products, supported by marketing skill, is required, such as in food and drinks or, less spectacularly, in industrial segments such as electronics and data processing, where the continuity from craft worker to engineer is less compelling (Sorge, 1991: 176).

But this argument is no longer as persuasive as it was in the recent past. The changes in the international division of labour, the greatly intensified competition and market volatility and the radical advances in several core technologies in recent decades have all acted to erode the boundaries between industries and undermine the plausibility of the mass/customised production distinction. Diversified quality production (Sorge and Streeck, 1988) and associated human resources and technology management requirements are gradually confronting all industrial sectors and call for more homogeneous management adjustment strategies across sectoral boundaries. The implications of this for British policymakers have now been widely recognised. But unless there is more widespread recognition of the social embeddedness of business systems, and reform becomes less piecemeal, success will continue to elude them.

### References

Allen, C.S. (1987) 'Germany. Competing Communitarianisms', in G. Lodge and E. Vogel (eds), *Ideology and National Competitiveness: an Analysis of Nine Countries*. Boston: Harvard Business School Press.

Altmann, N. and Sauer, D. (eds) (1989) *Systemishe Rationalisierung und Zulieferindustrie*. Frankfurt: Campus.

Berghahn, V.R. (1986) *The Americanisation of West German Industry 1945–1973*. Leamington Spa/New York: Berg.

Best, M.H. (1990) *The New Competition. Institutions of Industrial Restructuring*. Cambridge: Polity Press.

Best, M.H. and Humphries, J. (1987) 'The City and Industrial Decline', in B. Elbaum and W. Lazonick (eds), *The Decline of the British Economy*. Oxford: Clarendon Press. pp. 223–39.

Bosch, G. (1988) 'Der bundesdeutsche Arbeitsmarkt im internationalem Vergleich: Eurosklerose oder "Modell Deutschland"', *WSI-Mitteilungen*, 3: 176–85.

Cable, J. and Dirrheimer, M.J. (1983) 'Hierarchies and Markets. An Empirical Test of the Multidivisional Hypothesis in West Germany', *International Journal of Industrial Organization*, 1: 43–62.

Campbell, A., Sorge, A. and Warner, M. (1989) *Microelectronic Product Applications in Great Britain and West Germany. Strategies, Competence and Training*. Aldershot: Gower.

Casey, B. (1986) 'The Dual Apprenticeship System and the Recruitment and Retention of Young Persons in West Germany', *British Journal of Industrial Relations*, 24 (1): 63–82.

Chandler, A.D. and Daems, H. (1980) 'Introduction', in A.D. Chandler and H. Daems (eds), *Managerial Hierarchies*. Cambridge, MA: Harvard University Press.

Child, J. and Kieser, A. (1979) 'Organization and Managerial Roles in British and

West German Companies: an Examination of the Culture-free Thesis', in C.J. Lammers and D.J. Hickson (eds), *Organizations Alike and Unlike*. London: Routledge and Kegan Paul.

Dascher, O. (1974) 'Probleme der Konzernverwaltung', in H. Mommsen, D. Petzina and B. Weisbrod (eds), *Industrielles System und Politische Entwicklung in der Weimarer Republik*. Düsseldorf: Droste Verlag. pp. 127–35.

Doran, A. (1984) *Craft Enterprises in Britain and Germany*. London: Anglo-German Foundation.

Dyas, G. and Thanheiser, H.T. (1976) *The Emerging European Enterprise*. London: Macmillan.

Dyson, K. (1986) 'The State, Banks and Industry: the West German Case', in A. Cox (ed.), *The State, Finance and Industry*. Brighton: Wheatsheaf.

Edwards, J.S.S. and Fischer, K. (1991) *Banks, Finance and Investment in West Germany since 1970*. Discussion Paper No. 497, Centre for Economic Policy Research, London, January 1991.

Edwards, P.K. (1987) *Managing the Factory*. Oxford: Basil Blackwell.

Elbaum, B. and Lazonick, W. (eds) (1987) *The Decline of the British Economy*. Oxford: Clarendon Press.

Finlay, P. (1981) 'Overmanning: Germany vs. Britain', *Management Today*, August: 43–7.

Gallie, D. (1978) *In Search of the New Working Class: Automation and Social Integration within the Capitalist Enterprise*. Cambridge: CUP.

Gamble, A. (1985) *Britain in Decline*. 2nd edn, Macmillan.

Grant, W. (1986) *Why Employer Organization Matters*. Working Paper No. 46, University of Warwick.

Hall, P.A. (1987) 'The State and Economic Decline', in Elbaum and Lazonick (1987). pp. 266–302.

Hannah, L. (1976a) *The Rise of the Corporate Economy*. London: Methuen.

Hannah, L. (1976b) *Management Strategy and Business Development*. London: Macmillan.

Hannah, L. (1980) 'Visible and Invisible Hands in Great Britain', in Chandler and Daems.

Herrigel, G. (1989) 'Industrial Order and the Politics of Industrial Change: Mechanical Engineering', in P.J. Katzenstein (ed.), *Industry and Politics in West Germany*. Ithaca, NY: Cornell University Press.

Hirst, P. and Zeitlin, J. (eds) (1989) *Reversing Industrial Decline*. Oxford/New York: Berg.

Hirst, P. and Zeitlin, J. (1990) *Flexible Specialization versus Post-Fordism: Theory, Evidence and Policy Implications*. Working Paper, Birkbeck Centre for Public Policy, London.

Hofstede, G. (1980) *Culture's Consequences*. London: Sage.

Homburg, H. (1991) 'The "Human Factor" and the Limits of Rationalization: Personnel Management Strategies and the Rationalization Movement in German Industry between the Wars', in S. Tolliday and J. Zeitlin (eds), *The Power to Manage? Employers and Industrial Relations in Comparative Historical Perspective*. London/New York: Routledge.

Horovitz, J. (1980) *Top Management Control in Europe*. New York: St Martin's Press.

Hughes, A. (1990) *Industrial Concentration and the Small Business Sector in the UK: the 1980s in Historical Perspective*. Working Paper No. 5, Small Business

Research Centre, University of Cambridge, August 1990.

Janoski, T. (1990) *The Political Economy of Unemployment. Active Labour Market Policy in West Germany and the United States*. Berkeley, CA: University of California Press.

Kern, H. and Schumann, M. (1984) *Das Ende de Arbeitsteilung?* Munich: C.H. Beck.

Kocka, J. (1971) 'Family and Bureaucracy in German Industrial Management, 1850-1914', *Business History Review*, 45: 133-56.

Kocka, J. (1975a) *Unternehmer in der Deutschen Industrialisierung*. Göttingen: Vandenhoek und Ruprecht.

Kocka, J. (1975b) 'Expansion – Integration – Diversifikation. Wachstumsstrategien industrieller Grossunternehmen in Deutschland vor 1914', in H. Winkel (ed.), *Vom Kleingewerbe zum Grossbetrieb*. Berlin: Dunker und Humblot. pp. 203-26.

Kocka, J. (1980) 'The Rise of the Modern Industrial Enterprise in Germany', in Chandler and Daems.

Kocka, J. and Siegrist, H. (1979) 'Die hundert groessten deutschen Industrieunternehmen im spaeten 19. und fruehen 20. Jahrhundert', in N. Horn and J. Kocka (eds), *Law and the Formation of the Big Enterprise in the 19th and Early 20th Century*. Göttingen: Vandenhoek und Ruprecht.

Kotthoff, H. (1981) *Betriebsraete und Betriebliche Herrschaft*. Frankfurt: Campus.

Landes, D. (1969) *The Unbound Prometheus. Technological Change and Industrial Development*. Cambridge: Cambridge University Press.

Lane, C. (1989) *Management and Labour in Europe. The Industrial Enterprise in Germany, Britain and France*. Aldershot: Edward Elgar.

Lawrence, P. (1980) *Managers and Management in West Germany*. London: Croom Helm.

Levine, A.L. (1967) *Industrial Retardation in Britain, 1880-1914*. London: Weidenfeld & Nicolson.

Maitland, I. (1983) *The Causes of Industrial Disorder: a Comparison of a British and a German Factory*. London: Routledge and Kegan Paul.

Marsden, D.W. and Ryan, P. (1991) 'Initial Training, Labour Market Structures and Public Policy: Intermediate Skills in British and German Industry', in P. Ryan (ed.), *International Comparisons of Vocational Education and Training for Intermediate Skills*. London: The Falmer Press. pp. 251-85.

Maurice, M., Sorge, A. and Warner, M. (1980) 'Societal Differences in Organising Manufacturing Units', *Organization Studies* 1. 63-91.

Mowery, D. (1987) 'Industrial Research, 1900-1950', in Elbaum and Lazonick (1987). pp. 189-222.

NEDO (National Economic Development Office) (1987) *The Making of Managers*. Report on behalf of the MSC, NEDC and BIM. London: NEDO.

Plumpe, W. (1991) 'Employers' Associations and Industrial Relations in Postwar Germany: the Case of Ruhr Heavy Industry', in S. Tolliday and J. Zeitlin (eds) (1991) *The Power to Manage? Employers and Industrial Relations in Comparative Historical Perspective*. London: Routledge. pp. 176-203.

Pollard, S. (1965) *The Genesis of Modern Management*. London: Edward Arnold.

Porter, M.E. (1990) *The Competative Advantage of Nations*. London: Macmillan.

Prais, S. (1981) *Productivity and Industrial Structure: a Statistical Study of Manufacturing Industry in Britain, Germany and the US*. Cambridge: Cambridge University Press.

Prais, S. and Wagner, K. (1988) 'Productivity and Management: the Training of

Foremen in Britain and Germany', *National Institute Economic Review* (February): pp. 34–47.

Sabel, C., Herrigel, G., Deeg, R. and Kazis, R. (1987) *Regional Prosperities Compared: Massachusetts and Baden-Württemberg in the 1980s*. Discussion Paper of the Research Unit Labour Market and Employment, Wissenschaftszentrum Berlin.

Sabel, C. and Zeitlin, J. (1985) 'Historical Alternatives to Mass Production: Politics, Markets and Technology in Nineteenth Century Industrialization', *Past and Present*, 108: 133–76.

Saxenian, A.L. (1989) 'The Cheshire Cat's Grin: Innovation, Regional Development and the Cambridge Case', *Economy and Society*, 18 (4): 448–77.

Schumann, M., Bäthge-Kinsky, V., Neumann, U. and Springer, R. (1990) *Breite Diffusion der Neuen Produktionskonzepte – Zoegerlicher Wandel der Neuen Arbeitsstrukturen*. Zwischenbericht, Soziologisches Forschungsinstitut Göttingen.

Scott, J. (1985) *Corporations, Classes and Capitalism*. London: Hutchinson.

Siegrist, H. (1980) 'Deutsche Grossunternehmen vom späten 19. Jahrhundert bis zur Weimarer Republik', *Geschichte und Gesellschaft*, 6 (1): 60–102.

Simon, W. (1976) *Macht und Herrschaft der Unternehmerverbaende*. Opladen.

Sisson, K. (1987) *The Management of Collective Bargaining*. Oxford: Blackwell.

Sorge, A. (1991) 'Strategic Fit and the Societal Effect: Interpreting Cross-National Comparisons of Technology, Organization and Human Resources', *Organization Studies*, 12 (2): 161–90.

Sorge, A. and Warner, M. (1986) *Comparative Factory Organisation, An Anglo-German Comparison of Management and Manpower in Manufacturing*. Aldershot: Gower.

Sorge, A., Hartmann, G., Warner, M. and Nicholas, I. (1983) *Microelectronics and Manpower in Manufacturing. Applications of Computer Numerical Control in Britain and West Germany*. Aldershot: Gower.

Sorge, A. and Maurice, M. (1990) 'The Societal Effect in Strategies and Competitiveness of Machine-tool Manufacturers in France and West Germany', *International Journal of Human Resources Management*, 1 (2): 141–72.

Sorge, A. and Streeck, W (1988) 'Industrial Relations and Technical Change: the case for an extended perspective', in R. Hyman and W. Streeck (eds) *New Technology and Industrial Relations*. Oxford: Basil Blackwell. pp. 19–47.

Streeck, W. (1984) 'Co-determination: the Fourth Decade', in B. Wilpert and A. Sorge (eds), *International Perspectives on Organizational Democracy*. Chichester: John Wiley.

Streeck, W. (1986) *The Territorial Organization of Interests and the Logics of Associative Action. The Case of Artisanal Interest Organization in West Germany*. Discussion Paper, Research Unit Labour Market and Employment, Wissenschaftszentrum Berlin.

Streeck, W. (1990) 'On the Institutional Conditions of Diversified Quality Production'. Unpublished Research Paper, University of Wisconsin, Madison, July 1990.

Trebilcock, C. (1981) *The Industrialization of the Continental Powers 1780–1914*. London: Longman.

van Tulder, R. and Junne, G. (1988) *European Multinationals in Core Technologies*. Chichester: John Wiley.

Weimer, S. (1990) 'Federal Republic of Germany', in W. Sengenberger, G.W. Loveman and M.J. Piore (eds), *The Re-emergence of Small Enterprises*.

*Industrial Restructuring in Industrialised Countries*. Geneva: International Institute of Labour Studies.

Whitley, R. (1991) *Societies, Firms and Markets: the Social Structuring of Market Economies*. Paper prepared for the 10th EGOS Colloquium, Vienna, 15–18 July 1991.

Whitson, C. (1989) 'Rationalizing Foundries', in S. Tailby and C. Whitson (eds), *Manufacturing Change: Industrial Relations and Restructuring*. Oxford: Basil Blackwell.

Wilks, S. and Wright, M. (eds) (1987) *Comparative Government and Industry Relations*. Oxford: Clarendon Press.

Williams, K., Williams, J. and Haslam, C. (1990) 'The Hollowing Out of British Manufacturing and its Implications for Policy', *Economy and Society*, 19 (4): 456–90.

Wood, S. (ed.) (1989) *The Transformation of Work?* London: Unwin Hyman.

# 4

# European Business Systems: the Dutch Case

## *Ad van Iterson and René Olie*

The Netherlands has a strong image: seafaring, wooden shoes, permissiveness. Stereotypes, of course. But these stereotypes do seem to point to essential features of Dutch society and economy. In this chapter we will explore how dominant economic actors are organised in the Netherlands and how they are related to the specific institutional context. Rather than focusing on one or two aspects of industries, our aim is to draw a general picture of Dutch business and to compare it with other European business systems.

## Characteristics of the Dutch Business System

### Dominant Economic Actors

The contemporary structure of Dutch business resembles the shape of an hour-glass. On the one hand we see 16 enterprises employing more than 20,000 people, including very big multinationals with worldwide operations, such as Shell, Unilever, Philips, DSM and AKZO. On the other hand, we see a large number of small-sized companies. Especially striking is the small number of medium-sized firms.[1] In addition to their small share, Dutch medium-sized firms tend to be smaller than their counterparts in neighbouring countries, such as Belgium and Germany.

Although their contribution to the Dutch economy has gradually declined during the past years, the impact of the Dutch 'big five' (the five multinationals named above) remains substantial, particularly with respect to employment (55 per cent of all people employed by listed companies in the Netherlands: CBS, 1991: 234), R & D intensity and their dominating role on the Amsterdam Stock Exchange (a third of the effective turnover of all shares: CBS, 1991: 251).

The presence of several large multinational enterprises underlines the strong international orientation of Dutch business. Faced with a small domestic market, many firms in the Netherlands are dependent for their economic survival on foreign markets. Exports, for example, amount to 60 per cent of national income. The percentage of firms with more than 100 employees involved in export is nearly 50 per cent (Ministry of Economic Affairs, 1990: 42). The international orientation of Dutch business is further stressed by the fact that the level of the Netherlands' foreign investments is only surpassed by the United Kingdom and the USA (Van Nieuwkerk and Sparling, 1985).

Apart from the striking position with respect to the distribution of company size and the strong international orientation, Dutch business is also distinguished by its sectoral distribution. First of all, there is the strong focus on the agricultural sector. Although only 6.9 per cent of the Dutch working population is employed in this sector, agricultural products (dairy, meat, cut flowers) are Holland's second most important export commodities (18 per cent in 1989; machinery and transportation equipments 23 per cent, chemical products also 18 per cent) (CBS, 1991: 288). Second, the Netherlands' economy is marked by the prominence of the energy sector, especially mineral fuels and chemicals, and the disproportionate size of the trade (transport and transshipment) and service industry.[2] This can also be seen in Table 4.1. The top 16 Dutch companies in terms of employment, for example, comprise a large number of companies that are not manufacturing enterprises at all. The traditional strengths of the Netherlands seem to reside in the distributive and financial services, not in the areas of heavy industry. This lack of development of heavy industry is remarkable even for small countries. Belgium and Sweden, for example, have shown that small countries are able to develop a viable and varied heavy industry sector (Lawrence and Spybey, 1986).

## The Degree of Managerial Discretion from Owners

A further important characteristic of the Dutch business system is the considerable separation of ownership from control. Family-owned companies, especially among the larger firms, are not very common, although there are a few exceptions to that rule such as C & A, DAF, Vendex International, SHV Holdings. Additionally, a few large companies whose shares are traded on the Amsterdam Stock Exchange are still partly owned by the founding families, e.g. Heineken. Overall, though, Dutch family-owned businesses are not at all comparable in importance to those in Italy, for example, where powerful families have a dominant influence on the regional and national economy. State-owned companies are equally rare in the Netherlands. The Dutch state has (diminishing) interests in only a small number of companies: Internationale Nederlanden Groep, Fokker, KLM, DSM, Volvocar and Hoogovens.

The legal form which is used by most large Dutch firms is the so-called Naamloze Vennootschap, with limited liability and

Table 4.1 *The 16 largest corporations in the Netherlands (in terms of employment)*

| Corporation | Sector | No. of workers |
| --- | --- | --- |
| 1 Unilever | Foods, detergents | 301,000 |
| 2 Philips | Consumer electronics and industrial electronic equipment | 287,555 |
| 3 Royal Dutch Shell Group | Oil and petroleum products | 137,000 |
| 4 PTT Nederland | Post and telecommunication services | 95,370 |
| 5 AKZO | Chemicals, synthetic fibres, pharmaceuticals | 69,800 |
| 6 ABN AMRO Holding | Financial services | 58,165 |
| 7 Vendex International | Department stores, financial services | 56,900 |
| 8 Ahold | Supermarket chain | 53,388 |
| 9 Internationale Nederlanden Groep | Financial services | 49,620 |
| 10 Rabobank-groep | Financial services | 36,125 |
| 11 SHV Holdings | Wholesale and retail trading | 29,585 |
| 12 Heineken | Brewery industry | 28,908 |
| 13 KLM | Airlines | 28,589 |
| 14 Hoogovens | Steel, aluminium | 26,610 |
| 15 Nedloyd Groep | Transport | 26,185 |
| 16 DSM | Chemicals, energy, fertilisers | 24,850 |

*Source: Het Financieele Dagblad,* 'Jaaroverzicht 1990'.

quoted shares. The public limited liability company has been the dominant legal form since the beginning of this century (De Vries, 1985). As in Germany, Dutch public companies have a two-tier board system. At the top is a supervisory board, the Raad van Commissarissen, consisting entirely of non-executive directors, headed by a chairman (*president-commissaris*). Members of this board are appointed by cooption and not by the shareholders or by the workforce, as in Germany. Both the meeting of shareholders and the Enterprise Council have the right to propose or to reject new members. However, final decision-making power rests with the supervisory board. This disengagement from shareholders is necessary in view of the task of this board. Its role is to serve the interests of the company as a whole and not to represent the interests of one group in particular.[3] Therefore, a balanced board composition is usually pursued.

Interestingly, the executive board, the Raad van Bestuur, carries a similar task: that is to base its decisions on the general interest of the company. Dutch company law, with respect to joint stock companies (*het structuurregime*), therefore assumes that both supervisory and executive board act in the public interest of the company (Van der Geest, 1988: 465). They have to consider the interests of all stakeholders – suppliers of capital, management, workforce and the general public alike (Schreuder, 1981). It is also noticeable in this respect that the representative body of the workforce, the Enterprise Council (Ondernemingsraad), has a similar responsibility, apart from defending the interests of the employees.[4]

The Raad van Bestuur is appointed by the supervisory board and can also be removed from office by this same board, although this is very uncommon and is considered as an *ultimum remedium*. The relationship between the two boards is characterised by trust. Executives usually have a permanent appointment. Overall, the involvement of the Raad van Commissarissen in company policy is modest. It is the Raad van Bestuur which actually runs the company. The supervisory board intervenes only in non-routine cases, such as in a financial crisis, a crisis of confidence in the executive board, or when major decisions about the future operations of a company are involved. In general, one may say that control of the executive board by the supervisory board in Dutch firms is minimal, and consequently managerial discretion is high. Managerial discretion is further increased by the already mentioned permanent nature of the appointment of executives (in contrast to the German situation, for example).

The supervisory board is to some degree a 'prestige barometer' (Lawrence, 1986: 39). Leading companies usually have important board members. It is not uncommon to find former politicians, former senior company executives and leading dignitaries on this board, or executives of other important firms, although never from the same sector. Since board members usually lack specific knowledge of the industry in which the company operates and due to the part-time character of their function, interference by the supervisory board can only occur with respect to general policy and not with respect to daily operations (Van der Grinten, 1985).

Interlocking directorates can be found among larger companies in the Netherlands. They are usually filled by a relatively small number of people. A study of this phenomenon showed that two-thirds of 1200 connections between 250 big Dutch companies was maintained by no more than 68 people (Stokman et al., 1985). About 50 per cent of these 'big linkers' were board members in more than four enterprises.[5] These figures may seem impressive. However, as a result of the clear distinction between supervisory

and managerial board, the group of 'big linkers' has only limited
direct influence on management; their added value must be mainly
sought in their function as intermediaries of information.

We have already indicated that in Dutch public companies far-
reaching power rests with the executive board and that monitoring
of this power is exercised by the supervisory board only. A further
important characteristic of the Dutch business system is the very
limited market for corporate control in the Netherlands. Takeovers against the will of a company's management are almost
impossible. It is worth noting in this respect that both Dutch
employers and trade unions represented in the Social and
Economic Council (SER) are unanimously opposed to the
proposed 13th EC directive regulating public tender offers for
listed companies.[6] The directive is based upon the Anglo-Saxon
practice of giving priority to the interests of shareholders. This
runs counter to the Dutch and German approach, where shareholders and employees have about the same level of influence, and
management – which is required to look after the interests of all
those involved, shareholders, management, employees, customers
and suppliers alike – has more scope (Moerland, 1989: 11). The
proposed directive would allow unfriendly bids, thus opening the
door to raiders and equally would outlaw the legal protection
constructions.

This lack of a strong market for corporate control in the
Netherlands does not mean that shares are closely held by business
partners. Dutch company shares are usually widely dispersed.
Furthermore, banks and other companies hold few shares in
companies. In sum, as a result of Dutch company law and the
absence of a market for corporate control, managerial discretion is
fairly high compared to other European countries, the United
Kingdom in particular.

*Market Organization*
Relationships between Dutch firms are neither particularistic and
long-term, nor do they cover a variety of transactions. There is a
tendency towards short-term market relations. A kind of vertical
quasi-integration occurs in the dairy industry, and in the chemical
industry between producers of raw materials, processing industries
and end users. In the transport sector and coachworks industry
combined action is also noticeable between users and producers
(Ministry of Economic Affairs, 1990: 54). Overall, however,
'cooperation is not a very well developed characteristic of our
industrial culture' (ibid.). Even joint R & D efforts are fairly rare.
The cooperative attempts that can be found are mostly the result

of economic forces: divestment of non-core businesses, high R & D investments and shortening product life-cycles.

Although coordination of economic activities through clusters of companies is clearly exceptional, we see an increasing number of relationships between producers and suppliers develop as a result of the introduction of new technologies, such as CAD-CAM and JIT systems. The amount of cooperation and the type of relationship between company and supplying companies are, however, very much different from the Japanese model. While the Japanese model is known for its stable, long-term relations and a strict hierarchy among the supplying companies, the Dutch sub-contracting model (and probably the standard in many other countries) is characterised by instability. A hierarchy may be noticeable (main suppliers and sub-contractors), but this order often changes very quickly in subsequent periods.

As could be concluded from the sophisticated anti-takeover protection Dutch firms regularly use, financial linkages between companies, such as equity investments and cross-shareholdings, are fairly exceptional. Financial ties are primarily defined in terms of control. This is quite different from the situation in France and Italy, and to a lesser degree also from the business practice in Germany and the Scandinavian countries where strategic considerations often induce companies to take a minority share in other companies. However, these strategic cross-shareholdings will probably increase if the proposed 13th EC directive is implemented.

One exception to this general image may be worth mentioning. Collusion between firms is not strictly forbidden in the Netherlands (*Wet Economische Mededinging*). Although anti-trust laws exist, these are not as stringent as in many other countries. If companies are about to enter a cartel contract with a group of companies, they have to report this to the Minister of Economic Affairs, who decides whether such a cartel is harmful to the economy or to the interests of customers. If this is not the case, the cartels are allowed. These cartels are usually kept secret (de Jong, 1990b).[7]

*Authoritative Coordination and Control Systems*
As in the German two-tier system, the executive board and not the supervisory board bears complete responsibility. The board is presided over by the *president-directeur* or *voorzitter* (chairman). Unlike the American chief executive officer, the Dutch chairman is not the ultimate authority figure who actually leads the firm. A Dutch board is principally a team of equals. Responsibility for corporate actions is carried by the whole board. At the most the

*voorzitter*, usually the person who is the highest in seniority, may be considered as a *primus inter pares*, as in Germany. Consequently, decision-making in this board is characterised by consensus. It does not happen very often that chairmen use their decision-making power against the will of other board members. Consensus is highly valued (d'Iribarne, 1989). This may, of course, indicate that Dutch boards in comparison to their foreign counterparts are relatively slow in reaching agreements, which may include weak compromises where clear, tough decisions are to be preferred (Franke and Whitlau, 1979).[8] Charismatic business leaders do not seem to thrive in this system. In general, charismatic or heroic leadership is not a common phenomenon in the Netherlands, nor is it something considered worth striving for. Biographies of Dutch captains of industry are more or less non-existent, in sharp contrast to some other countries. 'Management has never been very spectacular. . . . In our history we do not know any popular heroes, nor any Sun Kings in the centre of an impressive household' (ibid.: 172).[9] If one asked several students in business administration to name the CEOs of the five largest Dutch enterprises, most of them would not be able to do so (see also van Hezewijk, 1987: 37, on the low profile of Dutch business elites).

Although a flamboyant leadership style is not to be expected, task-orientated, formal leadership is not emphasised either in the Netherlands (as, for example, in Germany). Persuasion power and expertise are the main bases for authority. On the one hand, the Dutch manager has to be a problem-solver and task-oriented. At the same time, his group expects him to be considerate and nurture group relations. 'The successful manager is always a good bargainer. A sound integrator. . . . He makes good manoeuvres, not Machiavellian, not just social integration, and certainly not just task oriented, but "handig"' (Lawrence, 1986: 67).

Loyalty and commitment of employees is elicited in several ways. Reward systems in Dutch organisations are primarily tied to position.[10] Only 19 per cent of the Dutch working population is paid by some kind of performance-based reward system, which is in sharp contrast with the situation in many other European countries (see e.g. Thierry, 1987: 804). Loyalty to the organisations' goals is therefore evoked primarily by fringe benefits and career paths. In this sense, larger companies like multinationals have an advantage over smaller companies in attracting managerial talent.

If labour market mobility is an indicator of company loyalty, then one should conclude that firm loyalty is reasonably high. Employees may change jobs frequently in the first few years of their career, but grow more security-minded afterwards. More than two-thirds of the top managers work in the same firm where they started their career 25 years ago. This loyalty is even more explicit in the manufacturing sector: three-quarters of all careers are internal; in services this is about 50 per cent (Metze, 1989). Frequent changes in career paths are generally regarded a sign of disloyalty and even ingratitude. Larger Dutch firms are inclined to promote internally (however, promotion occurs at a slow rate) and fill most positions in this way, including those in the executive board. Intercompany mobility is further reduced by the fact that changing jobs often involves a partial loss of pension claims.

Mobility between sectors is even more insignificant. Especially, mobility from public service to business, or vice-versa, as is frequently found in France, is more the exception than the rule, although some exchange of managers occurs with respect to the Ministries of Economic Affairs and Finance as well as the Agricultural departments. Mobility between large companies, notably the multinational firms, and the smaller Dutch firms, is equally rare. In this respect it looks as if distinct labour market circuits exist.

## Institutional Context

In order to explain the distinct business concepts in East Asia, Whitley (1991) emphasises the characteristics of dominant social institutions and the historical patterns of social development. The environment is summarised in terms of three interrelated features: the system of authority relations, the system for establishing trust and obligation relations between exchange partners, and, finally, the structure and policies of political and bureaucratic state elites. Interestingly, the dominant forms of business organisation in East Asia partly reflect the nature and interconnectedness of social institutions from the pre-industrial era. Whitley (ibid.: 22) argues that these factors may not be equally significant in explaining the business organisations in other industrialised countries, since industrialisation has evolved over a longer time span. Pre-industrial structures may be less relevant in explaining variations; more important, however, may be the role of intermediate institutions such as education and training.

### The Historical Context: Water, Trade and Calvinism

Dutch history is marked by three major interrelated features: water, trade and Calvinism (von der Dunk, 1980: 132; see also: Zahn, 1989). Water, first and foremost, defined Holland's economic position in the maritime sector and associated services such as banking, insurance and finance. The overseas carrying and transshipment trade brought the Netherlands its unprecedented prosperity in the seventeenth century. Even when the pre-eminent position of the Netherlands during its Golden Age was taken over by other European countries at the beginning of the eighteenth century, these remained the cornerstones of national economic wealth.

In comparison to the surrounding countries, the industrial era in the Netherlands developed relatively late: about 1880, at a time when the second industrial revolution (the introduction of the electrical and chemical industries) in England and Germany was about to commence. Mokyr (1976: 260) explains this in terms of the relatively high wage level at the time which would reduce the returns available on new investments. The situation does appear to have been compounded by a lack of entrepreneurial zest combined with a marked aversion to risk and the fact that the Dutch bourgeoisie viewed their nation primarily as a commercial nation with no future in industry (ibid.: 262). As long as trade and the transshipment of goods, combined with a highly productive agricultural sector, sustained the prosperity of the nation, the incentive for industrialisation remained relatively insignificant. Prosperity made the Netherlands rest on its laurels: while the upper class lived off their investments, the lower classes were greatly assisted by charity (Kossmann, 1976; Mokyr, 1976: 194). Together, these factors led to a situation in the eighteenth and nineteenth centuries in which incentives to industrial entrepreneurship were limited.

Although the industrial gap was closing by 1914, the characteristics of the pre-industrial nation are still felt in many ways. The Netherlands retained its initial strengths in distributive services and agriculture. Likewise, the position of the welfare state, or 'caring state' (De Swaan, 1988), and the lack of incentives for ambitious industrial achievements, seem to be as valid now as they were in the eighteenth and nineteenth centuries. From this tradition, trade on the one hand and a strong social concern on the other, a value pattern has evolved which in Hofstede's terms can be circumscribed as highly individualistic and feminine at the same time (Hofstede, 1980; in particular Hofstede, 1987: 4).[11] The Netherlands is not a 'winner takes all' society (Lawrence, 1986).

Next to water and trade, the third pillar in Dutch social development is the Calvinist tradition. The Netherlands found its national unity in the combat against the Catholic Spanish court (1568–1648). Calvinism was the ideology which fitted in with this struggle for freedom. At the same time, this tradition facilitated trade.

Commerce, for one thing, requires tolerance and sobriety. Trade is trade, even when it is with the devil himself (Von der Dunk, 1980). In Calvinism, these attitudes found a spiritual-religious legitimation (cf. Weber, 1976). The Calvinist tradition emphasises thrift, sobriety and a realistic attitude; glamour and showiness are to be avoided. Making money is not wrong in itself, as long as it does not imply decadence (cf. Schama, 1987). In spite of the trend in recent decades towards secularisation, the national character still seems to be impregnated by the dominant Calvinist ethic.[12] This ethic is reflected in management values such as the ethic of incorruptibility, of steadfastness, and of reliability, but also in the meticulous concern with details and proceduralism (Lawrence, 1986).

One can acknowledge a typical Dutch understanding of individuality: individualism because of the Calvinist moral accountability which is an individual responsibility, but not individuality in the sense of self-glorification and eccentricity: numerous proverbs condemn both (see again Schama, 1987; also Rentes de Carvalho, 1982).[13] The emphasis is on conformity rather than on individual excellence, which helps to explain the low emphasis on individual performance, the relative lack of a careerist attitude among managers, and the unpretentious leadership style. According to Phillips (1985), Dutch society is stifled by an overwhelming emphasis on bourgeois civility, and consequently spontaneity, individualism and creativity are suppressed by the pressures towards conformity. Bourgeois civility is not uncommon in a country where trade has brought prosperity to a nation and an aristocratic tradition is not established: 'their [the Dutch'] prosperity depended on merchants and guilds[14] instead of on aristocrats and militants' (Lewis, 1987: 251). Merchants have always been the dominant social class, under the Republic (1588–1795) as well as under the monarchy (1813 to the present). This, combined with the widespread rejection of the idea of excellence, the profound anti-elitist character of the Dutch, seems to explain not only the lack of personal authority and loyalty which are (also) characteristic of the Dutch business system, but similarly the emphasis on cosiness (*gezelligheid*) in the workplace.

Tolerance is seen as an integral part of the Dutch national heritage (Lewis, 1987: 259).[15] Tolerance was not only fostered by the reality of everyday trade, but was further reinforced by the proliferation of religious denominations and sects which fragmented loyalties. This religious division led to the development of separate life-spheres for different groups, the so-called pillarisation or *Verzuiling* (Goudsblom, 1967; Zahn, 1989). Pillarisation can be defined as the formal and informal patterning of social institutions such as schools, political parties, labour unions, broadcasting, as well as other aspects of social life, along confessional (Roman Catholic, several Protestant denominations, humanistic) and later along political (socialist, communist) lines. Pillarisation is a good example of institutional pluralism which has its origins in the pre-industrial era, albeit that pillarisation only 'evolved' during Dutch industrialisation. Although the *Verzuiling* has lost much of its fundamental sense, it still can be seen in the origin of universities, labour unions, hospitals, mass media and political parties. Most important, however, is that pillarisation has reinforced a tradition of compromise and consensus. Since neither of these different religious and ideological groups has gained absolute power, coalition building involving compromise seeking was to become another characteristic of Dutch society and lifestyle. At first glance, pillarisation seems to contradict consensus and compromise. However, pillarisation did not occur along class divisions, but ran counter to these, and has therefore reinforced the consensual spirit within these pillars. Even today, the Dutch political system is firmly pluralist. No party is ever able to achieve a majority in parliament on its own. The government is always formed by a coalition of parties (see also Albeda, forthcoming).

The significant features of the political system where proportionality and consensus dominate (Geddes, 1990) are reflected in the industrial sector. For example, in the operative and accepted codetermination system and in the prevailing conception of the firm as a nexus of stakeholders, where neither of the parties dominates, and a kind of coalition building is necessary to achieve certain goals. As we have seen, it is assumed that the two boards in a Dutch company pursue the public interest of the company, which surpasses the partial interests of stakeholders, suppliers of capital, management, workforce and the public. This commitment to the company's interest as a whole is even expected from the representative body of the work force, the Enterprise Council.

*State Commitment to Industrial Development and Risk Sharing*

Before the Second World War, a belief in the power of the free market determined to a large extent the role of the state in the Netherlands. This *laissez-faire* attitude changed into a more dominant role of the state in the post-war reconstruction. The state shifted from a complementary to a more developmental role which aimed at creating full employment and a modern welfare state. Throughout the twentieth century, however, the economic policy of the Dutch government has been characterised by a dislike of protectionism. Although state involvement in the post-war reconstruction can be called highly influential, direct involvement with companies remained low. Even during the concentration trend in the 1970s, where in many countries government-controlled agencies played an active match-making role (as in England and France), the Dutch state stood aside. State involvement primarily focused upon creating a favourable climate, while channelling firm behaviour by issuing a multitude of bureaucratic restrictions at the same time.

The post-war period of government involvement has clearly decreased since 1980. As in many other European countries, privatisation has supplanted nationalisation as the key industrial policy. The few state-owned companies left have mostly been privatised in recent years. The state's current withdrawal is further underlined by the abolition of investment premiums and other subsidies.

We must therefore conclude that active intervention by the state never was an enduring quality of Dutch economic state policy, irrespective of the political background of governments. Unlike in France, for example, the Dutch state has never really acted as a strong coordinator of economic activities, with respect to either trade or industry. This is not surprising in a country with a long trading tradition, a large export sector and with multinationals with major operations abroad. Economic planning and development is more a matter for provincial and municipal authorities than a role performed by the national government in the Netherlands. In the words of a report from the Ministry of Economic Affairs: 'The state must no longer direct, but rather "listen"; put in another way: be a "partner"' (Ministry of Economic Affairs 1990: 5).

*Capital Market or Credit-based Financial System*
In contrast to other continental European countries such as France and Germany, the Netherlands has a well-developed capital market, which means that the shares of public companies are usually widely dispersed. About 45 per cent of the shares of listed companies are in the hands of private owners. Because pension funds and life insurance companies invest only a small proportion of their funds in common stock,[16] they possess no more than 15–20 per cent of the shares of listed companies in the Netherlands (Rietkerk, 1991). In contrast to the surrounding continental countries, and also because of a restrictive policy on the part of the Dutch government, the Dutch banks were never engaged in large-

scale financial participation in national industry. Therefore, the amount of industrial participation usually does not exceed 2 per cent of their balance total (Immenga, 1975: 21; Rietkerk, 1991).

Dutch banks are first and foremost commercial banks specialising in short-term credit provision and trade finance. 'The fact that Dutch banks never developed into investment banks is a consequence of the orientation of the Dutch economy towards international trade and commercial activities, particularly those related to the Dutch colonies' (Stokman et al., 1985: 113). The main providers of long-term credit are the pension funds and insurance companies, as well as the saving banks (ibid).

Being important providers of capital in the Dutch system, the behaviour of these 'institutional investors' is of some significance. All large companies in the Netherlands have their own pension funds and smaller companies often participate in a pension fund for a whole branch of industry. The largest pension fund in the Netherlands (and in Europe) is ABP (*Algemeen Burgerlijk Pensioenfonds*), the civil servants' pension fund. Unlike the assertive policy often pursued by their counterparts in the USA and the UK, institutional investors in the Netherlands show a more reserved policy vis-a-vis management. They seldom exercise their formal ownership rights (Rietkerk, 1991: 121). Confrontation with a company's management is rather exceptional. There are two factors in particular that reinforce this policy. First of all, investment in shares is restricted by law. As a result, the amount of shares composes only a minor portion of the total amount of funds of a corporate investor. Secondly, membership of a pension fund is obligatory for Dutch working citizens. The constant influx of capital relieves the pension funds of the obligation to compete for these resources and press company management for higher returns on investment (Frentrop, 1991). Of course, this adds to the already observed managerial discretion Dutch management generally enjoys. The same kind of remoteness can be observed in the relationship between companies and banks. As we have seen, Dutch banks never developed into *banques d'affaires*, neither do they have deposit voting rights for private shareholders as in Germany. Demands for a change of policy or management only come up when interest or the repayment of loans is at stake (Frentrop, 1991).

*The Education and Labour Relations Systems*
Although equality may be a strong value in the Netherlands, the Dutch education system is marked by a high level of differentiation, not only along confessional lines or by state-affiliation, but

also according to educational level. In this the Dutch educational system is more similar to the German system than to the British one. Differentiation according to ability starts at the age of 12, the beginning of secondary school. The various types of secondary school feed different types of higher and further education establishments, such as universities and higher vocational schools. University graduates, for example, usually take VWO (a preparatory academic education) from 12 to 18 before they enter university. The universities themselves, however, are not organised into a strong prestige hierarchy. They have relatively low entry barriers and grants are easily obtainable. There is no Ivy League or Oxbridge in the Netherlands, although there are some minor differences of status and aura. An 'old boys' network' supported by prestigious universities is clearly absent.

Further, one can recognise a 'German-like' distinction between universities and technical universities (Delft, Eindhoven, Enschedé), but without the clear status differences which are characteristic in the German system. In some cases strong connections between university and business exist. Several of the established chemicals and antibiotics industries, for example, rely strongly on research being done at the universities in Leiden and Delft. An even stronger position in a whole network is taken by the agricultural university at Wageningen. These interrelations are not restricted to producers and university only, but an even wider network exists in which the Ministry of Agriculture and the agricultural board play a role too. This network functions as a closed system, where everyone knows everyone, mainly because they have the same educational background: the agricultural university. A similar tied network does not exist with respect to other universities.

Next to the widely supported government economic policy of wage control, the high level of institutionalised cooperation between unions, employers and government is often mentioned as the major factor which contributed to the striking rise of post-war Dutch wealth. Labour and management, in contrast to England for example, have traditionally been not in adversarial but more or less cooperative roles. Even in the polarized 1970s the strike rate in the Netherlands was quite low. In the 1980s and early 1990s the labour unions seem again to have taken a cooperative stance. A significant feature of the relationship between management and unions is the commitment to employee job security. Massive lay-offs, such as occur in the USA in order to adjust the labour force to the changing demands of industry, are not tolerated. In some ways, this commitment resembles the Japanese lifetime employment system.

In comparison to other European countries, wage claims are usually moderate, motivated by the policy of unions to link unemployment benefits to wage rises. This shows that Dutch unions focus on broader issues than the interests of workers alone; they consider all social and economic issues in Dutch society as their domain. Dutch labour organisations have a tradition of 'broad unionism'.

The relation between companies and unions is mainly indirect. Matters that are related to work and working conditions in companies are mostly handled by the Enterprise Council. The labour unions' main focus is working out collective labour agreements, the so-called CAOs. CAOs are legally established series of agreements which result from bargaining sessions between labour and management. Individual contracts must at least meet their standards, and again, negotiations decide what level beyond an existing CAO is to be reached. About 700 of these CAOs (at industry level or at company level) are concluded each year. These CAO-contracts concern mainly wages and benefits.

## Conclusions

If one has to describe a business system that is specific to the Netherlands, a few things stand out. First of all, the dominant international orientation of firms, and the emphasis on trade and the service industry (together with agriculture). Second, large Dutch firms enjoy a remarkably high level of managerial discretion, which is reinforced by permanent tenure of executives, the relation of trust with the supervisory board, the minor influence of shareholders and the failing market for corporate control. Third, and related to the previous aspects, is the dominant perception of the firm as a community of interests. The two boards, and even the company's Enterprise Councils, have to regard the interest of the firm as a whole. The concept of the firm as a nexus of stakeholders may not be different from the prevailing conception in many other European countries (for example, Germany), yet, in combination with the capital-based system, it is. Furthermore, we believe that in Dutch companies the idea of common interest instead of partial interest is more strongly emphasised. A unitary rather than a plural conception dominates. The sphere of compromise and consensus-building in Dutch firms is further underlined by the prevalent management practice of consensual decision-making as well the non-authoritarian leadership style.

In trying to explain these particular features, we have argued that the Dutch business system reflects to a large extent basic values and structures which developed in the pre-industrial era. As Shetter argues, 'the decision-making links within Dutch industry and business operate along traditional and socially accepted lines that probably continue some forms evolved in the seventeenth century, and it would not be too irresponsible to speak of a Dutch business "style"' (Shetter, 1987: 94). This may sound surprising, since Whitley (Chapter 1 in this volume) suggests that pre-industrial structures may be less relevant in explaining variations in Western European business systems. Nevertheless, it is striking that the pre-industrial emphasis on trade and agriculture still plays an important role in the Dutch economy, and that the early-developed practices, such as consensus-building among stakeholders, seem to continue unabated in current business practices and beliefs.

Apart from explanations derived from proximate institutions (Whitley, Chapter 1 in this volume), we have focused upon more immediate institutions, such as commitment of the state, the role of financial institutions, education and labour unions and labour relations. The reserved policy of governmental as well as financial institutions seems to add to the already existing managerial discretion as well as the reduced existence of company networks. Furthermore, the cooperative attitude of labour unions towards capital and management, instead of regarding them as their natural opponents, also reinforces the idea of the Dutch firm as a nexus of interests rather than as a collision of interests.

The accepted and prominent role of the unions and the Enterprise Council may explain why the considerable managerial discretion in the Dutch system does not automatically lead to a situation where management becomes too self-oriented. The aforementioned managerial discretion may be great with respect to shareholders, but not with respect to labour-related issues. It is also countered in other ways. Being a country with a strong international orientation, the challenge of foreign competitors must be met by Dutch industry. In this sense, the international marketplace operates as a countervailing power to management.

## Notes

This is the third revised version of the paper presented at the 10th EGOS colloquium in Vienna, 15–18 July 1991 (Working group 10: Business Recipes: National and Cross-National Perspectives).

The authors would like to thank Professor Dr W. Buijink, Professor Dr J. Hagedoorn, Professor Dr E. Kimman, Dr S. Maijoor, Professor Dr H. Schreuder, Professor Dr A. Sorge, Dr Ali Ben Reza Tourani Rad and Dr T. van Veen for their comments on the first draft.

1 In some cases, these medium-sized firms do, however, make up the structure of

a whole industry (as in transport), and have a considerable impact on supplier firms and on the dissemination of knowledge and technology.

2 Only in the United States is the percentage of service industry as compared to other industries bigger (Ministry of Economic Affairs 1990: 40). In the USA this proportion amounts to 3:1; in the Netherlands 2.5:1. The average for European countries is 2:1.

3 Artikel 2: 140, lid 2, Burgerlijk Wetboek.

4 By Dutch law (Council Act 1950, 1971, 1979), any company employing at least 35 people is required to have an enterprise council called the *Ondernemingsraad* (OR). The OR consists only of elected employee representatives, including qualified middle managers. Since the amendments of 1979, Dutch enterprise councils have had more extensive rights than in most other European countries (Teulings, 1987). They do not only have extensive information rights concerning all financial and economic results, they also have advisory rights with respect to strategic decisions of management and codetermination rights with respect to social policy.

5 Earlier studies by Stokman et al. of the 70 largest corporations in the Netherlands revealed a network of interlocking directorships (*commissarissen*) with a very centralised structure. The network of interlocks derived its structure mainly from the interlocks of financial corporations and institutions, particularly from those of commercial banks and insurance companies. For example, a centralised network was built around the two commercial banks ABN and Amro Bank (which were merged in 1990). A second cluster outside the overall centre of the network could be seen around the RABO, the third major bank in the Netherlands and strongly oriented towards the agricultural sector. The RABO Bank served as the nucleus of a local agricultural oriented cluster.

   In view of the central position of financial institutions in the network, the authors conclude that 'interlocking directorships should be seen primarily as channels of information and control for the aggregation and provision of credit and capital' (Stokman et al., 1985: 116).

6 See *Het Financieele Dagblad*, 13/15 October 1990; a committee of representatives of Dutch public companies, the so-called 'commissie-Van der Grinten' (1987), came to a similar conclusion.

7 It could be suggested that the recent merger wave and cooperative attempts could be explained partly from the growing internationalisation and EC measures that forbid these collusive practices.

8 See also Van der Velden, 1990; Rost van Tonningen, 1991.

9 Of course, there are exceptions to this rule. We only have to mention the three Antons: Anton Philips (Philips), Anton Plesman (KLM) and Anton Dreesmann (Vendex).

10 Noteworthy in this respect is the low status differentiation between managerial functions, which is reflected in low wage differentials between e.g. financial and production managers.

11 Hofstede explains the Dutch orientation on service from the feminine character of the Netherlands. Femininity has led to a national predisposition to rendering services (1987: 11).

12 Since Calvinism and trade have such an important place in Dutch history, the merchant and the preacher are often used as the two symbols of Dutch character. Note that '[t]he Dutch preacher is a Calvinist, even if he or she is a Catholic, Jew, Humanist, Communist or agnostic' (Hofstede, 1987: 4).

13 To mention only one: 'Steek je hoofd niet boven het maaiveld' (Do not put your head above the trench).
14 Dutch guilds, however, were already abolished in the early nineteenth century, in contrast to, for example, Germany.
15 We do agree with Zahn (1989: 38), who states that tolerance does not automatically imply an avoidance of conflicts. In Zahn's view, tolerance is not a characteristic of the Dutch people, but the outcome of series of conflicts. Conflicts of interest have become more regulated and are solved through widely accepted, institutionally embedded, rules of behaviour.
16 Whereas pension funds in the UK and the USA invest about 40 per cent of their funds in stock, this percentage for Dutch pension funds is only 13.5, of which 5.9 per cent is invested in foreign stock (Rietkerk, 1991: 114). A large share of risk-sharing capital is forbidden by the Dutch government.

## References

Albeda, W. (forthcoming) 'The Rebirth of Tripartism in the Netherlands', in E. Rosenstein and W.M. Lafferty (eds) *The International Handbook of Participation in Organizations*. Oxford: Oxford University Press.

Centraal Bureau voor de Statistiek (CBS) (1991) *Statistisch Jaarboek 1991*. The Hague: SDU.

Dunk, H.W. Von der (1980) 'Die Niederlande und Deutschland: Randvermerke zu einer Nachbarschaft', in H. Bleich et al., *Die Niederlande: Korrespondenten berichten*. Zürich: Hecht. pp. 131–49.

Franke, B.H.V.A. and Whitlau, W.A.C. (1979) *De Vennootschap Nederland*. Deventer: Kluwer.

Frentrop, P. (1991) 'Nederlandse aandeelhouder emancipeert', *NRC-Handelsblad*. 8 June.

Geddes, Andrew (1990) 'The Netherlands: a Paradigm of the Post-Industrial Society?'. Ph.D. dissertation, Loughborough University of Technology.

Geest, L. van der (1988) 'Onneembare vesten', *Economisch-statistische Berichten*. 73 (3656): 465.

Goudsblom, J. (1967) *Dutch Society*. New York: Random House.

Grinten, W.C.L. Van der (1985) 'De commissaris', *Economisch-Statistische Berichten*. 10–4 (3): 323–5.

Hezewijk, Jos van (1987) *De netwerken van de topelite*. Amsterdam: Balans.

Hofstede, G. (1980) *Culture's Consequences*. London/Beverly Hills, CA: Sage.

Hofstede, G. (1987) 'Dutch Culture's Consequences: Health, Law and Economy', *Research Memorandum 87–037*. Maastricht: Rijksuniversiteit Limburg.

Immenga, U. (1975) *Deelnemingen van banken in andere bedrijfstakken*. Brussels: Commissie van de Europese Gemeenschappen.

d'Iribarne, P. (1989) *La Logique d l'honneur*. Paris: Seuil.

Jong, H.W. de (1989) 'De overnamemarkt: protectie of vrije handel?', *Economisch-Statistische Berichten*. 74 (3726): 939.

Jong, H.W. de (1990a) 'De overnemingsmarkt in Europa', *Maandblad voor Accountancy en Bedrijfseconomie*. 64: 595–605.

Jong, H.W. de (1990b) 'Nederland: het kartelparadijs van Europa?', *Economisch-Statistische Berichten*. 75(3749): 244–8.

Katzenstein, P.J. (1985) *Small States in World Markets*. Ithaca, NY: Cornell University Press.

Kossmann, E.H. (1976) *The Low Countries*. Oxford: Oxford University Press.

Lawrence, Peter (1986) *Management in the Netherlands: a Study in Internationalism?* Report for the Technische Hogeschool Twente.

Lawrence, P.A. and Spybey, T. (1986) *Management and Society in Sweden*. London: Routledge & Kegan Paul.

Lewis, Flora (1987) 'Netherlands. Dear Father State', in Flora Lewis, *Europe. A Tapestry of Nations*. New York: Simon & Schuster. pp. 256–67.

Metze, Marcel (1989) 'De weg omhoog', *Intermediair*. 15 (25): 19–23.

Ministry of Economic Affairs (1990) *Economie met open grenzen*. 's-Gravenhage: SDU Uitgeverij.

Moerland, P.W. (1989) *De overnemingsmarkt: theorie, empirie en regelgeving*. The Hague: VUGA Uitgeverij.

Mokyr, Joel (1976) *Industrialization in the Low Countries 1795–1850*. New Haven: Yale University Press.

Nieuwkerk, van M. and Sparling, R.P. (1985) *De internationale investeringspositie van Nederland*. Monetaire monografie, n. 4. Amsterdam: De Nederlandsche Bank.

Phillips, Derek L. (1985) *De naakte Nederlander: kritische overpeinzingen*. Amsterdam: Bert Bakker.

Rentes de Carvalho, J. (1982) *Waar die andere God woont*. Amsterdam: De Arbeiderspers.

Rietkerk, G. (1991) *Onderneming en vermogensmarkt*. 3rd, rev. edn, Leiden: Stenfert Kroese. [1st edn, 1977].

Rijnvos, C.J. (1985) 'De bankier', *Economisch-Statistische Berichten*. 1–4 (3): 328–30.

Rost van Tonningen, M.G. (1991) 'Consensus en utopia', *NRC-Handelsblad*. 16 March.

Schama, Simon (1987) *The Embarrassment of Riches*. London: Collins.

Schreuder, H. (1981) *Maatschappelijke verantwoordelijkheid en maatschappelijke berichtgeving van ondernemingen*. Leiden: Stenfert Kroese.

Shetter, William Z. (1987) *The Netherlands in Perspective: the Organization of Society and Environment*. Leiden: Martinus Nijhoff.

Stokman, Frans N., Wasseur, Frans W. and Elsas, Donald (1985) 'The Dutch Network: Types of Interlocks and Network Structure', in Frans N. Stokman, Rolf Ziegler and John Scott, *Networks of Corporate Power*. Cambridge: Polity Press.

Swaan, Abram De (1988) *In Care of the State*. Cambridge: Polity Press.

Teulings, A.W.M. (1987) 'A Political Bargaining Theory of Codetermination: an Empirical Test for the Dutch System of Organizational Democracy', *Organization Studies*. 8 (1): 1–24.

Thierry, H. (1987) 'De effectiviteit van prestatiebeloning', *Economisch-Statistische Berichten*. 2–9: 804–9.

Velden, Ben van der (1990) 'Onze tegenspraakcultuur verbaast het buitenland', *NRC-Handelsblad*. 25 October.

Vries, Joh. de (1985) *Geschiedenis der accountancy in Nederland*. Assen: Van Gorcum.

Weber, Max (1976) *The Protestant Ethic and the Spirit of Capitalism*. London: Allen & Unwin. [1st edn in English, 1930].

Whitley, R.D. (1991) 'The Social Construction of Business Systems in East Asia', *Organization Studies*. 12: 1–28.

Zahn, Ernest (1989) *Regenten, rebellen en reformatoren*. Amsterdam: Contact. [Dutch translation of *Das unbekannte Holland: Regenten, Rebellen und Reformatoren*. Berlin: Siedler, 1984.]

# 5
# Strategies against Structure: Institutions and Economic Organisation in Denmark

*Peer Hull Kristensen*

The Danish business community is fragmented – in every sense of the word. Some observers blame it for being incapable of acting in concert; others praise its variability and high capability for adaptation. They agree that it is difficult to ascribe a 'system' to the Danish business community. This article argues that many of the well-known systems of business organisation are not found in the Danish business community, which can neither be viewed as a system of strong dominating economic agents, as a dual system nor as a system of regional industrial districts. In rejecting these ideal or stereotypes of business systems our argument outlines a Danish pattern of interacting strategies that explains the reproduction of fragmentation and shows how inherited life patterns and careers combine with and mutually reinforce corporate strategies and structures. In doing so we demonstrate that there is a 'system' which explains why the business community does not form a common system of business organisation.

## Historical Features of Fragmentation: Trusts against the Yeoman Republics, 1870–1914

The major reason for the fragmented Danish business community is the success of traditional classes in combining their efforts and establishing themselves in Danish society during the period of modernisation in the last quarter of the nineteenth century. After this period a small group of corporations competed continuously with a surprisingly widespread and well-organised yeoman republic for control over, and organisation of, the economy. All participating classes and groups saw their own fight for survival and prosperity as a fight for the national interest and reconstruction after the loss of Schleswig-Holstein in 1864.

For the small group of large merchants, brokers, private bankers and landowners who centred around the three major Copenhagen banks, prospects were especially favourable. In 1857 when the first bank, Privatbanken, was established with C.F. Tietgen as director, a financial crisis had defeated Hamburg's financial influence in banking and the Danish Parliament had restricted the guilds' influence on industry. Nothing seemed to impede Tietgen and his group from implementing his surprisingly strong vision of a system of modern production plants, established as stock-owned corporations and coordinated mutually through cartels, trusts or holding companies. This group restructured sugar refineries, distilleries, breweries, mining, shipping, shipyards, railways, telegraphs, telephones, etc. after the most fashionable American and British ideas (Kristensen and Sabel, forthcoming). The success of these financial and corporate groups was so great that 'important parts of our industry' were given 'a trust-like character, before trusts and cartels played any important role in the economic structure of other countries' (Willerslev, 1952: 233).

Most of this corporate community has survived until today. The three Copenhagen banks, trusts and stock companies from that period, together with a limited number of newcomers, will be represented in any report on the dominant agents of Danish industry. At the same time, any such report will demonstrate that these agents are mutually integrated through a highly complex set of overlapping membership of boards and directorships (see, for example, Andersen, 1966; Guldager, 1978; Johannsen and Olsen), and play a major role even in the current wave of mergers.

Through the establishment of a cooperative movement Danish farmers organised the dynamic that dominated the country's development (Senghaas, 1982) for the next 50 years, ascribing a subordinate part to the community of corporate groups in Copenhagen. A century of state reforms had prepared the farmers for this principal role. Since the agricultural reforms of 1788, legislation had prevented them from destroying each other by mutual competition. Concentration and centralisation of the control of land was simply impossible. Consequently, compared to many other nations conditions for continuous cooperation within village communities were very favourable. Constitutional reforms in 1848 gave the farmers political rights that turned them into a very self-conscious and politically active class. Based on these institutional foundations the concept of the yeoman farmer had a very special connotation, which manifested itself in the 'self-help-movement' through which the yeoman class constructed its own institutions. Their savings banks and building societies, organised from the middle of the nineteenth century, put them in control of the capital needed during the phase of establishing farmers' cooperatives. By establishing dairies, slaughterhouses and cooperatives, local groups of farmers organised and gained control over the individual farm's forward and backward linkages of the value chain and hence created the economic organisation that transformed Denmark into a mass producer and exporter of high quality butter and bacon.

This movement cut off the corporate community in Copenhagen from earning the profits which they would have obtained by controlling the value chain around farms. This value chain was continuously expanded through forward and backward integration of new business areas (for example cement plants, machinery shops for the production of dairy equipment, export, import), or the cooperative movement would use its bargaining power to buy inputs cheaply and sell outputs at high prices when doing business with corporate groups (for example in shipping). Banks and stock markets lost control over capital, as for example building societies played a very important role in financing both buildings and machinery.

Simultaneously the movement strengthened a counter-pole of economic organisation: the yeoman republics of railway towns. Local dairies and slaughterhouses were not 'separate units of economic decision making' (Whitley 1990: 50–1), they rather constituted physical plants representing 'cooperative networks and informal alliances' (ibid.) among local farmers. On the other hand, they also formed among themselves 'cooperative networks and informal alliances' in order to create a national system of cooperation (exporting, importing, producing, selling, buying, manufacturing). This system stretched across Denmark from the west to the east during the same decades as railways were constructed running from Copenhagen in the east towards the western part of the country, establishing an infrastructure that turned the whole country into one market. While the railways reinforced the creation of the well-known mass-producing corporations in the USA (Chandler, 1977), the fusion of railways and the farmers' cooperative movement created a fine-meshed network of tiny railway towns in the Danish countryside. These railway towns became service centres of neighbouring agricultural districts, offering cooperative instalments, shops, savings banks and other facilities.

Even though it is difficult to conceive the railway town as an 'authoritative unit of economic action' (Whitley, 1990) it is the proper unit for analysing the 'working logic' of an industrial strategy confronting corporations in Copenhagen. These tiny towns or villages viewed each other as competitors engaged in a rivalry to build up a society of their own which would not be dependent on a neighbouring village or town. As their means were the institutions of the farmers' cooperative movement, any improvement in one locality would, however, strengthen all other localities. In effect, by the end of the nineteenth century the Danish countryside was engaged in an enormous construction process, creating one of the richest societies in the world whose centre of prosperity was the individual farm.

For journeymen these railway towns and villages offered opportunities at a time when the prohibition of guilds combined with industrialisation cut them off from their normal careers in privileged towns and Copenhagen. By setting up small shops, working as dealers and repairing industrial goods, craftsmen from many trades provided the railway towns with a polyvalence of skills. Consequently, these small societies achieved a certain level of self-sufficiency and were able to adapt to industrial innovations. Furthermore, these craft shops were managed in a way that stabilised total employment in the small communities. By engaging in different combinations of construction and 'factory'-production, craft shops could even out the level of activity determined by seasonal conditions or business cycles, gradually adding specialised industries to the economic organisation of yeoman republics of railway towns.

Even though railway towns were necessary preconditions, additional measures were required to secure craftsmen a place in either the yeoman republic or the modern corporation in Denmark. In their attempts to save as much as possible of the guild system during liberalism, craftsmen in Copenhagen and the privileged towns created the institutions necessary to reproduce craftsmen as an expanding social class. Being unable to reconstruct the guilds, they imitated all the institutional and organisational innovations that they came across. They engaged in a self-help movement very similar to that of the farmers, tried to organise their own banks, cooperatively owned factories supplying intermediate goods and cooperative sales-houses for finished products, or bought common supplies, etc. Most of these experiments failed, as the crafts had no institutions to protect them from their mutual competition, and larger firms would use such cooperatives and trade associations to favour themselves rather than the craft in question. Most institutional innovations soon faded away and their associations became weak.

The greatest success of the craft movement, however, was the creation of a craft-educational system. The first experiments with craft schools started at the beginning of the nineteenth century when people with visions of enlightenment wanted to increase the skills of apprentices by teaching them technical drawing, mathematics, etc. and to read and write. But technical schools really became part of the craft movement when the guild system was prohibited in 1862. The schools were seen both as a counter-measure against proletarianisation – as a way of regulating their numbers – and as an imitation of the farmers' high-school movement. Initiated by local and national craft associations, a system was developed from 1870 to the 1930s based on 350 local technical schools furnishing each apprentice with basic training in disciplines such as drawing, mathematics, physics, etc. and a complex of national craft-specific schools, where they could finish their theoretical training. On top of this system a Technological Institute was created in 1907 to experiment with new technologies, to develop courses in new technologies for further training and to modernise the curricula of local and national technical schools. As a result of these efforts knowledge of new technologies was rapidly either integrated into existing craft education or, if totally new 'professions' were needed, these were integrated into the family of the craft-educational complex. Another effect was that courses and further training became an institutionalised practice among journeymen and entrepreneurs. Finally, by establishing their own engineering education (the Teknikum-engineer) around the time of the First World War, craft-workers were given the opportunity to compete with the academic (civil) engineers for the highest managerial positions within the hierarchy of industrial corporations. A highly diversified system of further training adapted craftsmen to changing technologies and modes of industrial organisation and thereby to new positions as technicians and managers. As in Germany (Maurice et al., 1986), the crafts had an important impact on the organisation of the whole corporation.

In Denmark, however the organising effect of crafts reached out to the whole corporatist structure. After some trial and error in the 1870s, Social Democratic union organisers learned to depart from the old guild divisions, and, by providing journeymen with services similar to the guilds, the Danish labour movement became one of the most successful in the world, as measured by the unionisation rate. Reinforced by this, employers' associations also divided along the traditional divisions among crafts and trades. This mode of organisation was formed by struggles during the last quarter of the nineteenth century, by strikes and lockouts, workers fighting for their professional pride and wages against masters feeling pushed to unite forces with colleagues in order to escape from *omgangsskruen* (the 'Whipsaw tactics' of the 'rolling strike'), which journeymen easily organised through their new unions. The fight was intense but very short. Denmark got its 'labour market constitution' as early as 1901, when the two parties recognised each other as negotiators and established rules of negotiation, committing each other to keep collective agreements and industrial peace between periods of negotiation.

For the railway towns, the craft-educational system implied a continuous supply of craftsmen to help the yeoman republic to survive and grow on the principle of a cooperating network of many small producers. State-regulated apprenticeships and technical schools made it easy for the craftsmen of railway towns to achieve full membership of their trades by sending their apprentices to the final examinations at the national craft schools in Copenhagen. At the turn of the century they began to compete with their colleagues in privileged towns by organising their own locally owned technical schools. 'Journey' in journeyman was again more than a connotation of tradition in the small railway towns, as they would travel all over the country both for jobs and further training, without a sharp distinction between the two. Horizontal and vertical mobility in the labour market instead of segmentation – either by locality or corporation – became tied to personal identity, and membership of unions and associations was a ticket to ride. In short, the craft system became national, and small or large shops in every corner of the country were 'rites of passage' for a transition to life in industry.

This mode of organising the labour market plays a major part in explaining 'the Danish system', which has prevented the business community from organising into an Anglo-American, a dual system or an Italian system of industrial districts.

## Railway Towns: from Agricultural to Industrial Districts?

The organisational architecture of farmers' cooperatives was a two-edged sword in local development. As long as initiatives were taken from the bottom, the cooperative superstructure supported growth in local economies. However, both the standardisation of quality within this decentralised system of mass production, and the external shocks of bilateralism in 1930s world trade, gradually gave power to a coordinating apex of technocrats and full-time managers at the top of this system. Their strategy – economies of scale and mass production – easily merged with the general philosophy of the cooperative movement, and even when it implied closing dairies and slaughterhouses during the 1960s and 1970s, the farmers did not use their controlling authority in favour of local economies against the coordinating apex's aspirations. By concentrating public institutions and closing railways and stations, the state seemed to reinforce a hopeless future for these small communities.

And yet, during the economic crisis in the 1970s and 1980s small towns in peripheral regions proved to be the only power centres of industrial growth while large towns and cities continuously declined (Maskell, 1982: 43; Planstyrelsen, 1990: 34). Traditional theories of industrialisation and development were facing a strange phenomenon: growth in employment primarily came from locally initiated enterprises (Hartoft-Nielsen, 1980; 1985). The firms were independent and family-owned, being a framework for self-employment rather than growth in size (Illeris, 1991). External control of business enterprises in the peripheral counties of Jutland was less than in any other counties (Planstyrelsen, 1990). These counties' industrial workforce was just as skilled as that of Copenhagen and even more strongly involved in further training (Maskell, 1982).

However, the phenomenon can easily be explained by the railway town's normal pattern of stabilising activities and employment in the yeoman republic of railway towns. Normally a small labour force was kept busy during spring and summer by sowing and building and construction, and during the autumn much labour was needed for harvesting and for jobs in slaughterhouses, in preservation firms, etc. During the winter, however, activities were low, posing both challenges and opportunities for craftsmen. They were forced to search for complementary businesses if they wanted to keep their apprentices busy and make sure that their good journeymen would not quit; but the winter time also offered the possibility of enrolling smallholders, farm workers and building workers into some kind of 'factory' production. And from these winter activities, some form of speciality production or subcontracting activities often evolved, gradually changing the businesses of the firm away from its original locally oriented activities towards industrial production for the larger national or international market. For small craft firms operating under such conditions any crisis, either in the general economy, in building and construction or in agriculture, poses an ideal combination of threat and opportunity: threat because they might risk losing business due to low demand for their original activities; and opportunity because they can recruit workers from a larger segment of the labour force.

During the crises of the 1920s and 1930s, the agricultural areas experienced a wave of new manufacturing SMEs which took advantage of protectionism and bilateralism in world trade, and the 1930s proved to be only second to the 1960s in respect of industrial growth. Consequently, after the Second World War an abundance of small shops and even larger factories competed with farmers and cooperatives for people and capital in small railway towns.

In the wake of the post-war agricultural crisis, the proportion of youngsters enrolling as apprentices in Western Jutland increased from 25 per cent to 49 per cent between 1950 and 1965. So crafts and craft-educational institutions became a means of transforming troubles into opportunities for a whole generation of young would-be farmers and craftsmen. Their yeoman inheritance gave them a strong impetus to create their own businesses, but now outside of agriculture. As such they were expressions of a self-reinforcing mechanism, as small craft-based enterprises have a high inclination to hire and educate apprentices, who in turn – especially in these regions – will often establish their own businesses.

During the 1960s and the 1970s this mechanism was primarily supported by a general boom in the building and construction industry and by investments in agriculture. Several crises during the 1970s and 1980s, however, made these small entrepreneurs look for complementary business. Cabinet-makers and carpenters started sub-contracting for furniture-makers, blacksmiths for machine-shops and factories, gradually evolving into industrial enterprises, leaving open the local market for building and construction, agricultural machinery and repair, to new generations of young entrepreneurs, who were later on to be caught in the same traps and to react as had their predecessors.

Consequently, the railway towns survived as entrepreneurial communities, increasingly based on manufacturing industry rather than services for agriculture. The basis for the evolving enterprises being small communities and crafts, this development reproduced the small enterprise structure within typically fragmented industrial branches, such as iron- and metal-working, furniture and the garment/knitting industry. In a few cases, groups of former railway towns have transformed into industrial districts of flexible specialisation (Kristensen, 1992), with some of the characteristics of their Italian counterparts (Pyke et al., 1991). The most pronounced example is the knitting/garment industry of Herning-Ikast, together with the furniture district of Salling in Viborg county. But the resemblance is limited.

The institutional formation of crafts not only affected labour markets, careers and entrepreneurship and supported the development of railway towns, but also impeded the latter's transformation into industrial districts. The craft-educational complex facilitated the horizontal and vertical mobility of journeymen. So it is not a 'world of fixity' (Sabel, 1990; 56), but rather a nationwide open 'landscape' in which modern 'journeymen' (Kristensen, 1990b) acquire the skills to transform themselves as in the old system (from apprentice through journeyman to master). But travelling in this system means crossing boundaries of firms, districts/regions, classes – often even crossing the institutional divide between the private and public sector, establishing contacts with many people and building a large personal network.

Consequently, entrepreneurs, managers or workers in enterprises do not feel committed to respect the limits of a narrow district, neither through membership of associations nor through the selection of sub-suppliers and customers. Apart from the knitting/garment district of Herning/Ikast, no district in Denmark has been able to establish a local institutional framework for regulating cooperation, to create common services and to develop a strategy for protecting itself as a business community. The field is open – so it seems – for producing either a dual structure of small firms sweating for large corporations, or of fragmented industries being structured by growing corporations through waves of mergers.

## Between Corporate Power and Industrial Districts: the Iron and Metal Industry

For a century the Danish iron and metal industry has been characterised by a small group of large producers at one end of the scale and a large group of small producers at the other end. This has posed an ideal setting for developing a typical dual structure in which small producers sweat and pay the costs of stable production during business cycles. Such a dual perspective may have been part of the explanation as to why the iron and metal industry has been the most dynamically growing industry in Denmark, increasing its share of total manufacturing employment from 31 per cent to 43 per cent between 1945 and 1979 (Hansen, 1983: 146; 1970; 20; Frøslev Christensen, 1981: 30).

This growth, however, is explained neither by national raw materials nor by a large dominating industrial group, mass-producing and marketing a significant product, such as cars or consumer electronics. Rather its role has been very heterogeneous, producing a wide range of the capital goods needed to modernise along the Danish pattern: agricultural machinery, food processing equipment, industrial machinery, measuring instruments and high quality well-designed consumer durables (Kjeldsen-Kragh, 1973: 29 ff.); and growth was achieved by an increasing number of enterprises increasing their average employment. The most permanently growing sector has been machinery shops and factories (employing

18 per cent of all manufacturing employment in 1979) (Frøslev Christensen, 1981: 30), due to increasing export rates (Hartoft-Nielsen, 1980: 125–6). In peripheral regions the iron and metal industry increased its share of total employment from 13.6 per cent in 1958 to 28 per cent in 1977. From 1972 to 1977 this industry on average grew by 60 per cent in the towns of the counties of Ribe, Ringkøbing and North-Jutland. By 1977, 40 per cent of the Danish machine industry were located in small towns of peripheral areas (ibid.: 134–8).

Cooperation between firms in this industry can be very important, as they allow *ad hoc* problems to be solved continuously. Such *ad hoc* patterns of cooperation seem to be very stable, though products or batches are often changing. On average, a study (Grøn, 1985) showed that firms were operating through seven forward and nine backward linkages (ibid.: 95 and 99). These surprisingly few and stable contacts comprised an interesting mix of regional, national and international relations, organising directly or indirectly the transactions of firms on different markets. For example, the supply of standardised components seems often to flow *through* local sub-contractors from the foreign producer to the industrial end-user, implying that the individual firm's 'internationalisation of production' is organised through its local or national network. Local subsidiaries of externally owned corporations seem to create important links to foreign sub-contractors, and, from the perspective of a local district, seem to organise the channels through which the district goes shopping in the international industrial market place. On the other hand, firms reciprocally connect each other to sales networks nationally and internationally. So though the individual firms have only a few contacts, these contacts are multiplied along the value chain within the wider local context.

Stability of contacts among producers is best explained by referring to the way these relations originate in a system where journeymen travel from one firm to another in their quest to end their careers as managers or entrepreneurs. During such a journey a personal network is gradually built, tying persons across the boundaries of individual firms to each other as friends and colleagues (see also IVTB, 1974: 88), and thereby also creating trust, which both protects against a dualistic structure and the transaction costs of business opportunism. Further, these characteristics of their external relations are reinforced by the firms' internal capabilities. Basing production on standardised machinery and skilled workers, internal flexibility allows them to engage in several relations (Kristensen, 1986). Most sub-contractors are careful not to become dependent on one customer and try to develop their own products to balance business cycles, while end-producers are partly serving as sub-contractors when their normal markets are in recession.

On the other hand, because of their internal characteristics enter-prises often engage in highly customised production. They employ 'teknikum-engineers' as sales people to assist the customer in defin-ing the problems to be solved by the producer and his supporting network. Interviews with development engineers indicate that machinery shops tend to cooperate in the same manner as different crafts do in building and construction (Kristensen, 1988). As a customer, the development engineer contacts a machinery shop or factory, representing a speciality of major importance to the product or machine he wants to construct. Then this machinery shop sub-contracts to other speciality-producers parts of the job, as it is part of their strength to know about other specialists. Through this sub-contracting to specialists, decisions about what to produce and what to buy as standardised components from the inter-national market are parcelled out to people who know what is the cheapest and most competitive solution.

In effect, the Danish business community seems to favour a prin-ciple of complementarity and increasing variability to a system of dualism and narrow, dependent specialisation. And the system seems to be self-generating, as it is an ideal setting for starting new small enterprises. First, if an entrepreneur starts out with the idea of a new product, his own role may for example be reduced to that of a seller, as he can subcontract any number of functions within production and gradually, as his savings increase, build up his own plant to do parts of the production. Second, in such an industrial market, some sub-contractors even develop production facilities for a whole series of firms, for which they do the whole product. Third, many entrepreneurs looking for a yeoman existence can easily set up a subcontracting plant specialising in a certain process. Often skilled foremen or workers, who have been responsible for specific production processes within existing firms, start their own business with promises of having their former firm as first customer, but looking for complementary customers.

The implication of this, of course, is reproduction on an extended scale of the fragmented character of a fragmented industry.

## Corporations at Bay: Internal Limits to Corporate Authority and Strategy

For corporations that strategically aim at creating an integrated industrial corporation through acquisitions, the Danish iron and metal industry seems to offer unlimited opportunities. Most independent enterprises operate in fragmented branches; they do business without the protection of formalised agreements, strong family ties or coordinating organisation. They are on their own in difficult times, and, specialising in narrow niches, they often shift between slumps and booms, both of which place them in a weak financial situation. Corporations are continuously offered the opportunity of buying cheap enterprises and – so it seems – put an end to the industry's fragmentation.

The combination of fragmented industries and powerful corporate groups usually constitutes a very short period in a nation's history. By taking control over an industry, corporate groups normally put an end to its fragmentation. The paradox in Denmark is, however, that powerful corporate groups and fragmented industries have now coexisted for a century.

Waves of mergers have occurred continuously, and within the iron- and metal-working industry they have been impressive during the 1960s, the 1970s and the 1980s. Mergers have been actively supported by the state as taxation has made mergers more favourable than to let a son inherit his father's business; and for many years, taxation has been considerably lower for foundations and limited corporations than for personally-owned firms. But even though corporations have merged and bought out entrepreneurs, they seem to have been unable to provide Danish industry with a clear structure and strategy. Rather, corporations seem to fall victims to the recipes of fragmented business logics of the surrounding business community of small and medium-sized firms.

Anecdotal evidence about how the large Danish industrial corporations have evolved (Bernhard, 1988) or an analytical investigation of a confined period of mergers (Madsen, 1983) invalidate expectations of unfriendly takeovers or corporate headquarters carefully watching independent business enterprises that fall victim to financial troubles. Rather, mergers often follow after a period of technical cooperation between corporations and smaller firms, and are often motivated by the corporation's wish to secure the supply of technical services in exchange for capital, by which the enterprise in question solves its financial troubles. Business units which are merged into the corporation by such means are only related to the corporation through small, and perhaps minor, parts of their activities. Consequently, the firms gradually merged through such acquisitions constitute a heterogeneous group, operating in very different markets. Some few sources of synergy may be identified, but the role of the strategic apex of headquarters is in no way comparable to that of the integrated

American corporation (Chandler, 1977). It is obvious that each business unit's strategy must be determined by its own technology, adapted to its very narrow and specialised markets and to what is happening among a small and very specific group of international competitors.

The role of the corporation becomes much more clear when we change our perspective to that of the individual business unit which has been merged into the group. From such a 'bottom-up' perspective, 'membership' of a 'group of business units' secures access to financial resources, assistance through slumps, financial support to expand production capacity during booms or, finally, the natural gradual modernisation of equipment and machinery.[1] From this perspective the whole group is rather to be conceived as a mutual insurance company in which the individual units, each operating in a narrow niche-market which continuously shifts between high and low demand, contribute to and receive from a common financial fund the necessary means for stabilisation and modernisation. The corporation is rather a holding company playing the same role vis-à-vis its business units as the Japanese combination of financial institutions and the *Shôkôkai* do towards small enterprises (see Friedman, 1988), but without its regional effects. In short, rather than being the end of fragmentation, corporations become a means to stabilise and modernise a fragmented industry. To form such corporate groups of mutual insurance, or holding companies, has never been a formulated strategy within the strategic apexes of these corporations.[2] It should rather be explained as a pattern, effected by a range of causes.

One cause is the strategies formulated in the strategic apexes of these holding companies. During the 1970s and 1980s, following international fashions, its core was one of diversification and organisational divisionalisation. But where their American colleagues typically divisionalised and diversified what had formerly been integrated, to make profit from several rather than from a single mass-produced product, Danish corporations imitated their strategy by acquiring firms in related sectors. These global fashions merged with Danish strategic discourses in the early 1970s: in the form of the 'niche strategy'; that is, the selection of markets which were too small to attract the interest of foreign mass-producing corporations rather than following the common wisdom to do the opposite. Taken together – diversification, divisionalisation and niche-strategy fit well into the rationality of forming corporations to function in concert with the mutual insurance or holding company.

Another cause is the power of craft-workers, perhaps the

strongest impetus behind the choice of the niche strategy (compare Industrirådet, 1974). To be able to keep or recruit skilled workers, business units had to choose products which would often be changed due to customer demand and therefore had to be produced in small batches; in short, products that would call for and be in harmony with skilled workers and a craft organisation of the factory.

The basic power of craft-workers rests on their national mobility by which they can deny an enterprise the institutional support of the craft-educational complex. But craft-workers also exercise power within a factory. Any corporate strategy which tries to ascribe to a craft-organised enterprise a structural role which is contradictory to its work organisation may soon discover a drop in profitability, while respecting and improving on such internal organisation may show up in increasing profits. This selective force works on the local enterprise manager, whom the workers have no formal power to hire or fire, but with whom they can help to realise high or low profits. This power to manipulate economic results works through several mechanisms.

Factories organised by craft principles disperse its basic industrial knowledge among skilled workers rather than among a technocratic apex of the enterprise. Such a factory (Kristensen 1986; 1990c) is rather a system of mini-factories or sub-contracting, highly discrete workers under one roof. In the individual cell of machinery the skilled worker integrates planning, programming, setting, operation, maintenance and even suggests new investments to further the productivity of his small 'shop'. Business in this system is normally conducted through a complicated set of negotiations involving several layers of the organisation (the production workers, foremen, shop stewards, the production manager, the sales and sometimes marketing manager). If trust is high and reciprocal relations are maintained, etc., the system is very efficient as everybody is responsible each for their highly discrete area and is able to act immediately. If, on the other hand, a managing director wants to impose a strategy on the internal organisation, neglecting the complicated routes of negotiation, damaging reciprocal relations or devastating trust, individual workers or foremen can respond simply by 'working according to the rules' and only act on explicit orders. Such a simple reaction has drastic effects, as the firm has previously profited from this organisation, allowing it to save on technicians and administrators. Now it may be simply impossible for managers to issue the necessary orders due to a lack of knowledge about the production technologies and procedures. Further, in the Danish welfare state, a regulated labour market comprising a complex system of general and union-specific, national and local agreements with factories of workers organised in unions for different crafts, for unskilled workers, for gender, etc., much power rests in the hands of shop stewards, as they are among the very few who acquire the experience necessary to work with the 'system'. If trust exists, the shop steward has the knowledge and power needed to make this whole complex collaborate with the firm in mobilising resources. He may do what is needed to ensure the formal acceptance of letting workers work overtime, secure that the workers are undergoing further training to help the firm install new technologies, and even mobilise political alliances needed for getting resources from different sources of the public sector to make new adventures possible for the firm. But if trust is low, reciprocity not sustained, and traditional patterns of negotiation are neglected, it will take an excellent manager to escape from the traps that shop stewards can organise: to be cheated in wage negotiations, to be cut off from keeping promises to an important customer as overtime turned out to be impossible, or to be proven to have broken formal rules, which may bring the manager before the Labour Court.[3] Facing such a situation in the plant he is managing, it takes an unusually determined Board to refrain from blaming the manager for losing orders from major customers, for causing headlines in newspapers, for increasing wage-bills as well as destroying labour relations and productivity. It is much more probable that in the end, the Board will forget about strategy and ask him to stabilise the situation if they do not choose the most simple solution: to fire the incompetent guy and hire another manager, whom they will probably ask to restore confidence and trust-relations to customers and workers rather than to resume implementation of the strategy which initially created the troubles.

## Competing Strategies: Paradoxical Coalitions

Merging craft principles with the principles of the modern capitalist factory, we have shown, has had great impact on the function of both. Rather than destroying the craft life-pattern – apprentice, journeyman and master – the modern factory has elaborated the content and meaning of this life-cycle. As a consequence, industrial factories and enterprises, rather than structuring the population into classes, are fields of class transcendence. This has an effect on the normal dichotomy between management and the workers and creates a field where the art of coalition building does not conform to our theoretical expectations. In particular, the openness of careers and high discretion in jobs on the factory floor do not combine to determine one typical management style; on the contrary. Two very different routes to managerial or technical white-collar positions illustrate the diversity of personal aspirations and of relations towards the labour force which, in part, determine the social psychology of managers.

The first route follows from the fact that career patterns have been established and are open. For that reason our first ideal-type person enrols as an apprentice, looking at the factory and the surrounding craft-educational complex from the perspective of personal advancement. He or she is chasing jobs on the factory floor with a high degree of challenge and prestige and is looking for evening courses and additional educational institutions, which might speed up his or her career opportunities. To him/her the strong position of the unions, group solidarity and the workers' collective actions against management, attempts from shop stewards to negotiate comparable conditions for good and bad jobs and to allocate workers to different jobs in a fair way, all seem to be working against his/her personal ambitions. For that reason s/he becomes increasingly isolated from the collective, and feels that s/he fulfils his or her goals in spite of the prevailing rules, roles and values.

When these ambitions are fulfilled and s/he reaches out for a management position after some years of experience as a skilled worker, s/he has inevitably become isolated from and suspicious of the collective of workers which s/he is now going to manage; s/he will look at the new world of management techniques and methods with admiration and find among them such techniques that will enable him/her to wage war against the workers. In his/her opinion, they need to be controlled, because s/he – for good reasons – suspects them of using any occasion to find ways of cheating. Therefore, s/he uses labour agreements at all levels to ensure that s/he will be able to put his/her workers and shop-stewards in a position that will make them, and not him/her, commit the formal mistakes if the situation comes to a head and is brought before the Labour Court. In short, s/he is extremely apt at playing the game by which skilled workers try to select among managers, and the game itself will confirm expectations and reinforce his/her psychology as a manager.

The other route is almost in every aspect contradictory to the first. Our second ideal-type person is typically a skilled worker whose primary ambition is to use his/her job to stay in a field which satisfies his/her great interest in technology. In his/her job, high discretion is a precondition and s/he sees the craft union as the protector of this right. S/he may be strongly engaged in union politics to support any pressure on management ensuring that s/he and his/her colleagues are guaranteed the right to further training and the right to carry out the implementation of new technologies. S/he feels that it is a personal obligation to ensure that his/her colleagues on the factory floor are offered further training and become involved in the introduction of new technologies. Consequently, even if it entails private sacrifices, s/he is the first one to respond to any request from his/her shop steward to attend further training, to be involved in the instalment and introduction of new machinery and equipment – and also because s/he enjoys to work with new technologies. S/he may even join evening classes during leisure time to further his/her understanding of a new type of technology, for example to learn programming in machine-coding. To his fellow-workers, he will function as a teacher and a competitor, to whom they can turn with a problem and whom they will inform of solutions to problems they might come up with. This friendly cooperation in the shop confirms that he is right about the skills and potentials of his fellow men. In front of management and the technical staff he is the hero, as he will always be able to beat the 'white collars' of the field in which he is presently engaged. Thus he symbolises the protection of the organisation of work through craft principles.

However, managers have strategies towards such persons. Both from fear of losing the competence he has gained if he accepts a better job in another firm, and because they want this competence to become part of management's ability to control the factory, they may make him an offer that he cannot refuse. They may tell him that they will advertise a job for a management position covering the tasks he is currently performing and if he applies for the job, he will get it. If he does not, they will be forced to reposition him in a less challenging job in the factory. In short, he becomes manager and has to leave the workers' collective, the protection and opportunities which his union and shop steward gave him. As a manager his heart belongs to the workers' collective, and he wants to behave in a way which does not reshape the conflicts, start the jokes and rumours which he only knows too well will be provoked by a standard management role. For the management group, he will make suggestions which depart from their wishes and from criticism raised by the workers' collective. He will initiate changes and shape projects that will secure him the participation and cooperation of the factory floor, and be able to cooperate informally with shop stewards. By selecting his projects in this manner, his successes will confirm his expectations and help to reinforce the psychology by which he manages.

Of course, these two ideal-type management personalities, styles and strategies are just two poles in a much fuller and more varied spectrum. The implications of such differences among the managers, however, are far-reaching. The split between what we could call universal ideals of management techniques and methods, the universalised principles of factory and enterprise organisation and idealised concepts of strategy and structure for industrial firms on the one hand, and craft organisation on the other, is no longer a split between managers and workers, but rather an intrinsic conflict of the functioning of both the management team and the workers' collective. A continuous competition has been revealed within the enterprise among two – or, most often, more – coalitions, neither of which respects the traditional patterns of coalition behaviour which in organisation theory have been connected to the advancement of departmental interests in the competitive game for resources.

Thus, the firm has institutionalised a competitive game among two groups capable of suggesting very different types of investment projects, reorganisations etc., which they will seek to advance whenever the shifting contingencies among top managers and boards allow it. And we have shown that contingencies will often change, for many internal and external reasons. In effect, any factory studied is shaped by a long series of small incremental investment decisions, often mutually incoherent, and a series of modifications through which the two management types and the two groups within the 'workers collective' have tried to beat each other. Consequently, the factory is characterised by a range of different work stations representing a history of shifting strategies. In other words, fragmentation is deeply rooted in the factories.

### Notes

1 These functions were repeated by some managers of local business units belonging to corporations in my investigation of medium-sized enterprises within the iron- and metal-working industry (see Kristensen, 1986).

2 These observations are, however, not due to careful investigations or interviews with corporate headquarters, but my impressions from following the business press during a decade.

3 The Labour Court is part of the institutional complex by which unions and employers' associations agreed to regulate the Danish labour market at the turn of the century. Though many agreements are still signed locally or at the level of individual crafts and industries, central institutions play a crucial role in setting national frames, sanctioning and the rhythm for doing agreements. To limit strikes and lockouts to the period when negotiations on central agreements are taking place, the Labour Court has been institutionalised to solve conflicts among the parties, and to impose a fine on the party who is convicted of having broken a legal agreement.

# References

Andersen, H. (1966) *Hvem ejer Danmark?* Copenhagen: Fremad.

Bernhard, B. (ed.) (1988) *Sådan skabtes Danmarks store virksomheder.* Copenhagen: Erhvervs-Bladets Forlag.

Chandler, A.D. (1977) *The Visible Hand. The Managerial Revolution in American Business.* Cambridge, MA: Harvard University Press.

Friedman, D. (1988) *The Misunderstood Miracle: Industrial Development and Political Change in Japan.* Ithaca, NY: Cornell University Press.

Frøslev Christensen, J. (1981) *Erhvervsstruktur, Teknologi og Levevilkar*, vol. 2. Copehagen: Lavindkomstkommisionens Sekretariat.

Grøn, J.H. (1985) *Arbejde-Virksomheder-Regioner.* Esbjerg: Sydjysk Universitetsforlag.

Guldager, J. (1978) *Monopolkapital i Danmark i begyndelsen af 1970'erne.* Viborg: Politisk Revy.

Hansen, S.Aa. (1970) *Industri og håndværk.* Copenhagen: GAD's Forlag.

Hansen, S.Aa. (1983) *Økonomisk vækst i Danmark, vol. 2: 1914–1983.* Copenhagen: Akademisk Forlag.

Hartoft-Nielsen, P. (1980) *Den regionale erhvervsstruktur- og beskæftigelsesudvikling.* Copenhagen: Lavindkomstkommisionens Sekretariat.

Hartoft-Nielsen, P. (1985) 'Industriens regionale udvikling i Danmark', in Illeris and Pedersen (1985).

Illeris, S. (1991) *The Herning-Ikast Textile Industry: an Industrial District in West Jutland.* Working Paper, Roskilde University, typescript.

Illeris, S. and Pedersen, P.O. (eds) (1985) *Industrien – koncentration eller spredning.* Copenhagen: AKF.

Industrirådet (1974) *Industrivirksomhedens produktpolitik.* Copenhagen: Industrirådet.

IVTB (1974) *Erhvervsudvikling i Nordjylland. 2 del-rapport: Industrien i Små Nordjyske byer.* IVTB, Danmarks Tekniske Højskole, Lyngby.

Johannsen, B. and Olsen, P. (undated) *Magtkoncentrationen i Dansk Erhvervsliv – de store koncerner, banker og dagblade belyst med hensyn til magtkoncentrationen.* Arbejdsnotat no. 14 (Working Paper), Specialarbejderforbundets vækstkommision, Copenhagen.

Kjeldsen-Kragh, S. (1973) *Specialisering og konkurrenceevne.* Copenhagen: Nyt Nordisk Forlag.

Kristensen, P.H. (1986) *Teknologiske projekter og organisatoriske processer.* Roskilde: Forlaget Samfundsøkonomi og Planlægning.

Kristensen, P.H. (1988) 'Virksomhedsperspektiver på industripolitikken: industrimodernister og industriens husmæend', *Politica.* 2 (3): 282–97.

Kristensen, P.H. (1990a) 'Denmark's Concealed Production Culture, its Socio-historical Construction and Dynamics at Work', in F. Borum, and P.H. Kristensen (1990) *Technological Innovation and Organizational Change – Danish Patterns of Knowledge, Networks and Culture.* Copenhagen: New Social Science Monographs. pp. 165–88.

Kristensen, P.H. (1990b) 'Education, Technical Culture and Regional Prosperity in Denmark', in Sweeney (ed.) (1990), *Education, Technical Culture and Regional Prosperity.* Dublin: SICA.

Kristensen, P.H. (1990c) 'Technical Projects and Organizational Changes: Flexible Specialization in Denmark', in Warner et al. (eds), *New Technology and*

*Manufacturing Management. Strategic Choices for Flexible Production Systems.*
Chichester: Wiley. 159–90.

Kristensen, P.H. (1992) 'Industrial Districts in West Jutland, Denmark', in F. Pyke
and W. Sengenberger (eds) *Industrial Districts and Local Economic Regeneration.*
Geneva: IILS, ILO. pp. 122–74.

Kristensen, P.H. and Sabel, C.F. (forthcoming) 'The Trusts and the Yeoman
Republic: the Organization of Small Scale Production in Danish Industry and
Agriculture' in C.F. Sabel and J. Zeitlin (eds), *Worlds of Possibility: Flexibility
and Mass Production in Western Industrialization.*

Madsen, O.Ø. (1983) *Virskomhedsovertagelser og fusioner i dansk industri.*
Copenhagen: Nyt Nordisk Forlag.

Maskell, P. (1982) *Industriens regionale omlokalisering 1970–1980.* TTR,
Copenhagen Business School, Copenhagen, typescript.

Maurice, M., Sellier, F. and Silvestre, J-J. (1986) *The Social Bases of Industrial
Power.* Cambridge, MA: MIT Press.

Planstyrelsen (1990) *Tendenser i den regionale udvikling i Danmark.* Copenhagen:
Ministry of the Environment.

Pyke, F. et al. (eds) (1991) *Industrial Districts and Interfirm Co-operation in Italy.*
Geneva: IILS, ILO.

Sabel, C.F. (1990) *Skills without a Place: the Reorganization of the Corporation
and the Experience of Work.* Address to the Plenary Session of the British
Sociological Association, April 1990, typescript.

Senghaas, D. (1982) *Von Europa Lernen. Entwicklungsgeschichtliche
Betrachtungen.* Frankfurt-am-Main: Campus Verlag.

Whitley, R.D. (1990) 'Eastern Asian Enterprise Structures and the Comparative
Analysis of Forms of Business Organization', *Organization Studies.* 11(1): 47–74.

Willerslev, R. (1952) *Studier i dansk industrihistorie, 1850–1880.* Copenhagen.

# 6
# A Dominant Business Recipe:
# the Forest Sector in Finland

*Kari Lilja, Keijo Räsänen and Risto Tainio*

## Finland as a Forest Sector Society

In the European context Finland has been used as an example of how backward starting conditions for industrialisation and raw-material-based exports need not lead to a monocultural exclave economy (Senghaas, 1985: 72). Instead, Finnish forest firms have been able to create a dynamic growth path with a constantly widening scale of exports and, especially since the 1960s, with foreign direct investments in order to establish a European-wide production and distribution system. At the present time Finnish corporations are leading exporters in many paper product groups worldwide. How can this be explained?

We claim that the underlying reason for the sustained competitive advantage lies in the characteristics of the Finnish forest sector. This sector is constituted by forestry, mechanical forest industry (sawmills, plywood and particle board etc.) and chemical forest industry (pulp and paper), and several related supplier industries (energy, chemicals, machines, maintenance services etc.) and customer industries (paper converters). Through the interest organisations of these economic fields and their relations to the political parties and the state, the forest sector is also part of the political core of the Finnish society. Thus it is no wonder that Finnish social science has generated many accounts of this complex whole (Seppälä et al., 1980; Koskinen, 1983; Raumolin, 1984). The existence and importance of this sector has mostly been taken for granted, although its precise nature and its boundaries have remained ambiguous and most studies have been concerned with its specific aspects. Our own research in the field of management studies has continued this tradition (e.g. Lilja, 1989; Räsänen, 1989; Räsänen and Kivisaari, 1989; Tainio et al., 1989; Lilja et al., 1991).

Recently, several organisation and management researchers have started to redefine the object of their research towards broader, and at the same time looser, entities (e.g. Child, 1988). Attention is shifting from single organisations to configurations of markets and firms, to the ways in which business activities are organised within and between firms in different historical and national contexts. This shift of focus is very helpful for our attempts to understand Finnish firms and their management. New conceptual innovations have been made which highlight the relevance of our old research object, the forest sector, and relate it to similar or analogous phenomena in other countries.

Richard Whitley (1990; 1991) is one of those who have launched new concepts to describe the nationally specific features of economic action. His notions of the 'national business recipes' and more recently the 'business system' are instrumental in opening up new perspectives for country-specific and comparative studies. Although the meanings of these notions are still evolving and somewhat ambiguous, they are still useful in setting up new research questions, and in the Finnish case they provide a way to describe and interpret the old story of the forest sector in a new way.

The purpose of this chapter is to explain the international success of the Finnish forest corporations from their sectoral foundations. We will first demonstrate that Finnish forest industry corporations have, indeed, been able to create and sustain a strong position in worldwide international markets. Second, we turn to the description of the wider network of actors and institutions which have secured the long-term international success of the Finnish forest industry corporations. We outline the business recipe of the Finnish forest sector and the ways in which it has been possible to mobilise diverse actors, even with opposing interests and rationalities, into a huge collective project – this has occurred generation after generation from the construction of the first mill sites to the current stage of operating internationalised corporations. In the final section, we will discuss the implications of this Finnish case. The main lesson is that the success of the Finnish forest industry corporations cannot be understood without the resources created collectively by the exceptional history, shape and national position of the forest sector.

## The International Success of the Finnish Forest Corporations

The heavy emphasis on the forest industry in Finland dates back to the founding period of the Finnish forest industry in the 1860s. Around that time inventions were made which allowed the use of wood chips in the making of paper. This changed the value of forests completely. At that time Finland was part of Russia as a Grand Duchy. The Russian markets formed a large home market for the Finnish forest firms, which could expand their capacity for exports behind the shelter of a customs barrier unlike the competing Western European paper companies. The railway connections to Russia were excellent for transportation from the south-eastern part of Finland. Thus, besides the abundance of raw materials, the closeness of a large home market was the major inducement for the specialisation in the forest industry in Finland.

The sustained success of the Finnish paper industry corporations at the international level can be demonstrated by the statistics on the market share of world exports in paper products. As to the market share of world exports between 1960 and 1989, Finnish firms have kept a very stable market share in paper and board amounting to 14.4 per cent in 1989. The overall picture shows that the market share has fallen in the more standardised products and grown in the more high-value-added products. There is a rather dramatic drop in the market share of world pulp exports: in 1960 the share was 16.6 per cent and in 1989 6.5 per cent. This is due to the increasing vertical integration of the production system. In sawn goods the trend has been similar: decreasing from 13.6 per cent to 4.6 per cent over this 29-year period. The most remarkable point is that in printing and writing papers the market share of Finnish firms has remained the highest: in 1960 21.5 and in 1989 30.5 per cent. About 80 per cent of the total production in the forest industry is exported.

Rather few large corporations lie behind these figures. The largest are the following: Repola (which owns United Paper Mills), Kymmene, Enso-Gutzeit and Metsä-Serla. They produce a wide range of pulp, paper and board products. Moreover, they have all specialised in a couple of product groups where they have an internationally significant position. Thus, for instance, Kymmene has specialised in lightweight coated (LWC) printing papers, for which it has a Europe-wide production system. In Finland there are two mill sites where LWC is produced with three paper machines. It has built greenfield sites in Germany and the UK and bought a French company (Chapelle Darplay), which has been strong in LWC production (see Table 6.1). In 1990 Kymmene was the second largest producer of LWC paper in the world with a capacity of about one million tons. The largest producer was Feldmuhle (*HS*, 29 May 1990) (acquired by the Swedish corporation Stora). Similarly, United Paper Mills is the largest producer in the world of supercalendered (SC) printing papers. It is also the second largest producer in the European newsprint market with a Finnish

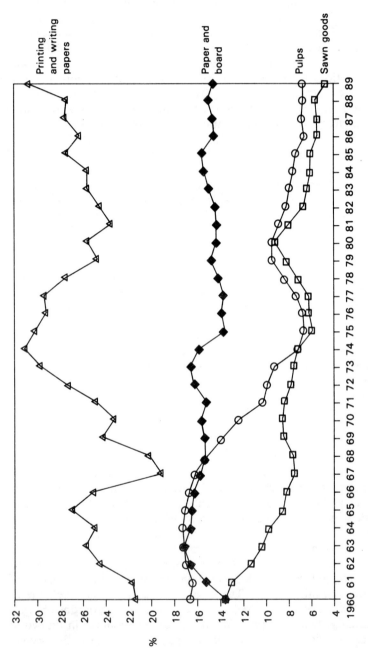

Figure 6.1   *The Finnish forest industry's shares of the world market, 1960–89 (Source: CAFFI, Annual Statistics, 1990)*

Table 6.1   *The capacity of coated printing papers of*
*Kymmene in different European countries*

| Country | Mill | Number of machines | Grades | Capacity |
|---------|------|--------------------|--------|----------|
| Finland | Kaukas | 2 | LWC, MWC | 430,000 |
|         | Voikkaa | 3 | MFC, LWC | 250,000 |
| U.K. (Caledonian Paper) | Irvine | 1 | LWC | 210,000 |
| France (Chapelle Darplay) | Rouen | 3 | LWC | 250,000 |

LWC/MWC = coated mechanical printing papers
MFC = machine finished coated.

*Source*: Kymmene Oy, Annual Report, Kymmene Paper Chain, 1990, 1991

home base at Kaipola and Kajaani combined with two paper machines in the UK (Shotton) and one in France (Stracell). Enso is a large producer of liquid packaging carton board and its fine paper division (Tervakoski, Varkaus and Kaukopää) has internationalised through its majority share of the Berghuizer paper company in the Netherlands. Metsä-Serla has been a large exporter of chemical pulp and became the largest producer of tissue papers in the Nordic countries with the acquisition of Holmen Hygiene (now Metsä-Serla AB).

In addition to these internationalised divisions in the main product groups of the pulp, paper and board industry, there are some nich-players which have been able to acquire a significant market share worldwide or in Europe in a narrow product segment with an internationalised production and distribution system. The most notable of these is Ahlstrom's special paper division, and especially its position in the filter paper markets. The production system covers, besides a Finnish mill in Kauttua, mills in Italy (Cartiere Bosso), Germany (Kämmerer), South Korea (Ahlstrom Korea Co.) and the USA (Filtration Sciencies Inc.). In the label business Raflatac and in release papers Lohjan Paperi, both owned by United Paper Mills, have taken similar steps like Ahlstrom on the European scale, being in the leading strategic groups of the respective industries.

It is true that the forest industry corporations are not the only Finnish corporations that have successfully internationalised. There are interesting examples from other industries, but a considerable part of the other corporations operate as suppliers to the forest

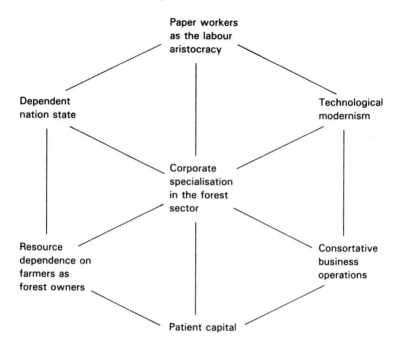

Figure 6.2    *The business recipe of the Finnish forest sector*

industry. In forest industry machinery businesses the Finnish corporations can show similar or even larger market shares on the international scale than the chemical forest industry divisions of the Finnish firms. Thus, for instance, in 1988–9 the market share of Valmet Corporation in paper machines was 22 per cent, clearly the largest of all companies in that business. This is a rather recent phenomenon stemming from the 1970s and 1980s and was based on the large home market created by the exceptional concentration of forest industry firms in Finland.

The continuing success of the leading Finnish paper industry companies on the European scale sets out the questions: how has it been possible and what are the underlying mechanisms for the success? In order to answer these questions a business recipe for the Finnish forest sector will be described and its evolution discussed.

### The Forest Sector Recipe as a Foundation for Competitive Advantages

On the basis of our earlier studies and other related research on the Finnish forest sector (Seppälä et al., 1980; Koskinen, 1983;

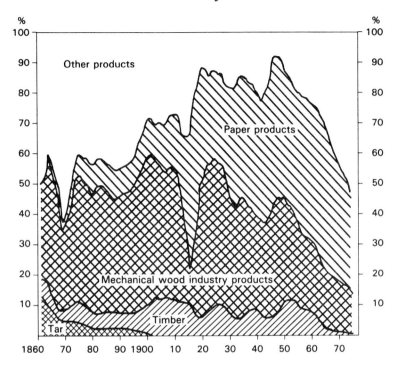

Figure 6.3 *The value of exports of forest industry products as a percentage of total exports in Finland, 1860–1977* (*Source*: Seppälä et al., 1980: 10)

Raumolin, 1984), we suggest that it forms a totality which can be described with seven characteristics (see Figure 6.2). In these aspects Finnish firms and Finnish institutional conditions differ considerably from those of other nations.

*Corporate Specialisation in the Forest Sector*
When looking at the list of the largest Finnish manufacturing corporations we find a disproportionate amount of corporations which have their main business in the forest industry. In 1985, there were 41 manufacturing corporations among the top 100 firms, of which 18 (44 per cent) originated from the forest industry (Räsänen, 1989: Appendix A). Because 90 per cent of the inputs of this industry come from Finland, the industry has huge multiplier effects to the economy as a whole. Until the end of the 1950s about 90 per cent of export incomes came from the forest industry. Even in 1988, 38 per cent of Finnish exports came from the forest

industry, of which 69 per cent was paper products (*Paper and Timber*, 1990: 87–8). Such specialisation is not uncommon in other small or underdeveloped countries, but the forest sector is nowhere else the economic engine of the country.

Because saw mills, pulp mills and paper mills were established by the side of rapids and along the waterways, far from the towns, the forest industry companies had to create the whole infrastructure for the mills and for the community. Thus the forest industry has had a decisive impact on community formation in Finland (as well as on other patterns of habitation, especially in the periphery, because of the need for part-time forestry workers). The leadership shown in the formation of new communities led to a mill-village and company-town tradition which emphasised the self-sufficiency of the company and community. One consequence of this was the tendency to diversify into new businesses. The maintenance shops were developed into engineering firms, the power plants supplied electricity and energy to the communities, the construction department took care of housing needs etc. From such a perspective it can be understood that at present the forest sector covers a very wide set of activities in Finland: besides forestry and forest industries it contains supplier and service industries such as parts of the energy, machine-making and chemical industries, as well as the maintenance and consulting services.

It has not, however, always been evident that the forest industry would have such a dominant position in the Finnish economy. In the nineteenth century the textile industry was most of the time larger than the forest industry. Since the 1960s firms in other industries have been able to export their products, and during the 1970s and 1980s the metal and chemical industries internationalised rapidly (Räsänen, 1989). Thus during booms there has been a general belief that Finnish firms could be competitive in world markets in other industries as well as the forest industry. Even the forest industry companies have diversified into other industries. But in the recessions, which have hit the forest industry very heavily, these corporations have been compelled to fortify their core businesses and withdraw from other industries.

One of the latest challenges to the forest-industry-led economic system came from Nokia and its charismatic CEO, Kari Kairamo. Kairamo launched a campaign which advocated a vision that Finland should become an 'information society' instead of a forest sector society. The latter was labelled as being old-fashioned 'smokestack industry'. Nokia itself had become the largest private corporation in Finland, with a considerable position in the electronics industry on a European scale (Lovio, 1989). The contest was won by the forest industry during the long boom at the end of the 1980s. Their investments in modern machines and in the product development paid off. They were also able to get their message across that the modern paper industry is in fact a science-based, high-technology industry. Nokia in turn had difficulties in consolidating its acquisitions in consumer electronics in Germany and Sweden. It was compelled to sell its computer division to ICL. Its size is not sufficiently large to become a developer of new technologies in the electronic industry, and the supporting infrastructure in the form of a 'Silicon Valley' is missing from Finland.

Thus the specialisation in the forest industry in Finland has resulted in a high concentration of internationally competent paper industry corporations which have mills and mill communities geographically close to each other. This has led to a keen competition for upgraded products and production processes. There are several mechanisms which enable the rapid diffusion of innovations across company borders despite attempts to keep improvements as business secrets. These mechanisms include the closeness of the mills to each other, networks derived from the educational institutions, a joint R & D research institute, professional societies, consulting firms, suppliers of machines and systems and career paths from one corporation to another. Companies which have failed in their modernisation efforts have found a safety network in the industry because they have been acquired by firms with stronger resources.

*Patient Capital*

The forest industry is capital-intensive, with long pay-back periods for investments. There are heavy fluctuations in demand and prices for forest industry products which make the income streams of the industry very volatile, and the long-term profitability of the industry is not high. In Finland these features of the industry were first learned by the private investors who started the businesses in the 1860s. They recognised very early that they had to establish commercial banks which would pool resources from a wider public and then lend these resources on a long-term basis to the forest industry firms. In this way the financial system became credit-based. The forest industry firms have been closely connected to certain banks and currently we can characterise the Finnish forest industry firms as being linked to three bank groups: to an originally 'Swedish-speaking' commercial bank, to a 'Finnish-speaking' commercial bank and to a cooperative bank group originating from the farmers' economic activities. Besides these there is a fourth group: the state-owned forest industry corporations.

The banks have acquired an in-depth expertise on the nature of the forest industry. Their CEOs sit on the boards of the forest industry corporations. However, this dependence is reciprocal, since the banks are also dependent on their key customers. These complicated relationships have taught both the private investors and the banks that the forest industry can survive only with patient capital.

The linkage of the forest industry firms (as well as other large industrial firms) to the bank groups in Finland bear a resemblance to the situation in Germany, where the industrial firms are also connected to 'patient' banks (cf. Chandler, 1990). Banks and institutional investors treat their shares in the core firms as strategic investments where benefits are reaped from the long-term growth of the value of the holding. The taxation policies of the state also support long-term investments. Thus the financial institutions in the Finnish case differ very much from the Anglo-American financial markets (Zysman, 1983). An additional explanation for the long-term involvement of the banks is that personal savings were supported by the state by allowing tax-exempt deposit accounts. The interest rates for savings and lendings were regulated, which secured a favourable margin and automatic profits for the banks. But there was also a mechanism which created 'forced' savings by the great majority of the population. The housing system has been based on family ownership and the market for renting a house or an apartment has been very limited. Because there has been a constant flow of labour force from the countryside to towns, and recently to the larger towns, there has been a need to constantly build and buy new houses. The housing market has been financed almost totally by the banks. Until 1987 the rules for lending money were very strict: the borrower had to save a considerable part of the capital needed for an apartment or a house. For this reason the rate of savings in Finland has been one of the highest in the world after the Second World War, reaching the level of Japan for long periods of time.

During the years from 1985 to 1990 Finland experienced a development towards a capital-market system. The pursuit for short-term profits from operations in the stock exchange or in global financial markets became routine practice not only for banks but also for corporations operating in manufacturing and trade. Foreign capital was also attracted to buy Finnish stocks. The forest industry was, however, relatively little affected by this finance-driven phase in the Finnish economy. The ownership structures of the Finnish forest industry corporations were protected as a national property and the cash flows were very favourable for that industry, especially between the years 1986 to 1989. With the current recession there is again a dramatic return to the credit-based financial system.

## Technological Modernism

Until very recently, the career of a university-educated engineer has been highly esteemed in Finland. Thus the competition to get into the technological universities has been very keen and this field of knowledge has attracted bright young men. It has also been a widely shared dream of the craft-workers that their sons could become engineers. The Finnish educational system has supported this type of upward mobility.

The forest industry has been one of the major employers of engineers. It is also typical that the forest industry has been led by engineers in Finland. They have been the bearers of a belief in technological modernism. This means a constant search for the most updated technological solutions irrespective of where they have been invented. Such a search has been backed by an education in technological universities where a broad, science-based view of *Technik* in the German style is linked to specific problems of the forest industry (cf. Child et al., 1983). This enabled the transfer of up-to-date technology into Finland and little by little its own Finnish-based solutions have been created. By the 1960s the Finnish engineering companies had become competitive in world markets for supplying machines to the forest industry. This was helped by the demanding domestic markets, while in Finland the rate of investment in the pulp and paper industry has been one of the highest in the world. The programme of technological modernism has been carried out in practice. Finnish know-how and consulting expertise on forest industry is competitive on a worldwide scale. The best known companies are Jaakko Pöyry Oy and Ekono Oy.

The pressure for this orientation which we have called 'technological modernism' stems from the fact that Finnish paper mills are far away from the customers located in other European countries. To overcome the bigger transportation costs and the distance disadvantage compared with the continental European countries, the Finnish mills have to lower their unit costs by economies of scale and scope (cf. Chandler, 1990). This has led to the construction of integrated mills which can use all kinds of wood as raw material, which is bought and transferred to the mill site. Thus the integrated site contains saw mills, pulp mills and power plants, and after the paper production phase in the value-added chain there may be paper converting factories. Integrated mill sites have special advantages in logistics. This is important because transport costs are 17 per cent of all costs in the forest industry (*Paper and Timber*, 1990: 88, Fig. 5).

Another indicator of the technological modernism of the Finnish paper industry is the way Finnish firms have accomplished their internationalisation. Finnish firms have in several cases built completely new mills in foreign countries instead of buying existing mills. For instance, United Paper Mills has had a special mill construction and start-up team which has completed seven machine projects during the 1980s both in Finland and abroad.

Though the Finnish forest industry has been aggressive in its investments in completely new establishments, there has been also a constant drive for the upgrading of capacity and product range. This has required constant incremental improvements in the production process by removing bottlenecks and experimenting with new production technologies (Lilja, 1989). One of the main innovations in this respect has been the introduction of on-line coating for paper. Today coated papers contain about 30 per cent of minerals and chemicals. The role of wood chips has thus rapidly diminished.

*Consortative Business Operations*
Perhaps in no other country are there so many types of cooperation and pooling of resources as in the case of the Finnish forest industry. There is cooperation and joint ventures in all kinds of business operations. The most significant form of cooperation has been the joint sales associations for the various forest industry products. This cooperation was started for the Russian markets in the 1880s and has continued until the present day. In this way the Finnish firms have established good visibility in the markets; they have been able to have sales offices around the world and these offices have been able to offer a full set of pulp and paper products to the customers. In contrast, the Swedish firms have had their own sales offices. Only after 1987 did Enso and, since 1991, Kymmene completely withdraw from the sales associations. Other fields where there has been cooperation include wood procurement, transportation of raw wood and export deliveries, process and product development, regulation of investments, etc.

*Resource Dependence on Farmers as Forest Owners*
In Finland the main owners of the forests are the farmers. In Sweden the forest industry firms own a third of the forests and in

Canada the forests are owned mainly by the state, which then gives the forest industry firms rights to take the raw wood into production. In Finland the production of forest industry products is possible only if the farmers sell their woods. By their control of the critical raw material the farmers have been able to lift the price of the raw wood to the highest in the world. This situation has created unique institutions, like national price negotiations for the raw wood, state-supported forestry programmes, wide-scale research on forestry which in the 1960s led to the cultivation of forests, and so on.

It was not clear at the beginning that the farmers would remain the forest owners when the 'green gold' began to be valuable. Firms and entrepreneurs rushed to buy land from farmers and this became a hot political issue. However, because farmers had a strong position in the parliament which was elected after 1906 on the basis of general suffrage, they were able to introduce a law in 1915 which prevented firms from buying land from farmers, and because firms could use middlemen in their deals a new and stricter law was issued in 1925. This law ended the struggle between farmers and forest industry firms, to the benefit of the former, and their strong bargaining power became established.

The dispersed ownership structure of the forests had a profound influence on the domestic economy because the main export industry did not form an enclave in society. On the contrary, it was integrated backwards even to the most remote countryside. These areas were kept inhabited via land reforms after the First and Second World Wars in order to secure part-time labour for forestry. The incomes from the raw wood and from forestry work have kept the countryside alive in a thinly populated country. But the farmers have not only stayed in the periphery: they have integrated forward into the forest industry and to banking via their cooperative movement. Through their interest organisation and political party they have held a strong position in the power structure of the Finnish society. It is unique in an industrialised country and can be understood only from the point of view of the forest ownership.

The high price of raw wood is clearly a disadvantage to the Finnish forest industry, but it has contributed to innovations in forestry management. Since the 1960s scientific methods have been applied in the cultivation of forests and investments are made in forests although they benefit only the next generation in the owning family. The result of this has been that the productivity of forests has grown and Finnish forest industry firms have been able to carry out their investments to expand their production capacity.

Because of the high price of the raw wood, innovations have to be made in the buying of wood, in forestry work and in its transport. This has led to the development of new forestry machinery and the mechanisation of forestry work. Forestry workers have, to a great extent, been replaced by private machine-owners. The high price of wood has also promoted the internationalisation of the Finnish forest industry because corporations have established mills in countries with lower raw wood prices.

### Paper Workers as the Labour Aristocracy

The continuity of the production process is the key factor in the capital-intensive process industry. The skills of the workforce and their willingness to cooperate in the management of the mills are necessary conditions for the usage of the production capacity. This has given the key paper workers a bargaining power which is well acknowledged by the employers. For this reason they have paid special attention to the terms of employment of the critical craft-workers in the pulp and paper mills.

Paper workers as a whole have not always been a labour aristocracy in Finland. It was only the machine tenders at the top of the career ladder who had an employment contract, which was beyond the reach of ordinary manual workers. This tradition came about in Finland during the founding period because at that time the key craft-workers were imported from foreign countries with their masters and technical directors. After one generation the key positions were taken over by Finnish workers. The difference between wage-labour in general and that of the paper workers was that the continuity of the contract was much more stable in the paper industry communities than elsewhere. The well-being of the workers in the paper industry communities was based first on a paternalistic concern of the employer to secure a stable labour force (see Koskinen, 1987). With the automation of control processes the number of workers has decreased. This has facilitated the broadening of benefits among the work force. For this reason the status differences between different jobs in the control rooms have also decreased. Employers maintain that workers have lost their motivation to learn new jobs because promotions do not improve the wages very much. To avoid this problem some employers pay the workers according to the number of jobs they are able to perform.

At the end of the 1960s the paper workers were able to introduce a system of productivity bargaining which allows them a share of productivity increases. This also explains the fact that workers have not resisted the technological modernisation of the pulp and paper mills. Since that time the increased benefits have been distributed more evenly across the whole labour force in the paper industry, and by the beginning of the 1990s workers as a whole in the paper industry appear as a labour aristocracy.

The Finnish system of industrial relations is based on industrial unionism and an exceptionally high density of unionisation. It has been characterised in international comparisons as being a conflict model. The strike-proneness of Finnish workplaces resembles that of Italy and France and deviates completely from the Scandinavian countries (Lilja, 1992). Thus it is very remarkable that the pulp and paper industry does not comply with the overall conflictual image of the Finnish industrial relations. For instance, there has not been an industry-wide strike related to collective bargaining in the paper industry since the beginning of industry-level collective bargaining in 1944. There have, however, been some industry-wide action days and it is also true that some paper mills have been bastions of working-class militancy (Kohtanen and Kauppinen, 1989). These workplaces, however, constitute an exception.

### Dependent Nation State

There are a number of different types of indicator which depict the dependency of the Finnish state on the forest industry. The strongest claim is that Finnish independence would not have been possible without industrialisation based on a domestically owned natural resource. Certainly the formation of all kinds of economic institutions were inspired by nationalistic ideas and they served simultaneously to strengthen the national identity. Finland differs from the Baltic states in that it has an economic engine which has been capable of exporting to the most developed countries in Europe. The dominance of the forest products in Finnish exports is astonishing: after 1920 and until 1960 it was on average above 80 per cent. Thus macro-economic policies have been forced to support the main export industry. A clear indication of this has been the periodic devaluations of the Finnish mark when the competitiveness of forest industry products have failed, mainly due to domestic cost pressures (Tainio et al., 1989: 101–2, 107, 110).

The Finnish political elite has arisen very much from the institutions of the forest sector. This is the case with several prime ministers and even presidents. Thus they have had an intimate understanding of the interests of the forest owners and the forest industry. For this reason the interest organisations of the forest sector have seldom launched visible public campaigns to further their interests. Good personal links have been enough to convince the government to look after the viability of the forest sector. One further reason for the strength of the forest sector at the national political level is the class alliance of the farmers and the bourgeoisie. As owners of forests, and increasingly of the forest industry, farmers have similar interests to the owners of the export industries. With their interest organisation and political party, currently called the Centre Party, the farmers have widened the social base of the politics which support the interests of the forest sector.

## One-Sector Dominance in the Finnish Business System

We have demonstrated that the leading forest industry corporations have achieved significant success in international markets for a variety of paper products and have maintained their position for over a hundred years and even expanded it. We have argued that the basis for the sustained development of the competitive advantage of the Finnish paper industry corporations is to be found in the business recipe of the Finnish forest sector. We suggest that the Finnish forest sector should be understood as an historically evolving whole of interrelated economic, social and political actions. The sector in its various forms of appearance has been an important mobiliser of economic, social and political resources to the forest industry corporations.

Nation states are formed by a variety of economic sectors which try to impose their business recipe for the national business system with its variety of institutions. Thus each national business system can be expected to have multiple, competing and internally contested sector-specific recipes simultaneously. The contested nature of the business recipes both inside the sectors and between the sectors constitute the dynamics through which national business systems evolve. Most large countries have many well-developed sectors and therefore the relevance of sectors in them is difficult to recognise. The methodological significance of the Finnish case is related to the fact that its national business system is dominated by one large and widely diversified sector. Thus Finland is a laboratory for the study of the evolution of a sector which has attracted firms from more and more industries (cf. Räsänen and Whipp, Chapter 2 in this volume).

The dominance of the forest sector is not based on a large quantitative contribution to the gross national product. It is based on economic, social and political mechanisms. The demand for domestic raw materials, export incomes and the multiplier effects to the Finnish economy reproduce its economic significance. Its social base is in the local communities, forest owners, professional networks and ethnic homogeneity of the Finnish people. These conditions contribute also to the political dominance of the forest sector within the nation state. Its political power is mediated by strong interest organisations and political representation, which has secured state support for the development of the forest sector.

Despite the established position of the forest sector in the Finnish society there have been attempts to impose alternative recipes for the national economy and the national institutions. An example of that was the vision to turn Finland into an information society with well-developed industries to support that recipe. If, even in the extreme Finnish case, the total dominance of one recipe has been questioned, then the competition of different recipes is an essential in the analysis of all national business systems.

## References

CAFFI (Central Association of the Finnish Forest Industries) (1990) *Annual Statistics*. 1990.

Chandler, A.J. (1990) *Scale and Scope: Dynamics of Industrial Capitalism*. Cambridge, MA: Harvard University Press.

Child, John (1988) 'On Organizations in "Their Sectors"' *Organization Studies*. 9 (1): 13-19.

Child, J., Fores, M., Glover, I. and Lawrence, P. (1983) 'A Price to Pay? Professionalism in Work Organiztion in Britain and West Germany', *Sociology*. 17 (1): 63-78.

*Helsingin Sanomat (HS)* 'Suurimmat Iwc-paperin tuottajat'. 29 May 1990.

Kohtanen, Jukka and Kauppinen, Timo (1989) 'Työtaistelut ja neuvottelusuhteet paperiteollisuudessa vuosina 1971-1984'. Helsinki: *Työelämän suhteiden neuvottelukunta*. 2/1989.

Koskinen, Tarmo (1983) 'Metsäsektori sosiaalisena ja sosiologisena kysymyksenä Suomessa', in T. Koskinen and K. Lilja, *Työ, talous, yhteiskunta*. University of Vaasa, Research Reports No. 92.

Koskinen, Tarmo (1987) *Tehdasyhteisö. Tutkimus tehtaan ja kylän kutoutumisesta tehdasyhteisöksi, kudelman säilymisestä ja purkautumisesta*. University of Vaasa, Research Reports No. 123.

Kymmene Oy (1990/1991) Annual Report, 1990, 1991, Kymmene Oy (1991), Kymmene Paper Chain.

Lilja, Kari (1989) *Epics and Epochs: Organisational Learning and the Kaskinen Pulp Mill*. Helsinki School of Economics, Working Paper F-232.

Lilja, Kari (1992) 'Finland: No Longer the Nordic Exception', in R. Hyman and A. Ferner (eds), *Industrial Relations in the New Europe*. Oxford: Blackwell.

Lilja, K., Räsänen, K. and Tainio, R. (1991) 'Development of Finnish Corporations: Paths and Recipes' in J. Näsi (ed.), *Arenas of Strategic Thinking*. Helsinki: Foundation for Economic Education. pp. 275-92.

Lovio, R. (1989) *Suomalainen menestystarina?* Helsinki: Hanki ja Jää.

*Paper and Timber* (1990) 'The Finnish forest industry – an overview', *Paper and Timber*. 72 (2): 86-98.

Räsänen, K. (1989) *Corporate Evolution in a Forest-sector Society: Sectoral Roots* and *Strategic Change of Finnish Corporations, 1973-1985*. Working Paper 89-11, EIASM, Brussels.

Räsänen, Keijo and Kivisaari, Sirkku (1989) 'Managerial Work and Corporate Innovation', *International Journal of Sociology and Social Policy*. 9 (5-6): 57-87.

Raumolin, J. (1984) *Metsäsektorin vaikutus Suomen taloudelliseen ja yhteiskunnalliseen kehitykseen*. Oulu: Oulun yliopisto. Pohjois-Suomen Tukimuslaitos C 51.

Senghaas, D. (1985) *The European Experience*. Leamington Spa: Berg.

Seppälä, H., Kuuluvainen, J. and Seppälä, R. (1980) *Suomen metsäsektori tienhaarassa*. Folia Forestalia, 434. Helsinki.

Tainio, R., Korhonen, M. and Ollonqvist, P. (1989) 'In Search of Institutional Management: the Finnish Forest Sector Case', *International Journal of Sociology and Social Policy*. 9 (5-6), 88-119.

Whitley, R. (1990) 'Eastern Asian Enterprise Structures and the Comparative Analysis of Forms of Business Organisation', *Organization Studies*. 11 (1): 47-74.

Whitley, R. (1991) 'The Social Construction of Business Systems in East Asia', *Organization Studies*. 12 (1): 1-28.

Zysman, John (1983) *Governments, Markets and Growth: Financial Systems and the Politics of Industrial Change*. Ithaca, NY: Cornell University Press.

# 7
# Small Country Business Systems: Australia, Denmark and Finland Compared

*Jane Marceau*

Discussion of business systems operating in the context of the nation state in different areas of the world – Asia, Europe, North America – is usefully supplemented by comparisons which highlight differences and similarities. Comparisons made in this chapter indicate the position and problems of three *small* industrial countries – Denmark, Finland and Australia. They indicate the business systems which have enabled these countries' development so far and which underlie both opportunities for and constraints on their further economic success.

Most small industrial countries have open economies and are too small to influence the international markets for their products. In Europe they have each developed particular strategies to cope with the increasing dominance of world markets for manufactured goods by the large countries, devising policies which combine free trade – an open economy – with strategies of domestic compensation for sections of their populations disadvantaged by the continual internal economic restructuring made necessary by changed international market circumstances. Katzenstein (1985) suggests that successful smaller economies have developed corporatist ('liberal' or 'social') domestic political arrangements, such as tripartite bargaining institutions and proportional representation voting systems, which generate 'low voltage' politics and through which each main social 'partner' is able to bargain peacefully as new issues arise. These systems generate high standards of living based on the free export and import of manufactured goods and services, good industrial relations and comprehensive social protection, especially covering the risks of unemployment. Australia, though equally a small industrial country, has generated a very different business system with differing social outcomes.

Small industrial countries – usually defined as advanced OECD nations with fewer than 25 million inhabitants – face particular problems in the emerging world economic order which may jeopardise the success of their business systems. First, as Andersen and Lundvall (1988), Walsh (1988) and others point out, major changes in the generic technologies of the new techno-economic paradigm (Perez, 1983) and the products in which they are embedded are increasingly dominated by large companies in large countries, disadvantaging the small. Speaking, for example, of Norwegian consumer electronics and telephone equipment sector, Fagerberg et al. sum up the situation as the 'standard small country pattern. Thanks to regulation from the PTT (Post Telegraph and Telephone Authority), there is a relatively large sector producing telephone equipment, but it is controlled by foreign multinationals. Consumer electronics virtually disappeared in the late 1970s' (1988: 128).

Second, the small countries are losing the markets once considered their own. Their niches are being threatened by developments in the Asian NICs, which competed first on labour costs but later on product sophistication and new process systems. This uncomfortable position is the 'small country squeeze' (Kristensen and Levinson, 1978). Not only economic, the 'squeeze' is also posing problems for the socio-political arrangements on which earlier social and political success was based as restructuring becomes faster, the outcomes less favourable, especially in the employment area, and the risk of permanent loss of local dominance in any one crucial area of technology greater.

Comparison of the business systems of small countries reveals not only that they differ quite considerably from those of their larger counterparts, especially in Europe, but also that they differ quite considerably among themselves (see, for example, Edqvist and Lundvall, 1990, in a paper which compares Swedish and Danish national systems of innovation). When analysis of a business system's operation moves from the macro level through the sectoral (industry) to individual firm levels many differences of strategy and functioning emerge.

This chapter focuses on Australia, a non-European country which has devised a system borrowed from its large counterparts in the Anglo-Saxon world despite being a small industrial nation and liable to face the same pressures as its European counterparts. Australia has a large geographical area but a small population (17.2 million) and is an Anglo-Saxon nation located in the Asian-Pacific region. The country must now use its heritage, its multicultural population and its social-democratic, federal political institutional structure to move from being a nation grown rich on the proceeds of a highly developed capitalist agriculture and minerals sector, creating only a weak, highly protected, foreign-multinational-owned industry, to become an open trading economy, rich not only in primary but also in complex manufactured products. Australia's ability to effect such changes is circumscribed by the dominance of a business system borrowed from elsewhere.

The discussion below has two emphases: first, the major characteristics of the dominant Australian business system are presented; second, in order to highlight diverse ways in which small industrial nations have ordered their portfolio of activities the focus is on some sectoral 'recipes' for the organisation of both production and innovation used in Denmark, Finland and Australia.

## Australia's Business Recipes

The first 150 years of white settlement in Australia saw the creation of a developmental state and a focus on 'colonial socialism' (Butlin et al., 1982). From the 1930s, however, the Australian state gradually retreated from this role, emphasising instead economic intervention through tariffs and quotas, a system now in turn being dismantled. The business system of Australia built on the country's 'natural' advantages of raw materials – minerals and agricultural. In contrast to the small European states, Australia developed a strong, efficient, low-cost, capital-intensive, world-competitive agriculture while its industries remained protected infants. While constraining ties with Britain were broken in the twentieth century, far from taking control of the industrial development generated by the isolation of the periods of the two world wars, the Australian state preferred, except in the immediate post-war period, to generate capital principally through direct foreign investment into the country and an open arms policy towards multinational corporations.

### *The Structure of the Economy*
The result of post-war industrialisation policies is very considerable concentration of industrial activity and a manufacturing economy polarized between large foreign firms and small Australian ones. In manufacturing in 1988, for example, only 4 per cent of all establishments employed 81 per cent of all personnel, and almost 50 per cent of employees worked in less than 1000 work-places (ABS, 1991). A similar concentration is apparent in the financial sector, although there the companies are usually Australian-owned, and in the minerals section of the primary sector. The importance of the service sector is now apparent and reflected in the occupational distribution, while tourism has become the single biggest export earner. These developments may see emerging a new group of players.

The structure of the industrial sector and its ownership are key elements in the understanding of the Australian business system, its organisational forms and the ideology justifying the operating recipes selected. The external influences on the economy push an essentially Anglo-Saxon mode of viewing the proper organisation of business and, especially important, the areas where government may offer support, largely explaining the creation and maintenance of a 'regulatory' rather than a developmental state, since the industrial 'partners' with whom the Australian government deals are powerful representatives of a quite specific Anglo-Saxon method of ordering business and business–government relations. The proponents of the business regimes dominating the UK and the USA – quite different from those both of continental Europe and Asia – have privileged access in Australia to public decision-makers. Thus, it is extremely significant – though never commented upon in this way – that the biggest business stake-holder in corporate Australia is the USA, followed closely by the UK. In 1986–7, these two countries alone accounted for almost 80 per cent of all foreign investment. In contrast, continental European firms altogether accounted for only 17 per cent of such funds sources (David and Wheelwright, 1989: 102).

A new and very powerful player is now entering the Australian arena, however. Japan, long established in Australia in areas such as automotive assembly, is now moving into other areas, including rural land, tourism developments and real property. By 1986–7, Japan contributed 21 per cent of foreign investment, a share growing fast, while other Asian countries contributed another 14 per cent (David and Wheelwright, 1989: 102–3). The Asian influence is thus clearly increasing in the economy but its impact will greatly depend on sectors entered and relationships developed with local companies, with multinationals from other countries, with financial institutions and with the government. So far, for example, the Japanese auto assemblers have proved more likely to adopt the locally dominant Anglo-Saxon business methods than to push local companies towards Japanese best practice (Marceau, 1990). This, however, may well be changing.

*Political Institutions*
The political institutional forms of Australia play a major role in shaping the business system because they limit the powers of public policy players while making nationwide policy consensus unlikely. Australia is a federation of six States and two Territories – created as the Commonwealth of Australia on 1 January 1901 – each having its own legislative and executive bodies with different

resource-raising and policy-making powers. Very short electoral cycles (mostly three years) mean governments almost continually face the electorate, either nationally or in one or more of the states, a situation militating against long-term policy development.

The constitutionally determined division of powers between federal and state governments gives the Commonwealth government only the blunter instruments of policy direction, notably the manipulation of tariffs, quotas, tax and interest rates and foreign investment review while the states control the more finely-tuned intervention levers. Governments in Canberra, moreover, while taking limited initiatives, publicly downplay strategic economic intervention.

Political intervention in the economy is further constrained by deep divisions within the business world. Farmers and miners, used to success on world markets, refuse to compromise their position by supporting a 'feather-bedded manufacturing section unused to the discipline of the market'. Recently, leaders of these sectors have been joined by those of the newly powerful and deregulated financial sector. In this context, suggestions for positive adjustment policies for the manufacturing sector look like special pleading.

*Capital Sources and the Market for Corporate Control*
Any business system relies on regular access to capital to expand its operations, or at least to maintain itself in times of economic downturn. Zysman (1983) has suggested that one crucial difference in industry development between countries results from the extent to which industrial financial requirements are met through a capital market or credit-based financial system. In keeping with its Anglo-Saxon orientation, Australia developed a capital market system, making 'patient' development money hard to find, in sharp contrast to the banking systems of Finland or Denmark. The Australian government's 1983 decision to deregulate financial markets, float the dollar and invite in 16 foreign banks made almost impossible national level strategic initiatives for *sectoral* economic development. Moreover, the inexperience of the banks in an open system, coupled to booming world stock markets and a tax regime which favoured overseas borrowing by excessively 'entrepreneurial' customers, has meant the creation of a potentially disastrous (private) foreign debt, now more than one-third of GDP.

*Education, Training and the Labour Market*
Whitley (Chapter 1 in this volume) has pointed out that in explaining the emergence of particular national business regimes certain

proximate institutions are crucial. In addition, to the state and the financial system, these are, particularly, education and the labour market. Historically, in different countries workers have grouped themselves for both market and political purposes in three main ways, building organisations and classifications based on craft or trade skills or on enterprise loyalty. In Australia, the union movement long followed the British model, basing organisation on craft and trade skills rather than industry or enterprise affiliation, and there has only ever been one central coordinating body, the Australian Council of Trade Unions (ACTU).

Comparing reasons for Australian labour's espousal of a work and welfare politics of 'domestic defence' rather than that of 'domestic compensation' favoured by its counterparts in the small European states, Castles has recently (1988) pointed to the timing and circumstances of the 'historic compromise' reached between capital and labour in Australia. In nineteenth-century Australia, unlike its European small-country counterparts, labour was scarce, was relatively wealthy and had a variety of alternative ways of earning a living, factors facilitating broad political institutions in which labour had a major share, the early granting of universal suffrage and the advent to power of Labor governments early in the twentieth century, indicating to labour the power of the vote. In the 1890s, labour and manufacturing industry, both adversely affected by economic slump, agreed to support population expansion and industrial development subject to the protection of labour by the provision of jobs (Castles, 1988). This agreement entitled employers to demand government protection for their activities so as to enable them to provide the jobs. The result was protectionist industrial policy and a unique judicial system of arbitration and conciliation of industrial disputes, notably those concerning wages. An essentially centralist and 'top down' national system of labour relations was thus created.

The outstanding feature of this bargain was the acceptance by both labour and employers of the notion of 'fair' wages, rather than wages based on a company's ability to pay with pay levels nationally arbitrated through a special court now called the Industrial Relations Commission. The system enshrines bargained outcomes in the 'awards' given to different categories of worker, each award covering all workers in a category regardless of the employing company's size, internal structure or market position. Although in times of labour shortages, workers in Australia bargain separately with employers for various levels of 'over-award' payments, the system is only now moving to enterprise bargaining.

The tribunal system also reinforced public beliefs in the labour market and in wage justice as the basis for social protection rather than reliance on a highly developed welfare system, as in many European small industrial countries. In particular, compensation for workers displaced by economic changes, which in a highly protected system were fairly slow, never came seriously onto the political agenda, again in contrast to small European open economies (Castles, 1988).

Australian workers operate principally on an external labour market where market power is gained through competences certified by independent educational institutions and enforced through national trade unions and a judicial apparatus which hears the views of all sides but 'legislates' independently. The result is the separation of the wage fortunes of workers from the economic health of enterprises and of groups of workers from each other. The separation of workers from each other is, of course, greatly reinforced by the multiculturalism of the Australian population (40 per cent born overseas or with a parent born overseas), which makes both communication and trust very difficult. In this system there is little to tie a worker to any enterprise and no obvious system for building 'trust' between workers and employers. Unlike their counterparts in Sweden, moreover, employers face few legal constraints on sacking workers at short notice.

The system encourages high labour mobility among workers, while many enterprises in Australia conduct little or no training (National Training Council/P.A. Management, 1987). To remedy this the federal government has recently introduced a compulsory training levy on all firms above a certain size, much on the model of the French recurrent education financing system. In addition, managers in Australia are relatively ill-educated and fewer have obtained tertiary qualifications than have their overseas counterparts (Lansbury and Quince, 1986). Moreover, in contrast to workers, managers tend to follow 'loyalist' careers, moving only seldom between companies, thereby limiting information flow on new managerial practices.

Again in contrast to Scandinavia, high-level technical education is also very underdeveloped in Australia. Most technical high schools have been phased out and TAFE (Technical and Further Education) has long been starved of staff and equipment, while technical universities and the engineers they produce have relatively low social status.

Change in the system was hastened in the 1980s with the influential ACTU report *Australia Reconstructed* advocating the introduction of multi-skilling and broadbanded categories of jobs for workers. Work-practice changes were also encouraged by political changes which in 1983 brought the ACTU directly into tripartite arrangements for creating and maintaining a successful incomes policy in a set of agreements known as the Accord. Modelled on the corporatist 'social pacts' familiar to Scandinavians and Australians, the Accord (now Mark VI) indicated a move away from Anglo-Saxon 'wage' policies (Mathews, 1992: 6) but that system is now changing again with the move towards enterprise bargaining.

### Organisational Outcomes in Enterprises

Most industrial and large service organisations in Australia have followed the Anglo-Saxon operating strategies which are often described as 'Fordist' or 'Taylorist'. Except in the financial sector, physical technologies are rarely state-of-the-art while decentralised managerial control strategies are evolving only slowly. As indicated above, work organisation remains largely trade- and craft-related, with specialised tasks and narrow demarcations, and companies conduct little formal training, undertake little research and less development (see DITAC, 1991), and employ few scientists and other high-level technical staff. Most major companies are part of multinational conglomerates and remain largely vertically integrated. As a result, the legal boundaries of economic actors (firms) still tend to coincide with the effective foci of economic activity much more systematically than is the case in the Asian economies, or indeed in some sectors of European economies as we shall see below. Inter-enterprise cooperation is marginal and Australian companies are only just beginning to shape and organise their markets on the Japanese model. They are far also from developing the new 'boundary crossing' organisational forms (Child, 1987), such as co-contracting, which are emerging elsewhere and from fostering close connections in operating rather than equity terms between large and small firms (Shutt and Whittington, 1987). The lag in Australian acceptance of Japanese managerial strategies for coordinating a wide range of economic activities through a kind of 'quasi' market rather than through either integrated hierarchies (very large integrated firms) or the haphazard conglomeration of equity holdings common in the UK and America means that many relationships between clients and suppliers are still determined by price considerations on the 'stress' model described in the automotive industry in Britain by Lamming (1987). Relationships of co-design, co-contracting or co-manufacture, built up over a long series of transactions, have as yet barely begun to emerge: the large core companies have been as slow in leading down this path as their suppliers have been to follow (see Marceau and Jureidini, 1992; Marceau, 1990).

Much of this pattern of individualistic organisation follows from the logic of the broader system of institutional arrangements. As we saw above, much was also borrowed from an earlier stage of development of a larger industrialised country on the other side of the world and transplanted to a country where for other reasons managers (owners) of capital and workers had been able to conclude a deal which encouraged protection of the weaker manufacturing sector and its support by an efficient set of farm and mineral production systems. The outcome was a business system owing much to Anglo-Saxon origins but with a vastly different material base and relationship to the surrounding world. Equally important, almost all major development activity has been 'top down', regulated by the government and carried out by large, usually foreign-owned, firms. The ideology attached to the system as the 'one best way' has proved very difficult to change.

*The Emerging Mix*

A new focus on deregulation, privatisation and a 'minimalist' ideology in relation to government involvement in economic development and exhortatory rather than more interventionist industry policy at federal level (the states may have to pick up the pieces and devise their own counter-measures) has recently become prominent. Deregulation of the financial sector is now almost a decade old but has proved only a limited success, with slow learning (NIEIR, 1990) by the banks causing massive distress to both manufacturing and service enterprise clients and to the banks themselves, which now report several billion dollars of bad debts and non-performing loans. Paradoxically, this apparent failure has not yet dampened ardour for further deregulation and privatisation and the government will soon have almost no levers to pull to effect direct and targeted economic change. The blunt nature of macro policy instruments available to federal governments may create political instability and is already threatening the Accord with the unions, risking a political backlash since in trying to develop an economy 'taxation and similar measures can only lead from behind' (Zysman, 1983).

Managing the economy through 'modernisation' has been accompanied by a focus on the operations of the proximate social institutions which impinge on the design of business systems. Recent public policy initiatives include the encouragement of industry training and the reform both of the TAFE sector and of the higher education system to make it 'more responsive to the needs of the economy'. The federal government has also reformed its own operations, emphasising a managerialist, rather than an expert, more policy-oriented approach. A new catchcry has been coined. Long the 'lucky country', Australia is now to become the 'clever country' through technological upgrading, the development of hi-tech sectors and the encouragement of an export orientation. Protection through quotas and tariffs has gone or is going (allowing a few adjustment years) and, much like the message put out by Mrs Thatcher in 1979, manufacturing in Australia is now to compete internationally or go to the wall. The constituent elements of the Australian business system thus seem to stand on the brink of major changes.

### Resource-Based Industries: Finnish Forests, Danish Design and Australian Wool

The outcome of the existing set of Australian institutions, population mix and public policies lies in striking contrast to those in other small countries, notably in Scandinavia. The comparisons can be seen at two levels in particular: the way in which the countries have developed a major national resource and the ways in which development nodes have been established and maintained, indicating alternative routes to transforming a productive system. The 'bottom up' development of the garment and furniture complexes in Denmark described in this volume by Kristensen (Chapter 5) had little chance of developing in Australia. Equally, the successful industrial take-off of the forest industries in Finland, also described in this volume, did not happen with the equally important wool resource base of Australia. This section uses sectoral data to illustrate the different 'recipes' used and their consequences.

### The Finnish Forest Sector

The Finnish forest industries, including wood, pulp and paper, and the Australian wool industry hold rather similar places in their host countries' economies. In 1989 in Finland forest industries accounted for 39 per cent of export income and in 1990 50 per cent of foreign currency earnings came from the 'narrow' forest sector (Ahonen, 1991). In Australia in 1988, wool was the biggest single export product (although it has slipped slightly since), accounting for 14 per cent of all foreign exchange earned from commodity sales, which in turn constitute by far the largest component of Australian export sales. Both the forest industry in Finland and the wool industry in Australia are clearly based on the abundance of a particular natural resource. There, however, the similarities end. The major differences between the two are seen in the fact that a major industrial complex has developed from the natural product (trees) base of the Finnish forest industry, emphasising the manufacturing transformation of the raw product, while in Australia 90 per cent of all wool sold overseas is exported as a 'raw' material, greasy wool. In the Finnish case, in contrast, the raw material provided the opportunity for the establishment of a world-class paper and pulp industry. In 1988 Finland held 26 per cent of the world market for printing and writing paper, while paper constituted 68 per cent of all Finnish forest-related export earnings (Ahonen, 1991). In addition, that industry was the basis for the development of a machinery industry which in turn is contributing to the forest industries' progress as well as to Finland's balance of trade. In Finland virtually all the wood produced is processed inside the country, by Finnish-owned companies, themselves operating internationally from their home base and exporting 80 per cent of their paper production.

The operations of the wood processors have also provided support to such industries as machine-building and, later, electronics. The natural resource, wood, has thus proved to be the basis of a series of industries, including the most hi-tech, and has provided Finland with support for technologically sophisticated R & D. It also long ensured secure employment and comprehensive locally-based services for the communities of rural Finland.

The business system which permitted this favourable result has been analysed by many observers (cf. Räsänen, 1989; Lilja et al., 1990; and Chapter 6 in this volume, Räsänen and Whipp, Chapter 2 in this volume; see also Lemola and Lovio, 1988 and Fagerberg et al., 1988). The essential ingredients seem to have been several. The industry benefited early on from a large quasi-domestic market arising from Finland's position within Russia until 1917. The paper mills, created from the mid-nineteenth century, were founded close to each other along lakes and rivers in a sparsely populated country. Put schematically, this combination of geographical isolation and yet propinquity led to 'complete' forest-industry communities, covering a range of activities, while at the same time the companies concerned were in constant competition with each other. Accounts by observers such as Lilja et al. (1990; and Chapter 6 in this volume) suggest that this competition was crucial in encouraging the companies to focus early on innovation and technological change, on production and process changes which encouraged the development of close user–producer relations and local specialist machinery producers. As the latter became more sophisticated, their search activities and the need for the forest companies to specialise in leading edge products, closely geared to end-user demands (because of competition with Sweden and Germany), even though markets were located geographically far away, became more acute and they created a virtuous circle of technological innovation, culminating in the early acceptance of computer-based equipment and an emerging Finnish electronics industry, often developed within the forest companies themselves (Ahonen, 1991).

From early in their history the forest industry giants gradually created supporting institutional links. The first problem, that of the huge capital investments necessary to the industry and a fluctuating income base, was overcome by banks providing a ready source of patient capital and the national government marshalling national savings (Finland was then a high-savings society). The two major commercial banks early became experts and closely involved in issues concerning forest industry development, while banks and mills jointly developed long-term strategies, including those for restructuring.

Given the importance of the forest industries to the whole economy, too, the Finnish state has long held close relations with forest industry actors. Early in the twentieth century land reform legislation ensured labour for the industry by confirming the existence of a population of small farm/forest owners. One major player was once also a state-owned company. As Lilja and his colleagues suggest in this volume, the farmers have both integrated forward to the forest industry and banking and held a strong position in the power structure of Finnish society. Many members of the Finnish political elite rose from the institutions of the forest sector, while intimate personal links secured government support for these industries. A strong set of education and technical training institutions, both publicly provided and created by the industry itself, also helped secure a permanent and loyal supply of skilled labour to all local development activities, while the workers in the paper industry itself have a system of bargaining which both assists flexibility and gives workers a worthwhile share of the increased productivity arising from technological modernisation. In addition, the dynamism of the industry provided demand for technical engineers who in turn provided further improvements and were rewarded with high social status. These engineers were created by the technological universities and backed by research institutes. As a result, Finnish consultants are in demand worldwide and the forest industry has thus spawned yet another arm, this time in the service sector.

The central players in the forest industry have also built strong support institutions on the sales side. Their distance from customers was initially overcome by their creation of joint trading houses which concentrated on the sale of the products of the industry as a whole rather than one firm. Lilja and his colleagues suggest (Chapter 6 in this volume) that in no other country are there so many types of *cooperation* – extending in Finland not only to sales but also to wood procurement, transportation, export deliveries, process and product development, regulation of investments and so on.

The Finnish forest sector thus shows a business system with clear dominant actors controlling the transformation of raw materials, a supportive system of public policies and high levels of technical education and innovation, ultimately spawning a wide range of new related industries, investment-aided by patient capital in the major development periods, a strong export orientation and close cooperation between major players at all levels of the production chain. While difficulties have emerged in some areas in recent years, the roots of the system are still strong (see Lilja et al, 1990).

### 'Bottom-up' Development: Rural Industrial Complexes in Denmark

The Finnish forest sector presents a contrast with the Australian wool industry notably because of the importance of the large-scale, corporately organised, industrial transformations of the raw material, the existence of patient capital and the high levels of technological change and cooperation at all stages of the production chain. The Danish rural business system contrasts essentially through the development of complexes from the 'bottom up', making considerable use of cooperative and small-business forms of organisation. As Kristensen (Chapter 5 in this volume) makes clear, and as other work by the same author and others (cf. Karnøe, 1991) suggests, an important element of the Danish national system involves harnessing local ideas, related to local resources, including raw materials, by local and usually small-scale initiatives. This is particularly clear in some sectors but evident, too, in others such as the agro-industrial development block (Edqvist and Lundvall, 1990). Even though recently some sectors sometimes seem to have been transformed by the emergence of dominant corporations of the kind found in most 'modern' economies, in practice these corporations are heavily influenced by arrangements already in place and differ greatly from, for instance, the archetypical American firm. In particular, as Kristensen (1990) points out, what appears to be major, unified corporations are in practice often little more than holding companies providing financial security and some common services for the activities of what are effectively small cooperating enterprises. Thus, rather than giving strategic direction from the top, the corporation's senior decision-makers find themselves having to choose among a variety of possibilities which are heavily constrained by the craft-workers who dominate production in the industries concerned and the small production units built around them, which have their own chosen directions. In this sense many sectors of Danish activity remain 'bottom up'. The Danish model, then, is one of local initiatives, cooperative forms of productive organisation, a very strong labour movement and a locally responsive Social Democratic state. Although Denmark (unlike Sweden) has in no sense a strong developmental state (see Edqvist and Lundvall, 1990; Karnøe, 1991), with little coherent industrial policy development, the orientation is one of 'public' conceptions of progress, favouring provision of a well-developed network of technical schools and other education facilities.

Struck by the continuing rise in employment in small and medium companies in the peripheral areas of Denmark in the 1980s, when the 'logic' of the dominant industrial system worldwide suggested that the reverse should be occurring, Kristensen and his colleagues found a series of flourishing local communities. Instead of 'rationalisation' into large companies and large productive units centrally located, they found a milieu which provided ideal opportunities for creating new businesses. Like the mill towns of Finland, the small railway towns of Denmark provide functioning industrial districts, not organised as in Italy but composed of networks of diverse companies, not collaborating in different stages of production in all cases but providing products and services essential to innovation. Thus, for instance, the small machine shops construct specialised tools, make up prototypes at short notice, solve technical production problems and produce experimental production equipment.

The railway system has long provided both a cheap and stable system for goods transportation and a *noyau* of skilled metal-workers who developed small-scale agricultural and industrial machinery workshops, notably making equipment for the dairy industry. A complex series of sub-contracting arrangements reduces barriers to entry for small entrepreneurs and facilitates skill development. The public provision of *technikum* engineers ensures higher-levels of skill and the widely dispersed geographical trajectories covered in the course of typical (spiralist, inter-company) careers build links with other areas and transfer ideas, while Danish design has become an element of success. Such local industries were so successful that by 1979 they employed 43 per cent of the total Danish industrial workforce.

This development was assisted rather than hindered by the larger corporations, which in some cases took them over because they adopted a strategy, contrary to many prescriptions advocating economies of scale, of aiming at niche markets and specialised products. Such strategies, as Kristensen points out in Chapter 5 in this volume, encourage investment in products, equipment and manufacturing practices appropriate to *small* markets and thus do not create organisational pressures to move towards the 'Fordist' model. The success of this 'bottom up' approach has been illustrated again in the development of the Danish wind turbine industry, which now has a considerable share of the European market and a foothold in the United States.

Not all businesses in Denmark operate on such a 'bottom up' principle, however, and the other side of the picture, emphasised by Edqvist and Lundvall (1990), is a modified 'top down' system where the moving forces are conglomerates of export firms and agencies set up by the farmers' cooperatives. These big firms are perhaps less responsive to members concerns than may sometimes appear (Annerstedt, 1991). The Danish business system, while characterised by the dynamism of small entrepreneurs, cooperatives and 'simple' but sophisticated design technologies created by the practical engineers created by the orientation of important sections of the education system, does not always escape the pressures created by the presence of other powerful interests and forms of organisation.

### Australian Wool

The wool industry in Australia could hardly be organised more differently from the two resource-based examples given above. Wool in Australia, despite the fact that Australia produces a third of the world's wool and 85 per cent of the world's fine wools, has remained a primary industry. Wool growing, selling and transporting are its essential elements. While three-quarters of the wool in the woollen[1] system is scoured, 85 per cent of all Australian wool enters the worsted system, where only 15 per cent receives even primary processing in its country of origin. The number of wool (worsted system) processors located in Australia is tiny and the firms are not large. There are only 20 scouring units, six carbonising and five combing units, while only five wool top-making firms, six worsted spinning firms, three weavers and five machine-knitting yarn-makers process to final stage. In the woollen system there are barely more processors, again mostly small and foreign-owned (Thomas, 1991: 1).

The basis of the industry is the roughly 70,000 stations, running an average of 6,000 sheep each, scattered over New South Wales, Victoria and Western Australia and outback Queensland. This kind of geographical pattern indicates the first reason for the differences with Finland and Denmark. Sheep production is an extensive agricultural activity, very different from pig raising or dairy production, and the product is light and easy to transport, unlike trees. Sheep grazing does little to generate flourishing local communities, especially when carried out on very large properties, often of hundreds, thousands and sometimes hundreds of thousands of hectares, frequently almost self-sufficient, supplied by capital cities as much as by tiny rural towns. The few permanent workers live on the properties, doubling as everyday machinery repairers, while much work is seasonally intensive (dipping, shearing, lambing) and generates bands of itinerant specialists rather than a stable community. Moreover, unlike those of metal- or wood-workers, the skills of the sheep-shearer are too specialised to turn to other uses. The few major auction centres could perhaps have generated processing activity, and indeed have done so in a few areas, but most processors remain small and scattered, have no links with each other and are no match for the well-organised farmers who developed – in concert with the government, itself much influenced by the National (originally Country) Party – national marketing and promotion organisations to keep wool prices stable and, if possible, up. These organisations, essentially representing only farmers, have been very slow to push technological change (Centre for International Economics, 1990) and long gave little thought to developing new technologies for different stages of the chain of production, despite the CSIRO's (Commonwealth Scientific and Industrial Research Organisation), world dominance of wool research, or to ways to reconcile farmers' demands for high income with processors' needs for a relatively low wool price. The overall long-time prosperity of the farmers persuaded them that they did not need to change their practices, while the banks provided no incentive to develop wool-related activities, remaining interested only in land and primary produce. The government similarly focused on protecting the industries centred on the few cities which have long provided a home for 80–85 per cent of the population, and thus for the majority of voters, apparently believing that the corporatist (government-farmers) marketing arrangements in place 'solved' wool production problems. Only the recent wool price crisis and moves by overseas processors towards much greater use of synthetics have shaken graziers' complacency and pointed to new directions.

The recipe according to which the industry developed provided no base for spin-off activities. Although recently being transformed by technological advances at all stages of production from animal health to textile weaving, the industry has seldom provided the impetus for change itself. Innovations made have almost always come 'top down' from the publicly funded national science and industrial research organisation (CSIRO) (and occasionally from the more enlightened members of the Wool Council or Corporation and the International Wool Secretariat), which almost alone builds bridges between producers and industrial users, while final consumers have as yet almost no say at all. Even in 1991, our interviews show that most processors prefer to leave innovation to the 'experts' rather than invest in R & D.

**Conclusion**

The notion of 'business system' may be applied at national or sectoral levels or at that of the strategies of production and organisation of the individual firm (see, for example, Räsänen and Whipp, Chapter 2 in this volume). Each analytical 'lens' generates a rather different view of the activity of enterprises in a national context and would generate yet another if the international context, the relevant international business system, were also to be incorporated. It is impossible to understand the recent evolution of national business recipes, and *a fortiori* sectoral ones, without taking such international recipes into account. A particular domestico-international context, for example, both stimulated the initial development of the forest industries in Finland and shaped much of the direction of its later successful direction by providing particularly privileged export markets (in the 1980s 25 per cent of all exports went to the Soviet Union and Comecon countries).

Similarly, it is particularly evident that Australian business activities have always been shaped by the happenstance of the country's foundation and the consequent 150 years of dependence on policies developed in the industrial 'mother country', Great Britain, located on the other side of the world. Moreover, final rejection of that link by governments in the post-war period only turned attention to another 'protector', the powerful United States of America. Both these protectors' influence is still pervasive, operating to filter choices in public and private corporate policies and select only a narrow range of those apparently appropriate. Thus, whether examining the organisational and productive strategies at the heart of the corporate sector or cutting welfare payments, Anglo-Saxon countries remain the models, providing the discourse and publicly acceptable range of alternatives. In the corporate sector these countries are, of course, also the owners of significant parts of the economy and their influence is thus even more direct. Discrepancies between theory and practice in the UK and the USA, notably in the area of trade policies, and the evident inadequacies of social policies based on 'domestic defense' (Castles, 1988) in a period of fundamental restructuring are apparently still invisible to Australian policy-makers.

A new set of international influences on Australia has, however, now appeared. Asia is now Australia's major trading area, increasing its suggestive power, but the *public discourse* which both legitimates and influences decisions made is still far from taking on any shade of Asian philosophy. The Korean development path and Singaporean industry policy are not part of the public agenda. Caught in a 1980s time warp, the opposition Liberal Party still believes firmly in economic policies which have failed in the Anglo-Saxon West, while the implications of Japanese management practices have barely made a dent on their thinking or their business supporters' activities.

A national business system focus usefully illuminates overall similarities and differences between countries, while a sectoral analysis more clearly indicates the functioning of the system on the ground. At sectoral level, 'bottom up' or 'top down' influences on structuring and restructuring become clearer, as does the absence of particular kinds of institutions or even political will. These differences were especially clear in the discussion above. Over the next few decades, however, the Finnish forestry industry, Danish industrial complexes and the Australian wool industry are all going to be subject to global restructuring and the decisions of dominant corporate actors. Already, at least in Finland, there is some evidence that the limits of the forest industry model of development may have been reached, while the situation of that other Finnish success story, electronics and especially Nokia may also be faltering (see Chapter 6 of this volume. See also Ahonen and Stenberg, 1991). On the other hand, the 'bottom up' approach of Denmark may well retain its vitality: Karnøe's (1991) work on the development of high-tech wind turbines in Denmark, a technology now acknowledged to have beaten that of the international big players, indicates once again that the importance of close user-producer relations in successful innovation is no less now, even in a field of 'modern' technology where competition is worldwide, than it was in the days of development of local industries in Danish railway towns. Perhaps in the emerging era, too, where countries at least have the possibility of learning from each other's successes, the Australian business system in both political and corporate, public and private, components, will add some of the Scandinavian ingredients to its mix.

In doing so, Australia will face many problems, as indeed the Scandinavian countries are themselves doing. Many new forms of productive organisation are emerging worldwide and almost infinite rearrangement of the key elements of the portfolio of activities undertaken in the process of adding value to raw materials and developing and selling services may prove possible. Such variety of form may, however, be characteristic only of the early stages of the emerging techno-economic paradigm, and as the new paradigm becomes established the influence of the world's more powerful players – large firms or large countries – may well increase. Issues of *control* may become increasingly important for enterprises and probably ultimately for governments, causing immense problems for a small English-speaking nation on the Asian side of the Pacific Rim, squeezed between the world's biggest national players – one on each side of the Rim – as well as for small open European economies. The Swedish privatisation programme, the indebtedness of many of the Finnish forest industry companies and the high unemployment rate in Denmark may be portents of major changes in Scandinavian systems. While Australia's singular position may be changing, the small open economies of Europe may also have to rethink both their public welfare and their industrial policies.

Moreover, it is by no means clear that *any* country characterised by an efficient agriculture but a weak manufacturing sector can make the necessary transformation, the reverse of the great leap from weak agriculture to strong industry which is the standard world model. Australia may still become dependent on beds, beaches and holes in the ground (a 'quarry-resort' economy). It is even less clear how the 'politics of domestic defence', appropriate perhaps to an economy with strong centralised labour market institutions, can be turned into those of 'domestic compensation' which have been used to facilitate structural adjustment with such apparent success by the small European states, such as Denmark and Finland, with open economies. Having led deregulation of the economy as a whole with that of the crucial financial system, the government has lost much control of internal economic processes (NIEIR, 1990) while not being prepared to compensate generously those disadvantaged by economic restructuring. Once the analysis of business recipes is broadened, as it should be, to incorporate study of the relationships between business and the state, Australian experience appears as unique as its geo-cultural position in the world. Its singular position may perhaps be changing, however, as the small European states themselves may have to rethink their public welfare and industrial policies.

## Notes

1 The woollen system is the trajectory followed by coarse, short staple wools and is used for blankets, blazers etc. The worsted system is the smooth fabric-making system using fine wool and long staples.

## References

Ahonen, P. (1991) 'Personal Communication'. Dept of Administrative Studies, University of Tampere, Finland.

Ahonen, P. and Stenberg, E. (1991) 'Technology and Industrial Policy in Finland: a Perspective on Industrial Complexes'. Paper presented to the Conference 'Way out of the International Restructuring Race', University of Amsterdam 11–14 December.

Andersen, E. and Lundvall, B-A. (1988) 'Small National Systems of Innovation Facing Technological Revolutions: an Analytical Framework', in C. Freeman and B-A. Lundvall (eds), *Small Countries Facing the Technological Revolution*. London: Pinter. pp. 9–36.

Annerstedt, J. (1991) 'Personal Communication'. Dept of Political Science, Roskilde University, Denmark.

Australian Bureau of Statistics (ABS) (1991) *Manufacturing Industry. Details of Operations Australia 1988–89*. Catalogue No. 8203.0. Canberra: AGPS.

Butlin, N., Barnard, A. and Pincus, J. (1982) *Government and Capitalism*. Sydney: Allen & Unwin.

Castles, F. (1988) *Australian Public Policy and Economic Vulnerability*. Sydney: Allen & Unwin.

Centre for International Economics (A. Stoekel, B. Burrell and D. Quirke) (1990) *Wool into the 21st Century*. Canberra: Centre for International Economics.

Child, J. (1987) 'Information Technology, Organisation and the Response to Strategic Challenges'. Paper presented to the Eighth EGOS Colloquium, Antwerp 22–4 July.

David, A. and Wheelwright, E. (1989) *The Third Wave: Australia and Asian Capitalism*. Sydney: Left Book Club Cooperative.

DITAC (Department of Industry, Technology and Commerce) (1991) *Australian Science and Innovation Impact Brief 1991*. Canberra: AGPS.

Edqvist, C. and Lundvall, B-A. (1990) *Comparing the Danish and Swedish Systems of Innovation*. Paper prepared for the Columbia University project on National Systems Supporting Technical Advance in Industry.

Fagerberg, J., Dalum, B. and Jørgensen, U. (1988) 'Small Open Economies in the World Market for Electronics: the Case of the Nordic Countries', in C. Freeman and B-A. Lundvall (eds), *Small Countries Facing the Technological Revolution*. London: Pinter. pp. 113–38.

Karnøe, P. (1991) *Danish World Leadership in Wind Technology. The Result of a Danish Recipe?* Paper presented to the 10th EGOS Colloquium, Vienna, 15–18 July 1981.

Katzenstein, P. (1985) *Small States in World Markets*. Ithaca, NY: Cornell University Press.

Kristensen, P. (1990): *Industrial Districts in West Jutland, Denmark*. Paper presented to the conference 'Industrial Districts and Local Economic Regeneration'. International Institute for Labour Studies, Geneva.

Kristensen, P. and Levinson, J. (1978) *The Small Country Squeeze*. Roskilde: Institute of Economics, Politics and Administration.

Lamming, R. (1987) *Towards Best Practice: a Report on Components Supply in the UK Automotive Industry*. Brighton: SPRU and IMVP.

Lansbury, R. and Quince, A. (1986) *Management and Professional Employees in Large Scale Organisations: an Australian Study*. Unpublished paper, Macquarie University Graduate School of Management, Sydney.

Lemola, T. and Lovio, R. (1988) 'Possibilities for a Small Country in High Technology Production: the Electronics Industry in Finland', in C. Freeman and B-A. Lundvall (eds), *Small Countries Facing the Technological Revolution*. London: Pinter. pp. 139–55.

Lilja, K., Räsänen, K. and Tainio, R. (1990) *Strategic Continuity and Change in Corporations: the Finnish Way*. Paper presented to the Workshop 'Arenas of Strategic Thinking', Foundation of Economic Education, Tampere.

Marceau, J. (1990) *Oiling the Wheels: Technological Change in the Automotive Industry in Australia*. Unpublished report, Urban Research Program, Australian National University.

Marceau, J. and Jureidini, R. (1992) 'Giants and Dwarves: Changing Technologies and Productive Interlinkages in Australian Manufacturing Industry', in J. Marceau (ed.), *Reworking the World*. Berlin: W. de Gruyter.

Mathews, J. (1992): 'An Australian Model of Industrial Restructuring', in J. Marceau (ed.), *Reworking the World*. Berlin: W. de Gruyter.

National Training Council/P.A. Management (1987) *Report of a Pilot Study on Investment in Training in the Non-government Sector*. Melbourne: National Training Council.

NIEIR (National Institute of Economic and Industry Research) (1990) *Australian Economic Focus*. No. 5.

Perez, C. (1983) 'Structural Change and the Assimilation of New Technologies in the Economic and Social System', *Futures* 15 (4): 357–75.

Räsänen, K. (1989) *Corporate Evolution in a Forest Sector Society*. Working Paper 89–11, European Institute for Advanced Studies in Management, Brussels.

Shutt, J. and Whittington, R. (1987) 'Fragmentation Strategies and the Rise of Small Firms: Cases from the North West', *Regional Studies*. 21 (1): 13–23.

Thomas, A. (1991) '*Adding Value to Australian Wool*'. Paper presented to the National Agricultural and Resources Outlook Conference, 1991. Canberra: Australian Bureau of Agricultural and Resource Economics.

Walsh, V. (1988) 'Technology and the Competitiveness of Small Countries: a Review', in C. Freeman and B-A. Lundvall (eds), *Small Countries Facing the Technological Revolution*. London: Pinter. pp. 37–66.

Zysman, J. (1983) *Governments, Markets and Growth: Financial Systems and the Politics of Industrial Change*. Ithaca, NY: Cornell University Press.

# BUSINESS SYSTEMS, INDUSTRIAL SECTORS AND STRATEGIC CHOICES

## Introduction

### Richard Whitley

Dominant social institutions constrain and direct the sorts of business systems that become established in particular contexts through the development of distinctive rules of competitive activity that structure, and are reproduced by, effective firm behaviour. The greater the variety of institutions and the weaker their cohesion within national boundaries, the more likely are different ways of organising economic activities to emerge and distinctive 'recipes' for strategic choices to develop. Additionally, the growing internationalisation of production in some industries has been seen as weakening the impact of national institutions and encouraging the development of distinctive sector-specific beliefs and competitive norms. The chapters in this part explore the relative significance of nation states, cultural systems and industrial rationalities, and their changing interrelationships, in accounting for variations in forms of economic organisation and activities.

The importance of 'industrial wisdom' is emphasised by Hellgren and Melin in their discussion of the Swedish pulp and paper industry as a critical factor in explaining changes in firms' strategic choices during the 1980s. They suggest that the role of national institutions in structuring prevailing beliefs about appropriate strategies declined as markets became more internationalised and worldwide competition intensified. New ideas about diversification and takeovers contributed to the development of a revised 'industrial wisdom' which led to major strategic changes in some firms. Presumably this was assisted by the deregulation of some capital markets which also seems to have affected parts of the Finnish paper industry.

In contrast, the significance of state structures and policies is emphasised by the studies of the financial services sector in Italy, Britain and France by Knights, Moran and Murray and O'Reilly. The actions of the Italian state and the associated role of political parties in dispensing patronage and mobilising support have clearly constrained the development of the personal financial services industry in Italy and, together with traditional familism and other attitudes to financial security, generated its distinctive post-war structure and practices. Equally, as Knights et al. show, recent changes in elite attitudes and interests within the political system and among dominant groups in closely related sectors, such as large-scale manufacturing, arising in part from the financial burdens of the present system, have generated considerable pressure to change the current structure which will probably result in new forms of economic organisation developing in this sector in the 1990s. These new forms will, of course, bear the marks of the circumstances and institutional context surrounding their emergence and are not going simply to replicate the pattern found in other European countries such as Britain or Germany. This case illustrates the point that particular configurations of firm–market relations which developed as a result of certain combinations of dominant institutions that structured economic activities in one period can change in later periods; but it also emphasises the crucial role of institutional changes and conflicts in effecting and structuring such developments.

The role of the state is also critical in structuring the 'rules of the game' in retail banking in Britain and France. As O'Reilly shows, restrictions on the use of part-time workers in France, together with lower levels of state support for child-rearing in Britain, have encouraged French banks to develop higher levels of 'functional' flexibility among their workforce than their British counterparts. Additionally, the generally higher level of education of younger workers in France has facilitated this strategy and, of course, the state has generally played a dominant part in the French banking system since the war, both through ownership and regulation. Differences in the structure and actions of state agencies in Britain and France have produced major variations in the organisation of the banking industries of those countries.

Finally, the crucial role of institutions and cultures in shaping firms' strategies and the development of industry structures is highlighted by Nishida and Redding in their discussion of the Japanese and Hong Kong textile industries. Major differences in state policies, the organisation of the financial system and the labour system have combined with considerable variations in trust relationships and levels of collective commitment to non-kin to produce quite distinct rules of the game in Japan and Hong Kong. As a result, the strategic choices made by leading firms and their structuring of market relations over time have been substantially different so that the organisation and functioning of the whole industry display marked differences between the two economies. This analysis shows very clearly how institutional contexts shape modes of economic organisation and effective paths of development for firms so that the 'same' industry assumes quite distinct forms in different settings and 'rational' strategies can diverge significantly between institutional environments.

# 8
# Business Systems, Industrial Wisdom and Corporate Strategies

*Bo Hellgren and Leif Melin*

The background to this chapter is a long empirical interest in the Swedish pulp and paper industry in general and particularly in one of its dominant actors, a Swedish printing paper company (Melin, 1977; Hellgren and Melin, 1991). In order to further develop our understanding of this industry we started to identify the role of possible business recipes, influenced by Grinyer and Spender (1979). However, we soon found that 'business recipe' is a rather loose and still evolving concept, with various meanings and inter-pretations. Compared with Spender's (1989) interest in 'industry recipes', Whitley (1990; 1991) represents a different stream of research on business recipes, clearly shown through his notion 'business system'.

Generally, the growing interest in business recipes represents a shift in unit of analysis from the single organisation to a broader context, such as sectors and nations. Furthermore, behind the two notions 'industry recipe' and 'business system' we can identify two more general theoretical perspectives with the common objective of capturing contextual structures in which organisations are embedded and explaining the impact of these contexts on the way of organising at the company level.

The first perspective emphasises the cognitive dimension of organisations and organisational fields. Different industries are seen as cognitive constructions, where collective belief structures may regulate collective behaviour. (See, for example, Huff, 1982; Porac et al., 1989; Spender, 1989; and Fombrun, 1986). The second perspective emphasises the dominating role of the broader social and institutional context of which organisations are an integral part. This perspective is represented by a number of scholars who have introduced different but related institutions approaches (see, for example, Etzioni, 1988; Di Maggio and Powell, 1983; and Whitley, 1990). The purpose of this chapter is to apply the two identified meanings of business recipe – the recipe as a collective cognitive structure and the recipe as an institutional context – to our empirical field, the pulp and paper industry.

Thereby we want to show how different dimensions of this industry will be visible, depending on which recipe-perspective we apply.

There are different ways of defining the boundaries of an industry. We choose to apply the institutional perspective to the Swedish part of the pulp and paper industry, defined by the territorial boundaries of Sweden. This means that we try to describe the pulp and paper sector as (part of) a Swedish business system. On the other hand, when we apply the cognitively focused recipe to the pulp and paper industry the system boundaries will not be delimited by the national territory of Sweden. We will focus on the international extension and character of the industry, but restrict our analysis to one significant product field within the whole industry, printing paper.

In order to illuminate how the two types of recipes are related to the organisational level, we will also introduce the case of a Swedish pulp and paper company and discuss its relationship with the specific recipes we describe. The concluding section of the chapter contains a comparative discussion of the two types of recipe-related concepts in order to further clarify the different meanings of these concepts and to argue for the need in organisation studies of both perspectives that these concepts represent. The development of different kinds of organisational structure and practice in different contexts require understanding in terms of those contexts (Whitley, Chapter 1 in this volume), and also the structural properties of organisation must be understood as symbolic representations and interpretations that are collectively shared by organisation participants (Fombrun, 1986: 406).

## Business Systems and the Pulp and Paper Industry

In this section, we will first introduce and discuss the notion of 'business system' in general. Thereafter, the focus will be on one type of business system, that is the business system that develops in the national setting. Empirically, we will illustrate this kind of business system in terms of the Swedish pulp and paper industry in its nation-based context. (The business system of the Finnish pulp and paper industry is characterised in Chapter 6 of this volume.)

### The Notion of Business System
According to Whitley (1990), a business system is a distinctive configuration of market–hierarchy relations that becomes established in its specific societal context. A business system institutionalises different economic rationalities and is the result

of the institutional environment in which it is developed. For example, there seem to be significantly different business systems in East Asia. Dominant economic actors established in Japan, South Korea, Taiwan and Hong Kong are remarkably similar within their institutional environments but distinctively different between them (Whitley, 1991). This implies an institutional structure that is influential regarding enterprise structures and their patterns of development. Institutional factors of importance for which business system will be established are the political and financial systems (Whitley, 1990). Besides institutional systems, social structures such as historical patterns of authority, trust and loyalty may also explain differences between business systems (Whitley, 1991).

Although the notion of business system is applicable on different system levels, there are several arguments for why the nation state is a proper level of analysis at which to identify significant ways of organising business. These arguments could be summarised in the following way: structural variations in terms of political, social and economic systems and the history and dominance of different economic sectors between nation states produce distinctive forms of business systems (cf. Whitley, 1990; 1991); this means that the context created by institutional and social conditions in a nation (or another defined region) shapes a dominating way of organising business in the nation in question. However, the nation state as the basic level of such analyses has been questioned.

Lilja et al. (1990; and Chapter 6 in this volume) argue for a sectoral perspective in order to understand national business systems. The background is their search for a dominant business system in Finland, *the* Finnish way of managing corporations and their business units. According to them, a nation's business system consists of multiple and competing sector-specific business recipes. The competition between and inside sectors is the dynamic force through which a national business system changes; a business system that consequently can be rather heterogeneous. Like Lilja et al., Porter (1990) is interested in the influence from the national environment on industry sectors. He suggests that we can identify national characteristics in many industries, but that these are overshadowed in actual competition by industry-specific circumstances.

### A Nation-based Business System – the Swedish Pulp and Paper Industry

We will here illuminate some features of the Swedish pulp and paper industry in order to present a broad outline of its nation-based business system. The point of departure will not be the sectoral level. Instead, we will start on the national level and exemplify some characteristics of what one may call a common Swedish business system. The pulp and paper industry has for at least two centuries played an important role in the Swedish economy as the major industrial sector (together with the mining industry) and has for long been the largest net exporter. It is therefore a plausible assumption that the Swedish pulp and paper industry both influences and is influenced by its national setting and that a search for this sector's business system should start on the national level. We will argue later on that the importance of the national setting for this sector has started to decline. The national arena seems to have been replaced by a more internationalised arena in which several Swedish pulp and paper firms are significant actors.

According to Katzenstein (1985), Sweden – as well as other small European market economies – is liberalist in its market orientations and corporatist in its political orientation. Sweden's small size makes it dependent on world markets and protectionism is therefore not a workable option. Instead, Sweden strives to smooth the turbulence created by international markets through arrangements to secure domestic cooperation. The need of flexible adjustments to meet international challenges has developed a spirit of political cooperation and active state intervention including incomes policy, a large public sector, and high social welfare expenditures. Important actors in the political arena in Sweden have been not only political parties but also the employers' national federation and the labour movement. Recently, there has been some sign of a weakening of both the employers' federation and the labour movement, and of an increasing tension between them; but historically, these two organisations have since the mid-1930s been homogeneous, centralised and powerful organisations that have interacted in a spirit of harmony and collaboration.

Another feature of the Swedish business system is the willingness of the business community to compete globally (a striving that is supported by the labour movement and the politicians). This international orientation among Swedish firms is not only the result of small domestic markets and influential support from politicians and the labour movement, but partly also a result of managerial attitudes (Sölvell et al., 1991). It is common among Swedish businessmen to be trained or to live for a long time abroad before returning home. Accordingly, foreign assignments have not been destructive to career opportunities. On the contrary, it has been a significant step in the career ladder. In this respect, Sweden differs from many other industrialised countries (ibid.). Compared with other small European market economies, another distinct aspect of the Swedish business system is this combination of an international business orientation and a strong, centralised and supportive labour movement (Katzenstein, 1985).

The industrialisation in Sweden was supported and led by a few powerful banks, industrialists and financiers (Glete, 1987). These initial relations have developed into long-term and stable connections between banks and industry, with a concentration on long-term rather than short-term credits facilitating business development and restructuring of troubled corporations (Sölvell et al., 1991). Two commercial banks – SE-banken (for long dominated by the Wallenberg family) and Svenska Handelsbanken – have had, and still have, close connections with a dominant part of Swedish industry, including two of the major Swedish pulp and paper corporations (Stora and SCA). In the pulp and paper industry, these two financial spheres are supplemented with a third sphere, the forest owner federation. This third sphere has been rather divided but still powerful because of its important possession of huge forest areas.

There are not only long-term and stable relations between banks and industry. Owners and managers also tend to stay committed to the nowadays matured industries where they once started. Instead of diversifying and leaving their original core business, the big Swedish corporations have developed into international and even global firms.

So far, we have broadly outlined some characteristics of what could be seen as parts of a common Swedish business system and thereby also pinpointed some features of the pulp and paper industry in Sweden. We shall now more directly focus on this industry in its Swedish context. The large Swedish pulp and paper corporations of today (three very big and four medium-sized) all have a history of being companies with a significant mill character, dominating the industrial communities where they were, and in several cases still are, located. Furthermore, they were big owners of the bases for major productive factors such as forests and hydroelectric power stations. Up until 1980, the industry was notably domestic-based in its production structure – with almost no production facilities abroad. Compared with its export sales share, the internationalisation of its production has been remarkably low. This industry was a true example of the traditional theory of foreign trade, regarding comparative advantages: the basis for the international market position of Swedish pulp and paper industry was the superior supply of pulpwood of good quality.

The Swedish pulp and paper industry does not, on the national level, show a high degree of product specialisation as a whole. Instead, the historical pattern has been that different companies have concentrated their activities on two or three product groups each. Some are very big in pulp, others in printing paper or tissue paper etc. This complementary characteristic of the product range of Swedish companies is perhaps one reason (besides the role of the financial spheres mentioned above) for the rather high degree of market collaboration which the Swedish part of this industry has shown, with close supplier–buyer relationships, R & D collaboration, organised negotiations about prices and mutual information on new investments. However, Swedish firms have not, compared with their Finnish competitors, coordinated their sales of pulp and paper as much. In Finland, there is a long tradition of forming joint product-wise sales organisations which operate worldwide through their sales offices (Lilja et al., 1990). Another difference compared with the Finnish pulp and paper industry is that the Swedes, as mentioned above, have not left their core business. Their Finnish competitors have diversified both to other forest products and engineering industries for machines and equipment used in the forestry and pulp and paper industry.

Understandably, from the description given above, this industry has been rather influential in the political decision process in Sweden. The investments in nuclear power plants were actively supported by the pulp and paper industry association. The fact that all manufacturing industries in Sweden pay a lower price for electrical energy than other consumer groups is much connected to the pulp and paper industry. It is the biggest electrical energy consumer in Sweden which has been using its negotiating power, further strengthened by the industry's role as being the dominant net exporter in Sweden. The list below summarises this overview of the business system in the Swedish pulp and paper industry.

Table 8.1 *Some characteristics of the established business system in the Swedish pulp and paper industry*

- International dependence – export orientation
- A domestic pattern of production plants
- 'Stick to the knitting' and product specialisation
- Powerful owners with a long-term interest in the industry
- Autocratic authority structures within firms
- Collaboration between domestic competitors
- Vertically integrated firms (from raw material to refined products)

To conclude, the Swedish pulp and paper industry forms a

nation-based business system with rather specific characteristics. However, the homogeneity of this recipe has been weakened during the last decade, not so much because of changes in the Swedish institutional environment but as an effect of changes in the more industry-specific recipe of the more and more globalised pulp and paper industry.

## Cognitive Recipes and the Pulp and Paper Industry

In this section we will present a number of recipe-related concepts that all focus on the cognitive dimension of inter-organisation structures. The conceptual discussion will end up with a definition of one notion, industrial wisdom, that will be used to represent this recipe category henceforth. This notion will be illuminated through a description of the industrial wisdom of the printing paper sector of the international pulp and paper industry.

### A Cognitive Perspective on Business Recipes

Industry structure is a multidimensional phenomenon. An inter-organisational structure cannot be understood without considering the 'superstructure' dimension, that is the ongoing social construction of meaning, the interactive sense-making and the shared values of this organisational collectivity (Fombrum, 1986: 405). Child (1988) suggests that a sector has a collective cognitive frame of reference and that a sector accordingly can be seen as a cognitive field. According to Huff (1982), an industry is even defined by shared metaphors and world views, behind which there are taken-for-granted assumptions characteristic of the industry in question. Spender (1989) found sector-specific recipes in his studies of three British industrial sectors. However, despite the divergences, the recipes express ideas about the same themes, for example how the market is segmented, how business units must relate to its market, the reciprocal patterns of influence and obligations and how these are sustained and protected from internal disorder and external competition (ibid: 157). One of Spender's essential points is that managers draw their judgements of appropriate structures and strategies from a shared pool of knowledge, unique for a sector. He labels this shared pool 'industry recipe' and defines it as 'the shared knowledge base that those socialized into an industry take as familiar professional common sense' (Spender, 1989: 69).

The industry recipe is a group-level concept and is a major contributor to how managers construct their theory of the situation. Spender regards an industry recipe as the business-specific world-view of a 'tribe of industry experts' visibly articulated in 'rituals, rites of profession passage, local jargon and dress' (1989: 7). Lilja et al. (Chapter 6 in this volume) define the business recipe of a certain industrial sector as the historically evolving logic of action. Based on the enactment metaphor (Weick, 1979; Bougon, 1983; Smircich and Stubbart, 1985), Goodman and Newell (1989) stress that managers make sense of the industrial environment through their own cognitive frameworks. One collective framework that influences the way managers see their environment is the 'industry wisdom', defined as the common set of assumptions held about the world by most actors in the industry (Goodman and Newell, 1989).

To summarise, there seems to exist a significant pattern of managerial beliefs at the industry level (Grinyer and Spender, 1979). Each industry is characterised by distinctive corporate languages, constructs and frameworks (Whipp and Clark, 1986). Such a collective cognitive frame of reference may guide member organisations into specific forms and activities (Child, 1988). We have found such a collective belief structure in our own studies of the cognitive dimension of industries (Hellgren and Melin, 1992a). This mental structure, the *industrial wisdom*, expresses shared beliefs about the competitive rules of the game and the structural freedom of action within an industry. In other words, the industrial wisdom is a shared conventional wisdom, about appropriate structure and action, that is held by most firms in an industry.

### Industrial Wisdom – an Industry-based Recipe

Industrial wisdom gives expression to cognitive characteristics of an industry. However, the proper boundaries of an industry are not easily defined (cf. Brooks, 1991). We have found that distinguishable parts within the whole pulp and paper industry have their own particular industrial wisdom (see Hellgren and Melin, 1992b). In this chapter, we present some results from our analysis of the industrial wisdom in the *printing paper sector*. We have identified the industrial wisdom in this international sector (with focus on its European part) at two different periods, about 1980 and about 1990.

At the beginning of the 1980s, the European part of the global sector of printing paper was rather delimited, just marginally interacting with the other dominant part – the North American arena. Furthermore, the sector was characterised by the domestic orientation of production plants. Only one of the ten largest producers in Western Europe had a production site outside its country of origin, while their sales had a strong export orientation.

Over 40 per cent of the world consumption of newsprint was exported from Scandinavia and Canada.

An important feature of the industrial wisdom at this time was long-range thinking. Investment plans, when investing in new machines, forests or hydroelectric power plants, were based on real long-range forecasts and, for business firms, unusually long pay-off times.

A general trend in the pulp and paper industry was to reduce dependence on chemical pulp for sale through vertical integration. However, as wood-containing printing paper is based on thermo-mechanical pulp this issue would not lead to increased investments in paper machines. Furthermore, the long-range demand for printing paper was predicted to diminish from 2.5 per cent per year during the 1970s to less than 2 per cent during the 1980s. The response to diminishing growth was to start to upgrade the product range, for example to lighter newsprint qualities and super-calendered paper qualities. A high price and a predicted scarcity of pulpwood was another important issue in the field. Use of alternative tree species and of waste paper were both discussed. Although the technology for use of waste paper was well developed in some other parts of the pulp and paper industry, and the potential economic advantage was visible due to the high price of pulpwood (and pulp), actors in this sector undertook a wait-and-see policy. The investment policy for new newsprint machines was to locate them where the raw material (i.e. pulpwood) was available and to close down or convert small sites. Profitability was seen as being created in the paper mill through bigger and faster machines and continuous 'trimming' of existing plants.

The 1980s was a decade of far-reaching changes. For example, there were changes regarding the set of newsprint and magazine paper producers and the localisation pattern of their production, indicating that the sector had become more boundless and global. Behind these and other changes we can identify a changed set of opinions, beliefs and ideas about how to act in the printing paper sector. Our interpretation is that changes in the industrial wisdom during the 1980s have mainly emerged from within the sector itself and from transnational changes such as EC 1992, and not at first hand from changes in national institutional structures.

In about 1990, the climate in the printing paper sector, as in other parts of the pulp and paper industry, was increasingly competitive. Large companies that are highly internationalised and which have relatively complete product portfolios dominate the field. The production orientation and cost-reduction efforts that were dominant in about 1980 are nowadays supplemented with an increased market and customer orientation, implying that the customer is regarded as a much more significant actor than before. Ongoing structural changes in the customer market towards fewer and bigger publishing groups, and changes in customers' purchasing policies towards a reduction in numbers of suppliers, force the producers to be more customer-oriented. Furthermore, both acquisitions and aggressive greenfield investments are necessary in order to reach the required size as a leading printing paper producer, capable of competing in a more competitive climate. The most interesting localisation for greenfield investments is within the EC, and in the future – when the expected growth in demand arrives – in Eastern Europe. The reason behind this localisation strategy is not trade limitations. Former barriers of trade have already been reduced during the 1980s. Instead, one reason is that the market in Western Europe is predicted to continue to grow at an annual rate of 4 per cent, and that the growth will be higher in Europe than in North America, where the USA is expected to have reached its saturation point in the demand for newsprint. But the main reason as to why the EC countries provide the best localities for new plants is perhaps the use of waste paper in the production of newsprint.

The belief in waste paper as the major raw material for newsprint is, quite suddenly, very strong. It is today a necessity to mix waste paper with virgin wood fibres. The environmental aspect is becoming increasingly important, even supported by a law in the USA on the minimum share of recycled paper. Furthermore, the price of pulpwood is still regarded as high. Together with improvements in the processing technology of waste paper, the environmental and price aspects make waste paper the most important domestic raw material within the EC. 'Nowadays, the big forests are found in London and Paris!' The increasing role of waste paper is challenging the traditional localisation pattern for competitive production of newsprint in countries such as Canada, Finland and Sweden.

Finally, it is necessary – in order to stay competitive – to further upgrade the product portfolio. New grades – improved newsprint and lightweight newsprint – are predicted to grow very fast during the 1990s. This leads to an initial removal of the boundaries between different parts of the pulp and paper industry, such as wood-containing printing paper and woodfree paper. The new industrial wisdom that emerged during the 1980s in the printing paper sector is summarised in Table 8.2.

Table 8.2   *Some characteristics of the new industrial wisdom that emerged during the 1980s in the printing paper sector*

---

- A belief in continued growth in demand for printing paper during the 1990s
- A belief in mergers and acquisitions as means to growth, replacing the earlier belief in organic growth
- A belief in customer-orientation as a supplement to an earlier dominating production orientation
- A belief in upgrading of products in order to remain competitive
- A belief in waste paper replacing the earlier belief in virgin wood fibre as a superior raw material in production of printing paper
- A belief in a new localisation pattern implying that new plants will be located where the customers are rather than where the traditional raw material is available

---

## The Influence of Institutional and Cognitive Structures on Individual Firms

In organisation studies the growing interest in understanding outer context(s) can to a great extent be explained by the influence of firms' structure and behaviour that these contexts are assumed to have. In this section we will discuss the ruling and framing role of the two contexts we have described and illustrated in earlier sections – the 'business system' type of institutional structure and the 'industrial wisdom' type of collective cognitive structure. To illuminate the role of these contextual structures we will here relate Swedish business system as presented earlier and the industrial wisdom of the international printing paper sector to an individual firm, a Swedish company in the pulp and paper industry. The following description of the company, Holmen AB, is based on a four-year in-depth and longitudinal case study of this company's strategic development during the two last decades, including an analysis of the development of its competitive environment, the paper industry, during the 1980s.

In 1968, Holmen AB was in a slight crisis, with a declining and unprofitable textile unit and a still profitable pulp and paper unit with very old production machinery. Based on systematic strategic analyses, a major decision was soon made to wind up the textile operations and to concentrate development offensively on wood-containing printing paper. The new business idea was to supply the market with newsprint and magazine papers and to grow with the market. Between 1970 and 1984, Holmen fulfilled its expansive concentration strategy with investments in three new machines for printing paper, which led to its position as the largest producer of newsprint in Europe. The company made some small efforts to diversify during this period, efforts oriented towards product areas outside the forest industry. But the main plan was to build increased capacity through investments in new paper machines. At the same time, the strategy was not offensive in relation to the competitors. The idea was to retain market share in a growing market.

This epoch of development in Holmen, the period from 1968 to 1984, was very much in line with and influenced by the prevailing industrial wisdom of the 1970s, such as the belief in organic growth, in domestic localisation of new machine investments and in the advantage of locating the paper mill near the raw material, in this case the forests. One factor that perhaps increased this influence was that the then CEO came to Holmen from a job as president of the industry association for the pulp and paper industry, an organisation that surely represented shared beliefs of the industry. However, in one respect Holmen was challenging the industrial wisdom. At this time, a leading recipe for future success was to grow through vertical integration and related diversification (horizontally). Here Holmen went its own way through its – for that time – unusual and powerful concentration on growth in just one vertical layer of the integrated production and in just one product segment.

Holmen was very much a historic product of the business system in the Swedish pulp and paper industry. Several characteristics of this business system also characterised Holmen during this epoch. The ownership structure was very stable from the 1950s. The authority structure was typically Swedish – a very centralised internal power structure combined with a rather paternalistic atmosphere and mainly cooperative relations with the local unions. Furthermore, an interesting consequence of the institutionalised business system was a rather strong respect for the overall structure of the Swedish pulp and paper industry, meaning that the relatively smaller companies, like Holmen, did not challenge the two biggest companies, which were dominated by the two biggest ownership spheres in Swedish industry.

After 1984, the business idea and main strategies of Holmen changed significantly. The new business idea was still based on a growth philosophy, but now more aggressively expressed: Holmen would become one of the leading Nordic companies in the pulp and paper industry, with each of its main business areas among the forefront of European suppliers. The strategy was to expand in at least two business areas, printing paper and hygiene products. Holmen had rather different market positions for these two areas, which also became apparent in the company's strategic activities.

In the product range of printing paper, Holmen decided to grow extensively, not only in the newsprint area but also in magazine paper (both uncoated and coated). Especially interesting was lightweight coated paper (LWC), at that time the fastest growing printing paper quality in the whole industry. For LWC paper, the strategic intent was to create European opportunities through a new strategic alliance. In this situation Holmen was contacted by a West German firm, a big producer of LWC paper, about possible collaborative arrangements. Important strategic possibilities of a partnership were obvious, especially as the West German firm had started to build a new paper machine for LWC qualities, which would make it the largest producer of this grade in Europe. In January 1987 Holmen acquired a stake of 25 per cent in the West German firm, with an option to double its stake. Through this acquisition Holmen had found a solution to its LWC investment problem and also a way into the Common Market.

Holmen's market position in its new business area, hygiene products, was rather weak even in the domestic market. The strategic intention for this business area was to restructure the domestic market before facing the Common Market. After the first acquisition in this business area in 1985, the new Hygiene Division of Holmen was announced as a growth area. The meaning of the strategic intention was that Holmen Hygiene had to reach a more powerful position in Scandinavia before they made any direct strategic movements into the EEC. It was regarded as impossible to increase the market share in Scandinavia through organic growth. The only way was a takeover of a competing firm. In 1987, Holmen acquired MoDo Consumer Products from a major Swedish competitor, the MoDo Group. This acquisition made Holmen Hygiene the third biggest producer of tissue in Europe, and a significant step in the restructuring of the Scandinavian market was taken. However, the end of the story of Holmen as an autonomous company occurred suddenly, when the company was acquired by the remaining MoDo Group in 1988.

While the earlier epoch was characterised by a rather defensive strategy to grow with the market in one business area, this strategic epoch, 1984–8, expressed a much more offensive dominance orientation, including related diversifications and evident ambitions to take an active part in the restructuring of the industry. To undertake this more aggressive strategy, Holmen gave up the earlier dominating idea about internal growth. The new strategy implied a strong belief both in far-reaching alliances and in acquisitions.

The 'strategic changes' in Holmen during this period occurred at the same time as the industrial wisdom in the printing paper sector changed radically. The change pattern of Holmen very much follows ongoing changes in the industrial wisdom. This seems to imply that Holmen adopted some of the new collective beliefs rather early, such as the strong belief in acquisitions instead of organic, internally driven growth. On the other hand, it also illustrates our assumption that changes in the industrial wisdom may be initiated not only by external forces but also by new beliefs and actions emerging in companies within a particular industry. New interpretations, thoughts and actions within firms that break with an existing collective belief structure in an industry may produce new collectively shared beliefs, and thereby contribute to the reproduction or transformation of prevailing industrial wisdom.

During the last decade we have seen changes in several Swedish pulp and paper companies that may indicate both that the nationally based business system (described in an earlier section) is in transition and that its influential role is decreasing. The type of changes that we refer to, and which we also have observed in the Holmen case, are hostile changes regarding ownership and less collaborative relations between Swedish competitors. The fact that a number of political decisions made in Sweden since 1990 are changing the overall 'Swedish model' in many respects also gives support to the current transitional state of the business system that we have studied. Furthermore, some strong Pan-European forces – EC 1992 and the 'opening' of Eastern Europe – will probably result in cross-national business systems that will replace some, until recently rather integrated, national business systems. Another factor that may diminish the ruling effect of nationally based business systems such as the one we have studied is the increasing autonomy of big industrial corporations in general. New structural forms of big multinational enterprises, such as the multi-domestic form, can hardly be understood as routed in a specific nationally based business system. Instead, these new forms indicate that we should look for the emergence of new cross-national business systems. The institutional environments that will generate the most distinctive business systems of the 1990s in Europe will presumably not be equivalent with the nation state (cf. Whitley, 1991).

**Institutional Ruling and Cognitive Framing**

In this chapter we have defined and illustrated two different concepts with a recipe-related content. In this concluding section we will further compare the meaning of these two concepts –

business system and industrial wisdom. Furthermore, we will argue for the need of both concepts in organisation studies. They and their inherent perspectives can supplement each other in a fruitful way and thereby lead to further development of our understanding of outer contexts that may influence the structure and functioning of organisations in different environments.

### Institutionalised Configurations and Ideational Structures

Recipe-related concepts, used to characterise the business setting, can be given theoretically divergent meanings and describe different dimensions of structuring. A 'business recipe' can describe a specific configuration of relations within and between organisations, such as authority relations, size of organisations and type of formal structures that dominate in a given context. The shape of a specific configuration, for example a national business system, is seen as the result of the institutional environment (a nation, a region or an industry) that the configuration is embedded in and a history of this specific environment. Institutional factors of importance may be the financial system, the political system, and the legal system, to mention just three. A 'business recipe' can also describe a pattern of commonly held beliefs about organisational issues (including structure, strategy and management style), beliefs that are shared within an organisation community. This cognitive content of recipes (giving 'cognitive' a broad meaning) focuses on the role of ideational structures in different organisational settings. With this structuring dimension we try to understand each structure as a vehicle for interactive sense-making (Fombrun, 1986). Relating these two meanings to our two recipe-notions, the business system describes mainly an institutional configuration, while industrial wisdom describes the ideational and cognitive structure of an organisational context.

Another difference is that business systems, when applied in empirical studies, are often defined from a territorial perspective and therefore describe institutionalised characteristics related to a specific geographic arena. The system boundaries of an industrial wisdom is instead functionally defined, which means that the system is constituted by the organisations that are involved in a vertical and horizontal market system (see Friedman and Weaver, 1979, and their discussion about 'territory' versus 'function'). A business system is derived from the context of a surrounding institutional environment, which often implies that the geographic boundaries for the chosen environment determine the characteristics found for the focal business system. Many industries may contain clusters of organisations that can be seen as nationally based 'development blocks' (Dahmén, 1988) or 'diamonds' (Porter, 1990). But these clusters are often strongly dependent on cross-national relationships within the whole industry, on foreign suppliers, foreign competitors in alliance relationships and on foreign customers. This means that the industrial wisdom is shaped by the industry-specific environment and context. The boundary in any territorial (geographic) sense is of less interest for the industrial wisdom, as this recipe expresses the core characteristics of the shared beliefs and knowledge within the focal system itself.

## A Final Comment on the Two Recipe-Notions

As indicated, our conclusion is that organisation studies could gain by using both notions of business recipe dealt with in this chapter. They are not mutually exclusive but instead complementary. Through focusing business systems, often-forgotten contextual characteristics of organisations can be described. On the other hand, this perspective can be given the same critique that Fombrun and Abrahamson (1989) articulate regarding other institutional perspectives when studying organisation communities. 'Current analyses . . . tend to overemphasise the conformity of organisations to economic and institutional forces within populations at the expense of the direct and indirect participation of those organisations in the construction of their environments' (ibid.: 27).

To understand organisations in their context we also need a cognitive perspective that focuses on sector-specific and cross-national business recipes. When arguing for an organisation-in-sector perspective, Child (1988: 17) wanted to see more research on 'sector cognitive fields', in our words studies focusing on industrial wisdom. As well as single organisations being socially constructed through the interactions and sense-making of human actors (Berger and Luckmann, 1966), organisational fields are also structured by the ideational dimension, which express collective thought structures and industry norms (Fombrun, 1986).

To summarise, we have illuminated two recipe-related notions with different meanings. Together they are complementary. Simultaneous analyses of business system and industrial wisdom in organisation studies could create a true contextual approach (Pettigrew, 1985). A conceptualisation of different recipes should consider the role of *both* institutional ruling *and* cognitive framing in the structuring of organisations.

## References

Berger, P.L. and Luckmann, T. (1986) *The Social Construction of Reality*. New York: Doubleday.

Bougon, M.G. (1983) 'Uncovering Cognitive Maps: the Self-Q Technique', in G. Morgan (ed.) *Beyond Method*. Beverly Hills: Sage. pp. 173–88.

Brooks, G.R. (1991) 'Defining Market Boundaries: Two Approaches'. Paper presented at the 11th Annual International Conference of the Strategic Management Society, Toronto.

Child, J. (1988) 'On Organizations in their Sectors', *Organizational Studies*. 9: 13–19.

Dahmén E. (1988) 'Development Blocks in Industrial Economics', *Scandinavian Economic History Review*. 34: 3–14.

DiMaggio, P. and Powell, W.W. (1983) 'The Iron Cage Revisited: Institutional Isomorphism and Collective Rationality in Organizational Fields', *American Sociological Review*. 48: 147–60.

Etzioni, A. (1988) *The Moral Dimension – Toward a New Economics*. New York: Free Press.

Fombrun, C.J. (1986) 'Structural Dynamics within and between Organizations', *Administrative Science Quarterly*. 31: 403–21.

Fombrun, C.J. and Abrahamson, E. (1989) 'Producing Cognitive Environments: the Superstructure of Corporate Communities'. Working Paper, New York University.

Friedman, J. and Weaver, C. (1979) *Territory and Function. The Evolution of Regional Planning*. London: Edward Arnold.

Glete, J. (1987) *Ägande och industriell omvandling. Ägargrupper, skogsindustri, verkstadsindustri 1850–1950*. Stockholm: SNS Förlag.

Goodman, R.S. and Newell, S.E. (1989) 'Industry Wisdom: an Aid to Formulating Strategy or Harmful to Firm Performance?'. Unpublished paper, York University, Toronto.

Grinyer, P.H. and Spender, J.C. (1979) 'Recipes, Crises and Adoption in Mature Industries', *International Studies of Management and Organization*. 9: 113–33.

Hellgren, B. and Melin, L. (1991) 'Corporate Strategies in Nordic Firms Facing Europe – Acquisitions and other Collaborative Strategies', in B. Stymne and L.G. Mattsson (eds), *Corporate and Industry Strategies for Europe*. Amsterdam: Elsevier. pp. 327–51.

Hellgren, B. and Melin, L. (1992a) 'The Role of Strategists' Way-of-Thinking in Strategic Change Processes', forthcoming in G. Johnson and J. Hendry (eds), *Leadership, Strategic Change and the Learning Organization*.

Hellgren, B. and Melin, L. (1992b) 'Structure and Change in Industrial Fields – a Contextual Approach', forthcoming in D. Sharma (ed.), *Advances in International Marketing*.

Huff, A.S. (1982) 'Industry Influences on Strategy Reformulation', *Strategic Management Journal*. 3: 119–31.

Katzenstein, P.J. (1985) *Small States in World Markets – Industrial Policy in Europe*. Ithaca, NY: Cornell University Press.

Lilja, K., Räsänen, K. and Tainio, R. (1990) 'In Search of the Dominant Economic Agent: the Finnish Case'. Paper presented at the Workshop on the Study of Dominant Economic Agents, Helsinki.

Melin, L. (1977) 'Strategic Purchasing Actions – Organization and Interaction'. PhD dissertation, Linköping University, Linköping [in Swedish].

Pettigrew, A.M. (1985) 'Examining Change in the Long-Term Context of Culture and Politics' in J.M. Pennings (ed.), *Organizational Strategy and Change*. London: Jossey-Bass. pp. 269–318.

Porac, J.F., Thomas, H. and Baden-Fuller, C. (1989) 'Competitive Groups as Cognitive Communities: the Case of Scottish Knitwear Manufacturers', *Journal of Management Studies*. 26: 397–416.

Porter, M.E. (1990) *The Competitive Advantage of Nations*. London: Macmillan Press.

Smircich, L. and Stubbart, C. (1985) 'Strategic Management in an Enacted World', *Academy of Management Review*. 10: 724–36.

Sölvell, Ö., Zander, I. and Porter, M.E. (1991) *Advantage Sweden*. Stockholm: Norsteds Juridikförlag

Spender, J.C. (1989) *Industry Recipes – The Nature and Sources of Managerial Judgement*. Oxford: Blackwell.

Weick, K.E. (1979) *The Social Psychology of Organizing*. Reading: Addison-Wesley.

Whipp, R. and Clark, P. (1986) *Innovation and the Auto Industry*. London: Pinter.

Whitley, R. (1990) 'Eastern Asian Enterprise Structures and the Comparative Analysis of Forms of Business Organizations', *Organization Studies*. 11(1): 47–74.

Whitley, R. (1991) 'The Social Construction of Business Systems in East Asia', *Organization Studies*. 12 (1): 1–28.

# 9
# Business Systems, Consumption and Change: Personal Financial Services in Italy

*David Knights, Glenn Morgan and Fergus Murray*

The idea that there are many different forms of effective business organisation is now commonplace. The search for the one universal model of management and business has been subjected to widespread criticism. The economic dynamism of East Asia with the very different organisational forms that exist there has been particularly challenging to the universalist approach. Even within Europe the continued prosperity of Germany and the expansion of Italy and France, all of which have distinctive business systems, provides further evidence of the diversity of effective forms. American dominance of management and business discourse, which was strongly associated with a tendency towards a single universal model of economic efficiency, has declined along with the reduction in American economic dominance. This has led to an appreciation of the diversity of effective business systems which exist and of their links to wider institutional processes (see the other contributions in this volume).

This chapter seeks to develop this approach by focusing particularly on the issue of change. As Whitley has shown in his analysis of the East Asian economies – especially Whitley (1990) and Chapter 1 in this volume, the emergence of particular business systems has complex historical roots. It is important to understand these roots in order to make sense of existing institutional arrangements, and also to uncover how they are changing. We are therefore concerned in this chapter to emphasise the dynamic nature of business systems analysis. In this sense, we take a somewhat different perspective to most of the other contributions in this volume, as our concern is to understand how a particular arrangement of institutional and business characteristics which has been effective over a lengthy period of time begins to disintegrate. We are therefore trying to understand elements of continuity and discontinuity in a process of system change. We believe that in a world economy where competition between companies and nation states is increasingly significant, the stability of nationally based business systems is threatened from many directions. It is therefore important that business systems analysis considers more explicitly the issue of change.

In order to illustrate this point, we examine the case of the personal financial services industry in Italy.[1] Our focus on the financial services industry arises for a number of reasons. First, the financial services industry seems to be organised along uniquely 'national' lines, in the sense that very different structures have developed even within countries that are in close geographical proximity, such as those of Western Europe. It therefore shows as strongly as any the importance of appreciating distinctive business systems. However, it has also been a dynamic industry, particularly over the last 20 years. It therefore raises interesting questions about how change occurs within business systems that have previously appeared to be stable. Second, the industry is important due to the character of its institutional relations. Often, the key relation that is considered here is to the industrial system via the provision of capital, where the varying nature of capital markets is seen as a significant determinant of the success of manufacturing industry (see, for example, Zysman, 1983). However, in our view there is an equally important set of institutional linkages which the business system approach points to and which is crucial in the case of the personal financial services industry, that is, the linkages between consumers, the state and the industry.

Finally, we have chosen to focus on Italy because it is a country which has changed quickly over the last 20 years. From being amongst the slowest developing countries in the European Community, it has grown rapidly. Much of this growth has been associated with the development of distinctive business systems in the industrial districts of the Third Italy (Piore and Sabel, 1984). This has prompted a great deal of debate concerning the nature of this business system and its generalisability. In turn, this relates to wider issues concerning the changing nature of Italian society and its political system. On the one hand, there are aspects of the 'Via Italiana' which are deeply embedded in long-term historical processes and appear resistant to change; on the other hand, major dynamic changes are occurring. How can the business systems approach help us to understand both these features? By focusing on developments in one particular sector over the post-war period, we seek to throw light on this question.

The chapter proceeds in the following way. First, we analyse the nature of the personal financial services sector in Italy as it developed in the post-war period through to the 1980s. In brief, we argue that, in comparison with other European countries, the industry was underdeveloped, and we explain this by reference to certain particular characteristics of Italian society and their effect on the potential consumers of such services. In the second part of the chapter, we seek to go beneath the relative stability of this system to uncover processes of change. We focus particularly on the growing fiscal crisis of the Italian welfare state and how this relates to wider social and political change in Italian society. In the third part, we present further data which show that although the Italian financial services industry lags behind much of Europe, it is expanding in its home market. We argue that this evidence of expansion can be understood by reference to the emergence of new groups of social actors (companies, consumers and political reformers) with interests in developing and expanding the personal financial services industry.

In conclusion, we argue that in order to understand the development of the Italian personal financial services industry in the post-war period, it is necessary to examine its location in wider social and political relations. Once we begin to do this, we see how the system that was developed in the 1950s is now being undermined and gradually replaced by a new set of relations, linking the industry to consumers and the state.

## The Personal Financial Services Industry in Italy

Our focus on the personal financial services industry as a business system is confined to considering its penetration of its home market and its overall size in relation to other countries. We begin, therefore, with a discussion of the market size and issues of international comparison.

Until the 1980s, Italians traditionally kept their money in as liquid a form as possible. Market research conducted in 1987 ('Multifinanziaria Eurisko', 1987), found that only 48 per cent of its Italian sample held current accounts with banks; 52 per cent of the sample had their wages and salaries paid in cash. On top of this, the Italian black economy operates primarily on the basis of cash, and participants generally seek to avoid transactions passing through banking institutions where legal requirements for disclosure might lead to tax liability. The preference for liquidity is further illustrated by the fact that in 1980, 70.6 per cent of non-cash household financial assets were in bank and postal deposit accounts, with only 29.4 per cent in shares, mutual funds or bonds. In the areas of life insurance and pensions, the Eurisko report showed similar low levels of uptake. Only 14 per cent of the sample had endowment life assurance; only 18 per cent had term life assurance; only 8 per cent had a company pension scheme and 5 per cent a private pension.

Table 9.1 *International comparison of insurance premiums in 1988*

|  | Insurance premium income as % of GDP | Ranking | Direct premiums per inhabitant (US$) | Ranking |
|---|---|---|---|---|
| Japan | 9.78 | 1 | 2310.9 | 1 |
| USA | 8.90 | 2 | 1751.3 | 2 |
| UK | 8.25 | 3 | 1208.4 | 4 |
| Germany | 6.69 | 4 | 1296.1 | 3 |
| France | 5.58 | 5 | 933.5 | 5 |
| Spain | 4.21 | 6 | 376.4 | 6 |
| Italy | 2.41 | 7 | 348.0 | 7 |
| Greece | 1.34 | 8 | 67.3 | 8 |

*Source:* Ania, 1990

This made the Italian financial services industry distinctive. On two different measures (premium income as percentage GDP, and premiums per inhabitant) Italy consistently comes very low in the international ranking of spending on insurance (see Table 9.1). In comparison with the UK, Italy consumes approximately between a third and a quarter less in terms of premium income as a percentage of GDP. With regard to premium income per inhabitant, Italians consume less than a quarter of the insurance products of the average UK citizen. Yet these countries have GDPs and populations of approximate equivalence. Again, it is of interest that Spanish citizens consume more dollars of premium per head than Italian citizens despite the higher standard of living in Italy.

As shown in Table 9.2, Italy is ranked fourth in terms of total insurance premium income generated in 1988, well below Germany, the UK and France.

Table 9.2 *Direct total insurance premiums in the EC in 1988 (millions US$)*

| | |
|---|---|
| Germany | 79,320 |
| UK | 68,973 |
| France | 52,154 |
| Italy | 19,995 |
| Holland | 15,054 |
| Spain | 14,698 |
| Belgium | 6,300 |
| Denmark | 4,823 |
| Ireland | 3,220 |
| Greece | 674 |

*Source*: Ania, 1990: diagram

In consumption terms, then, we can characterise the Italian financial services industry as one with a low level of usage of both bank accounts and insurance in comparison to other European countries at a similar level of economic development. This was reflected in the structure of the industry. Retail banking, in particular, tended to be heavily regionalised; only a few banks had a national presence. Bank ownership tended to take a variety of forms; private banks (that is, owned by a family or a group of families), mutual or savings banks and regionally owned banks have remained common. None of these have tended to have national ambitions nor have they had the capital to expand nationally through organic growth or takeover. Thus Italian banking has remained a patchwork of local and regional institutions where growth through acquisitions and mergers was also difficult to achieve because of these ownership structures. Thus in the late 1970s there were still 1069 banks in Italy, often having very localised cultures and ties (Manghetti, 1982).

The insurance sector was rather more concentrated, with the state insurer INA being dominant. Table 9.3 shows market shares of the Italian life insurance industry held by the top 10 companies. Clearly the market is dominated by INA (25.5 per cent) and Generali, which through its ownership of Alleanza controls 27.8 per cent of the life market. These two companies are followed by RAS with an 8.9 per cent share of the market. There are then six companies with between 4.5 and 2 per cent shares of the market. These are followed by 25 companies with market shares of between 1 and 0.25 per cent.

Table 9.3 *Market shares in life insurance (%), 1987*

| | |
|---|---|
| INA | 25.5 |
| Generali | 16.3 |
| Alleanza | 11.5 |
| RAS | 8.9 |
| Fideuram | 4.3 |
| SAI | 3.6 |
| Toro | 2.5 |
| Mediolanum | 2.3 |
| Fondiaria | 2.2 |
| Unipol | 2.1 |

*Source*: Mercantile and General

The life insurance industry has traditionally been heavily regulated. In order to conduct business, a licence must be granted by the Ministry of Industry and Commerce (MICA). This will only be granted after a detailed business plan has been submitted for the first three years of operation. All premiums and contracts have to be agreed with the authorities in advance. The industry has in the past had high levels of administrative and distributive expenses. However, regulatory barriers (and the informal influence of the major companies over the regulators) has meant that new entrants have been discouraged and competitive pressures to reduce costs and improve performance for consumers have been minimized. The consequence of this has been that there has been little drive to expand the market.

Taking deposit banking and the life insurance industry, then, we see that the personal financial services industry in Italy has a low level of development compared to most of its European neighbours. In the next section, we explore why this has occurred.

**Personal Financial Services and Social Relations**

Whilst there are undoubtedly a range of factors which could be adduced to explain the particular nature of the Italian personal financial services industry, we wish to argue that the low level of saving and investment that goes through formal financial institutions is related to the role which the family and the state has played in Italy in providing security to the citizenry. In order to explore this properly, we have to consider not just the family and the state but also how clientelistic relations tie the two together.

*The Family*
In a recent study which compared kinship and family patterns in Britain, the USA, Australia, West Germany, Austria, Hungary and Italy, Janet Finch observed:

> Of all the countries under study, Italy emerges with a particularly distinctive pattern of personal relationships and networks ... To Italians, relationships with both relatives and friends form a much more integral part of daily life than elsewhere. They are more likely to share a home with their relatives and also to have relatives living nearby. They are more likely to visit or telephone relatives daily and also to be in daily contact with a 'best friend'. Relationships between parents and children seem particularly important; children are less likely than in any other country to move out of the parental home before marriage and, in adult life, children are more likely to think of turning to their parents for practical assistance, or to borrow money. (Finch, 1989: 101)

Although there are considerable regional variations between the industrialised North (which is closer to other Western European countries in its family patterns) and the South (with its high dependence on agriculture and tourism), Italy as a whole appears distinctive. Membership of the *extended* family network has been a key part of social identity in the Italian context, overshadowing the marriage relationship itself, which is 'correspondingly less important, Italians being less likely than others to turn to their spouse for various types of assistance' (Finch, 1989: 101). In this sense, individual identity, separate from kinship ties, is less developed than in other European countries.

The significance of this needs careful consideration, for the Italian family is not an isolated entity. Rather it is connected to other social institutions through particular mechanisms of clientelism.

### Clientelism

As Eisenstadt and Roniger (1984) have shown, patron–client relations can vary in form in different societies. Underlying these variations, however, is a basic structure of exchange in which the patron offers diffuse help and protection to the client in return for particular services. Eisenstadt and Roniger argue that the relationship leads to:

> first, a rather peculiar combination of inequality and asymmetry in power with seeming mutual solidarity expressed in terms of personal identity and interpersonal sentiments and obligations; second, a combination of potential coercion and exploitation with voluntary relations and mutual obligations; third, a combination of emphasis on such mutual obligations and solidarity or reciprocity between patrons and clients with the somewhat illegal or semi-legal aspect of these relations. (Eisenstadt and Roniger, 1984: 49)

Clientelism has a long history in Italy, though its form has changed. Of particular importance, according to Eisenstadt and Roniger, has been the change from patronage being in the hands of the large landowners and manufacturers towards an increased importance of patronage exercised by political parties through the state. Common to both phases was the way in which access to a vast range of resources – economic, educational, legal and bureaucratic – was based not on universal rights and openness but on particularism, having the right connections with the right patrons. Nor was it the case that there was a simple differentiation between patrons and clients. Except for those right at the bottom of society who had no resources of their own and those at the very top who needed help from nobody, everybody could seek to be a patron for somebody and similarly would be likely to be somebody's client. In a clientelist society, nothing can be achieved without using the mechanisms of patronage and mutual obligation. Extended families work to advance the interests of their members through establishing a range of patron and client relations. In the Italian case, then, the security of members of the family is achieved through using these relations. Patrons look after their clients and in return the clients deliver patrons certain favours and services. In the period up to the 1950s, these relations were mainly local, based in Southern Italy particularly on long-existing ties between landowners and the landless. From the 1950s, however, changes occurred which brought the state more into the picture.

### The State
The defeat of fascism and the emergence of the Cold War in the late 1940s left the Italian political order in a state of turmoil. Anti-communist groups within Italy coalesced around the Christian Democrats supported by the Catholic Church, the landowners and the industrial and professional bourgeosie. Since this period, the Christian Democrats have maintained a stranglehold on political power and have used it deftly to sustain and nourish their electoral base. In particular, this has meant that state institutions, that is the civil service and bureaucracy, the judiciary, the nationalised industries, the regulatory bodies, have been thoroughly politicised in the sense that appointments to them have reflected the political interests of the party in charge (Corner, 1990). State institutions have not become autonomous from political and social interests. The complexity of this politicisation process has increased further since the 1950s as new factions have emerged within the Christian Democrats and other parties have grown more powerful and sought a share in power (such as the Socialists).

In the 1950s the Christian Democrats were determined to sustain their electoral base through creating clients, particularly in the less developed South. State funds were used at first in industrial and agricultural projects to create large numbers of jobs. This involved a transfer of funds from the industrialised North to the South, but it was supported generally as necessary to ensure that the divide between North and South did not deepen further. However, the Christian Democrats ensured that jobs and contracts were awarded in return for the political support of those who benefited. In return, local Christian Democrat political bosses expected to reap electoral rewards. This changed the nature of the clientelist structure since the old locally based patrons were sometimes bypassed by the installation of new party political bosses in particular regions.

In the late 1950s, the Christian Democrats extended this patronage further through expanding rights to old age and disability pensions to peasants, artisans and shopkeepers. This extension of pension rights was not based on the contributions paid by these sectors of the population. Nor were these rights universally available. As with jobs and contracts, access to the rights was controlled by political gate-keepers, who steered their clients through the system in return for political support. The extension of pension rights was another example of what Ascoli (1984) refers to as subordinating social policy to 'exquisitely political ends'. It was part of the Christian Democrats' strategy of developing and sustaining a social bloc willing to keep it in power (see also Corner, 1990).

The complexity of this process reflects and reinforces Baldwin's arguments that state welfare systems cannot be understood solely in terms of broad class categories such as working class and ruling class (Baldwin, 1990). On the contrary, patron–client relations went right through the Italian system of social stratification and thus the opening up and development of state institutions as providers of resources were pushed forward as much by certain elements of the middle class as of any other class. Ascoli (1984) argues that the post-war growth (1946–65) of the welfare state was aimed at bringing various categories of middle-class workers into the state-controlled system. According to Paci (1989), this created a system in which welfare benefits are provided to clients by patrons, the most important of which are now the political parties. The benefits of the system are potentially available to the middle class and well-to-do, as well as the working class and the peasantry. In return for political support, ranging from simply voting for a particular party through to more complex forms of support, the parties act as gatekeepers for all sectors of society which wish to partake of the welfare system. Given the complex coalitional system of Italian politics, it is difficult for any party to oppose these trends. Thus, far from disappearing with time, clientelist practices have been reinforced and enlarged with the extension of the provision provided by the welfare state and the complex nature of Italian politics.

These issues are illustrated particularly in relation to the Italian pension system (using this term to refer to disability and sickness pensions as well as old age pensions). The continued expansion of the pension system under the pressure of the political imperatives of clientelism meant that the number of pensions disbursed in Italy had risen to 17.9 million in 1985 compared with no more than 3.15 million in 1949 (Franco and Morcaldo, 1990: 108). Since people could draw more than one pension, as well as cumulate pensions to earned income, these figures do not reveal the actual numbers drawing pension, nor their dependence on pensions. According to

Franco and Morcaldo, the 1981 census results showed there to be 11.7 million people who had reached retirement age, thus indicating that 'there are several million cases of multiple pensions' (Franco and Morcaldo, 1990: 113).

The consequence of the large numbers of people involved in drawing pensions is that the Italian state devoted 48.4 per cent of its social expenditure to pensions in 1977. The only European country with a higher expenditure on pensions was Sweden with 52.2 per cent. The Western Europe average was 36.5 per cent (Ascoli, 1984). In the early 1980s pensions accounted for 25 per cent of public spending and 12 per cent of GDP; in 1950 the respective figures were 8.5 and 2.1 per cent (Ferrera, 1984). Pensions accounted for 3.8 per cent of the GDP in 1954, 8.4 per cent in 1973 and in 1980 they had reached 11.9 per cent (Regonini, 1984).

Disability pensions, in particular, were disproportionately important in the Italian context. In 1980 Italy's percentage of public spending on these was twice that of the EC average. This was because (a) they can be paid after only five years of contributions, and (b) the law states that disability is not governed by rigorous and objective criteria, but rather the state of the local labour market. Thus, Regonini concludes, 'For many years the law has been interpreted as an explicit invitation to concede with considerable indulgence disability pensions in areas where it was difficult to find work' (Regonini, 1984: 103). In 1980 in Southern Italy there were 290.5 disability pensions being paid per 100 people of pensionable age (this rose from a figure of 149.7 in 1970). Respective figures for Central and North Italy in 1980 were 179.8 and 72.8, and for 1970, 127.0 and 62.3. Franco and Morcaldo state that 'in the second half of the sixties and the first half of the seventies . . . disability pensions acted, in practice, as a substitute for unemployment benefits' (Franco and Morcaldo, 1990: 124).

Financial security in old age or ill health in Italy has been based on the art of *l'arrangiarsi*, the art of arranging for yourself and your family; of seeking security through various associative memberships (occupation, locality, party, ideology) and clientelist channels. The state is seen as the ultimate patron, as a legitimate resource on which people can draw to provide for their security. In this respect, the Italian state, its level of social spending and the expectations of its citizens appears unique. For example, in a recent comparison of these features between Britain, the USA, Australia, West Germany, Austria and Italy, Italy had the highest total social spending as a percentage of GDP (28 per cent) (Taylor-Gooby, 1989) and at the same time a very high percentage of people wanting the state to spend more, particularly on old age pensions

(76 per cent compared to 46 per cent in West Germany, the lowest of the countries analysed) and health (81 per cent compared to 52 per cent in West Germany: only Britain scored higher on health, 88 per cent wanting more spending). These attitudes were accompanied by high numbers believing that it was 'definitely the government's responsibility to provide health care for the sick' (86 per cent) and to 'provide a decent standard of living for old people' (82 per cent). Only the UK came close to the level of support for mass welfare programmes found in Italy, though here the significantly lower level of GDP spent on social spending (19 per cent as compared to Italy's 28 per cent; the UK was only 2 per cent higher than the USA) may help explain why British citizens wanted more spending.

It is important to note that this commitment to welfare is not embedded in the sort of overall philosophical commitment to the state as a superior moral actor to classes or interest groups which is characteristic of the Scandinavian societies (see, for example, Baldwin (1990) for a discussion of Sweden and Denmark). On the contrary, the state is a resource cynically used in the pursuit of family gain by many who avoid as much as possible meeting their tax obligations to the state. Italy is notorious for the size of its underground economy, in which goods and services are exchanged in ways that avoid meeting tax obligations. Similarly, the high number of self-employed in Italy have many ways in which they can avoid paying any personal taxation whatsoever, whilst at the same time enjoying the welfare benefits of the state. Thus middle-class groups, which in other societies are amongst the first to spend their disposable income on forms of financial security purchased from banks and insurance companies, are in Italy closely locked into the state welfare system.

In summary, Italian society in the post-war period has developed a particular system whereby the universal problems of security in old age, illness and disability are met through the family utilising its connections via political patronage to draw resources from the state. The idea that financial services companies such as banks and insurance companies could have a role to play in this has been absent (unlike countries such as the UK, the USA and Germany), so strong has been the connection between the family, the political parties, the state and welfare distribution. This is not to ignore that there are other factors which have militated against the development of the industry. For example, the connection between financial services companies and the state and its taxation system has led many of the self-employed to avoid using such institutions for fear of incurring tax liabilities. Also, the companies themselves (many of them being state-owned) are part of the patronage system and as such are not seen as totally trustworthy guardians of one's financial future. However, these factors themselves are not separate from the overall institutional context of Italian society. Together, they go to make up the unique 'Via Italiana' which has developed in the post-war period as a way of accommodating a complex, divided society to the stresses of unequal patterns of economic growth and income distribution.

**Changes in the Personal Financial Services Industry**

The previous section emphasised the way in which the consumption of financial services products was inhibited by the social relations of state, family and clientelism in which Italian consumers were embedded. In this section, we seek to reconstruct some of our arguments by looking at the process of change, the conflicts and contradictions which exist in the system.

Our initial starting point is the cost of the existing system. In the early 1980s a number of influential reports were published by the Bank of Italy-IMI-INA, Ania and academics. These identified and analysed a growing crisis in the state pensions system. Various parliamentary commissions were convened in the Chamber of Deputies and the Senate which deliberated on the problem and proposed various, largely piecemeal, reforms for the pensions system. (A list of these is provided in Moro, 1988.) One of the major reports produced was that sponsored by the Bank of Italy, IMI, and the state insurance company, INA. This highlighted the crisis of the state pension fund (INPS) and calculated that the number of pensioners to contributors would rise from 83.8 per cent in 1982 to 98 per cent in 2015. That is, by 2015 each wage-earner would be supporting one pensioner. This in turn implied raising the pension contributions from gross income of wage-earners to over 50 per cent. In the view of the report this spelt a terminal crisis for Italy's pension system, which was at the time already heavily in deficit (Moro, 1988).

This issue is particularly related to the question of who pays for the system. The Italian system is based on an intergenerational transfer from taxpayers to pensioners. It follows that those who can avoid paying taxes receive free-rider advantages when they become eligible for pensions. Since the large numbers of self-employed in Italy have traditionally been able to avoid personal taxation, the burden has fallen mainly on large businesses and their workforces, with the rest funded through the public sector deficit and the sale of short-term government bonds. For large industrialists this has meant a massive increase in indirect labour costs since the 1950s. In 1952, 9 per cent of the total salary bill went on pensions (employer 6.6 per cent; employee 2.4 per cent). By 1986, this had risen to 25.81 per cent (employer 18.66 per cent; employee 7.15 per cent), according to Moro (1988: 109). The continued escalation of these indirect costs was likely to damage the employers' international competitiveness. The large employers of the North, who in the 1950s and 1960s had willingly subscribed to the Christian Democratic strategy of building electoral support in the South through the use of the pensions system, were now having to cope with the fact that their taxation burden was continually increasing. In this context, reforming capitalists, both within the Christian Democrat Party and in other parties such as the Socialist Party, began to articulate the need to change the basis of the welfare state.

The growing tax burden was also contributing to a rethink on the part of the northern working class and its political leadership. The highly trade-unionised workforces of the northern manufacturing areas subscribed to a solidaristic ideology in which universal and high standards of welfare rights were accepted and approved. Nevertheless, the system has begun to create tensions both within and between unions, between those currently in work and shouldering the fiscal burden and those currently in receipt of pensions. This also reaches over into a regional conflict, between the North and the South, with separatist movements such as the Lombardy League gaining support from the northern working class on the grounds of what is seen to be an excessive redistribution of wealth and income to the South.

The funding of the deficit through government bonds has also begun to reach its limits. The inflationary pressure generated by this policy was only manageable through successive devaluations of the Italian lira, but once Italy entered the Exchange Rate Mechanism and sought to limit changes in the value of the lira, this option became less feasible.

These dissatisfactions led to a range of discussions in the 1980s concerning possible reform of the pensions system. The majority of reforms that were eventually proposed aimed to achieve one of two objectives: the reduction of the social assistential role of the state pension scheme and an expansion of the role of corporate and individual pension schemes (Ruozi and Paci, 1988b). In this respect, reform of the pensions system dovetails with wider reforms in the Italian system that are being proposed, particularly by the more dynamic elements of the capitalist class. Perhaps the most significant success of these reforms has been the separation of the central bank, the Bank of Italy, from political interference in its so-called 'divorce' from the Treasury in 1981. Since this period, the Bank of Italy has been central in the deregulation of the financial services industry and has pushed for a modernisation of this sector as well as the Italian economy more generally. As has already been noted, it has sponsored research on the accumulating impact of the pension system and has been a strong proponent of its reform. In its role as central bank, it has also sought tighter control over the monetary system, particularly once the lira was inside the Exchange Rate Mechanism. Thus, it has sought to curb inflationary pressures in general, and is committed to reducing the size of the public sector deficit. It has sought to persuade the government to reduce and rationalise welfare expenditure in the light of further moves towards European monetary union. It has also encouraged modernisation of the banking system as a whole in order to improve the financing of industry. This goes along with its attempts to improve the operation of the Milan Stock Exchange.

According to Martinelli and Chiesi 'In the last twenty years, the Italian capitalist class has moved from a position of weak political power and low legitimation to a position of strong political influence and widespread legitimation' (Martinelli and Chiesi, 1989: 109). The growing success of Italian capitalists from the North and the Third Italy during the 1970s has been significant in creating what Martinelli and Chiesi refer to as 'a shared culture favourable as never before to the capitalist values of market, efficiency and meritocracy' (ibid.: 126). They further state that 'Efficiency, freedom of enterprise, individual responsibility, professional competence and material reward are values gaining momentum and acceptance. They have oriented the restructuring of the economy, the recovery of most of the state-controlled firms and of portions of the welfare system and have timidly appeared even in the inefficient state bureaucracy' (Martinelli and Chiesi 1989: 133).

According to these authors, this does not indicate a wholesale change in Italian political and economic culture. Nevertheless, it is a significant change permeating all sectors of society as well as state institutions. One aspect of this is the crisis of the Italian Communist Party, struggling to maintain its position amongst a working class no longer drawn to revolutionary or socialist principles. The Communist Party is no longer so openly hostile to the accumulation of savings through private schemes – a change of position it shares with the Catholic Church!

This wider cultural change has implications for the operation of the welfare system. The role of clientelism, the extent of corruption, the unequal sharing of burdens and benefits, the consequences of economic performance – all of these are subject to critique by the modernising impetus of the new capitalists and their technocratic managers. As previously stated, this is leading to debate about the role which private schemes can take in the provision of welfare.

## The Growth of Italian Financial Services in the 1980s

At this point, we wish to argue that these changes are beginning to have an impact on the financial services industry itself for two reasons. First, the companies themselves see that the existing situation of dependence on the state for pensions cannot continue. Instead, it is likely that gradually the state will encourage consumers to make private arrangements for their security through establishing safe, long-term investments in financial services products, whether these are unit trusts, life assurance savings schemes or pension products. The companies have therefore begun to establish more attractive products that promote customer interest and demonstrate to the state the growing efficiency and professionalism of the industry. This has gone along with a restructuring of distribution channels. Traditionally, the selling of insurance and investment products in Italy has been in the hands of company agents who have been allocated a particular geographical area. The agents have been highly unionised and resistant to management attempts to make them take on new products or new selling techniques. In order to get round this, companies are following two tacks. One is to set up new direct sales forces paid on commission and with different terms and conditions from the existing agents. The second is to link up with banks to use their branches as sales outlets. In the past, Italian banks have not been allowed to sell insurance products, but this legislation is being eased and increasing numbers of banks are linking with insurance companies. Thus the companies are becoming more aggressive in their pursuit of business.

Second, certain groups of customers are beginning also to see that they need to supplement their state provision by private arrangements to insure themselves against major changes in state policy *and* to enable them to take advantage of capital growth that comes from long-term investment in stocks, bonds and property. These changes are reflected, for example, in the gradual growth of life insurance from its very low base. Life insurance has traditionally been the product which first of all establishes the principle of long-term savings with inbuilt capital growth. We therefore

Table 9.4  *Life insurance premium income*

| | As % of GDP | % Growth rate in real terms | % of total premium income |
|---|---|---|---|
| 1985 | 0.32 | 23.7 | 15.6 |
| 1986 | 0.40 | 30.0 | 18.3 |
| 1987 | 0.51 | 33.2 | 21.6 |
| 1988 | 0.58 | 20.3 | 24.1 |
| 1989 | 0.62 | 9.1 | 24.7 |
| 1990[1] | 0.64 | 8.6 | 25.0 |

[1] Estimate.
*Source*: Ania 1990

concentrate on this product to show the gradual growth of private long-term savings. Table 9.4 shows the development of life insurance sales from various perspectives. Between 1985 and 1990 life premiums as a percentage of GDP doubled. In the same period non-life premiums rose by only 11.6 per cent.

Since the 1987 Stock Exchange crash, the spectacular growth rates of the mid-1980s have declined, although in terms of the industry as a whole, life premium income continues to grow in importance. In 1979 life premiums were only 13.9 per cent of total premium income; by 1989 this figure was nearly 25 per cent.

Clearly, these figures still indicate the low development of life insurance in Italy. In 1988 life insurance as a percentage of total insurance premiums was 40.1 per cent in the USA, 75.2 per cent in Japan, 46.1 per cent in Germany, 59.2 per cent in the UK, 48.9 per cent in France and 48.7 per cent in Spain. In fact the only other European economies with a percentage of life premiums less than 30 per cent of total premium income were Belgium (29.6 per cent) and Portugal (18.1 per cent) (Ania, 1990: table 22).

However, what is most important is that there is a strong belief in Italy itself that these recent increases will continue. For example, econometric research recently conducted by Prometeia (1989) suggests that life insurance activity will grow by a yearly average of 17.9 per cent in the period 1989–95 and that a process of catching-up will be completed within the next decade or so. This is supported by market research studies which show a changing attitude on the part of the Italian consumer towards financial services products. The 1989 Einaudi Centre report on savers and saving in Italy concluded that private saving was on the increase. According to the Einaudi Report, the average Italian family was saving 12 per cent of its income in 1988, accounting for a third of all EC family saving, and at that time equalling those of France,

Table 9.5 *Motives for saving: first preference*

| | | Percentages | |
| | 1983 | 1986 | 1989 |
| --- | --- | --- | --- |
| Liquidity | 17.9 | 24.9 | 12.2 |
| Income | 20.4 | 20.6 | 28.0 |
| Security | 38.8 | 32.8 | 34.7 |
| Capital growth | 22.9 | 21.7 | 25.0 |

*Source*: Centro Einaudi 1989

Germany and the UK combined. The Einaudi Report also argues that there appears to be a change in savers' motives. They argue that there was a significant shift away from saving for 'almost obsessive' reasons of liquidity toward saving for income (*rendimento*).

What is also important is that the growth of these markets appears to be concentrated particularly in the northern, more prosperous parts of the country. Perhaps not surprisingly, per capita policy-holding and capital invested in the North is more than twice that in the South. The research conducted by Prometeia reported that in 1986 Piedmont and Lombardy accounted for 35 per cent of Italian insurance premiums (Prometeia, 1989) and northern Italy as a whole accounted for 62 per cent of premium income in 1986. Per capita regional insurance expenditure was 409,000 lire in Lombardy and only 99,500 in Calabria in 1986. Fifty per cent of life insurance policies in operation in 1987 were held by people in the North of Italy, with only 22 per cent held by people from the Centre and 21 per cent by clients from the South and the Islands (the percentage of insured capital was similar: 55 per cent in the North, 21 per cent in the Centre and 19 per cent in the South and Islands).

None of this is to deny the continued existence of inertial forces in the Italian system. Pensioners, for example, wield considerable political power through their votes (Regonini, 1984) and are likely to resist anything which reduces their existing benefits. The coverage afforded for lower-paid workers by the Italian state scheme is exceptional – 80 per cent of average salary over the last five years of employment – and the result of the political strength of the working class in the 1970s. These gains are not likely to be placed in jeopardy. Further, as has been argued, there are many parties who have substantial interests in seeing the system remain as it is – even Italian managers have recently seen the percentage of final salary they can receive from the state scheme rise massively: in 1988 percentage of final salary on an income of £125,000 rose from 12.39 to 47.73 per cent (NEWFIN, 1990: table 5a). This provision led to a fall in demand for private pensions. There will also be considerable opposition to the rationalisation of social security payments that might attack particularistic channels of clientelistic transfers.

Behind these phenomena remain the more deep-seated peculiarities of the Italian institutions: the extended family and the clientelist state. Both of these in turn relate to the fact that Italy did not undergo a thorough bourgeois revolution in terms of its political, economic and social institutions (Martinelli and Chiesi, 1989; Corner, 1990). It remains a hybrid society in which elements of Catholic traditionalism, socialist universalism, state corruption and bourgeois liberalism are still in complex antagonism.

### 'La Via Italiana': Summary

The Italian system of financial services developed a complex web of interconnections between the industry, the state and the consuming families and individuals. For many years, families have sought to protect themselves through linking to systems of political patronage. Whilst some have been excluded from this system, others have been able to trust the state to provide them with a form of financial security. This has meant that certain system disjunctures, most particularly the highly uneven economic development of the North and the South, have not generated social conflict. Instead, redistribution has occurred surreptitiously through the pension system. This situation has not been without its costs. State revenues have to come from somewhere and the fiscal crisis of the Italian state has emerged more threateningly over the last decade. This fiscal crisis has also started to rupture social cohesion since some groups are increasingly questioning the way in which redistribution occurs, who benefits from it and who is left out. Trust in the ability of the state to continue to meet these goals is starting to be undermined. Italians are beginning to look at private sector financial services products as a means of achieving security. The amoral familism (Paci, 1984; 1989) that brought them into the circle of state patronage is now leading Italians to consider the purchase of private financial services such as life insurance both as a means to protect their family and as a means to maximise their wealth and income. For long enough, Italians from all sectors of society felt their needs for financial security could be met by a combination of help from family, patrons and the state. During the 1980s that began to change. Certain powerful groups, particularly amongst the capitalist class and technocrat managers, have begun to seek alternative ways of gaining security. They have begun to look to the role of the private sector financial services companies. Elements within the state, the political parties, the large industrial employers and the Bank of Italy have also seen this as a potential way to reduce the clientelism, inefficiency and high cost of the state. The companies, in turn, have increasingly come under the influence of these reforming ideas and have begun to see new markets for themselves in a transformed Italy. They have begun to professionalise themselves and compete more actively for business, thus promoting increased awareness amongst customers of what is available. The imminence of the Single European Market and the gradual arrival in Italy of British, French and German companies eager to expand in what they perceive to be an under-insured market has also helped to concentrate the minds of the managers in these companies. They appear to have a brief window of opportunity in which they can establish themselves more securely in their home market before the full impact of the Single Market in financial services makes itself felt in the second half of the 1990s. Thus, what from certain perspectives might be deemed to be a 'virtuous circle of change' is being established. The detailed direction and speed of these changes is beyond our ability to predict, but the existence of change itself in a framework previously so tightly bounded and so deeply embedded is of major significance and draws us back to our overall theme – that the business systems approach must include the analysis of change.

## Conclusions

The peculiarity of the Italian case illustrates the central theme of the business systems approach that under different societal conditions, different institutional frameworks will develop which 'fit' together in distinctive ways. In our analysis of Italian financial services we have tried to illustrate this point. We have tried to show that the institutional arrangement of the Italian state, political parties, families and the role of clientelism has particular consequences for the distribution of wealth and income in Italy. As a result, it also has consequences for the way in which financial services have developed. However, the institutional arrangement is itself subject to change. The fiscal crisis of the state, changing family patterns (particularly in the North of Italy) and consumer expectations and changed political priorities amongst elite groups are undermining the stability of the system established in the postwar period. Central to this is the way in which consumer notions of how to achieve financial security and the institutional arrangements which can be trusted to provide it are developing. At present, they still remain centred on the state and its ability to provide such security. However, there are indications of some groups changing from this position and as they do so the political difficulties of creating a major overhaul of the system will perhaps lessen.

These changes are also part of a wider set of changes in financial services. Across Europe, there is a gradual redefinition of the boundaries between state and private provision in the areas of financial security. Particular pressure is being created through the wishes of the European Commission to create a base level of uniformity throughout the Community. The Commission is particularly wedded to the idea of a free market in all goods and services, and whilst this does not mean the dismantling of welfare state provision, it does imply the creation of an environment in which the sale of financial services can occur with relatively few restrictions, subject to an initial licensing process. These changes are not confined to Italy; they affect all European Community countries and are destabilising many traditional ways of working. New institutional patterns may begin to emerge. What appeared to be relatively settled business systems are now undergoing much more pressure for change than previously. In this case study, we have tried to show how in one particular area, complex changes at a variety of levels are occurring. As a general conclusion, we believe that it is important that the business systems approach takes up the issue of change. As well as understanding the causes of stability and continuity, we need to understand the process of change. The business systems approach with its focus on the complex interconnections of social and business arrangements offers the opportunity to do just that.

## Note

1. Our concern throughout the chapter is with *personal* financial services (as opposed to corporate or wholesale banking). Personal financial services includes products such as money transmission services (i.e. bank accounts and associated products), lending services (i.e. personal loans, mortgages and credit cards), and savings products such as life insurance savings schemes, unit trusts, and pension schemes.

## References

Ania (1990) *Relazione Annuale all'Assemblea dei Soci*. Rome, 27 November 1990.
Ascoli, U. (1984) 'Il sistema italiano di welfare', in U. Ascoli, (ed.), *Welfare State all'Italiana*. Bari: Laterza.

Baldwin, P. (1990) *The Politics of Social Solidarity: Class Bases of the European Welfare State 1875-1975*. Cambridge: Cambridge University Press.

Centro Einaudi (1989) *Rapporto sul risparmio e sui risparmiatori in Italia*. Rome.

Corner, P. (1990) *A History of Contemporary Italy: Society and Politics 1943-1988*. London: Penguin.

Eisenstadt, S. and Roniger, L. (1984) *Patrons, Clients and Friends*. Cambridge: Cambridge University Press.

Ferrera, M. (1984) *Il welfare state in Italia*. Bologna: Il Mulino.

Finch, J. (1989) 'Kinship and Friendship', in R. Jowell, S. Witherspoon and L. Brook (eds), *British Social Attitudes 6th Report: Special International Report*. Aldershot: Gower.

Franco D. and Morcaldo G. (1990) 'The Italian Pension System: Development and Effects on Income Distribution and Poverty' *Review of Labour Economics and Industrial Relations* Vol. 4, No. 2, Autumn, pp. 105-128.

Manghetti, G. (1982) *L'Italia delle assicurazioni: guida a un mondo di inganni, illusioni e poche sicurezze*. Milan: Feltrinelli.

Martinelli, A. and Chiesi, A.M. (1989) 'Italy', in T. Bottomore and R.J. Brym (eds), *The Capitalist Class: An International Study*. London: Harvester Wheatsheaf.

Moro, O. (1988) 'La previdenza integrativa in Italia', in Ruozi and Paci (1988)

NEWFIN (1990) 'Recente evoluzione della previdenza integrativa in Italia'. Università Commerciale Luigi Bocconi, Milan, mimeo.

Paci, M. (1984) 'Il sistema di welfare italiano tra tradizione clientelare e prospettive di riforma', in U. Ascoli (ed.), *Welfare Sate all'Italiana*. Bari: Laterza. pp. 297-324.

Paci, M. (1989) 'Public and Private in the Italian Welfare System', in P. Lange and M. Regini (eds), *State Market and Social Regulation: New Perspectives on Italy*. Cambridge: Cambridge University Press. pp. 217-34.

Piore, M.J. and Sabel, C. (1984) *The Second Industrial Divide*. New York: Basic Books.

Prometeia (1989) *L'evoluzione di medio periodo del settore assicurativo Italiano*. Bologna: Prometeia.

Regonini, G. (1984) 'Il sistema pensionistico: risorse e vincoli' in U. Ascoli (ed.), *Welfare State all'Italiana*. Bari: Laterza.

Ruozi, R. and Paci, S. (eds) (1988a) *La previdenza integrativa: esperienze e linee di riforma del sistema italiano*. Milan: Giuffre Editore.

Ruozi, R. and Paci, S. (1988b) 'Linee prospettiche della previdenza integrativa in Italia', in Ruozi and Paci (1988).

Taylor-Gooby, P. (1989) 'The Role of the State' in R. Jowell, S. Witherspoon and L. Brook (eds), *British Social Attitudes 6th Report: Special International Report*. Aldershot: Gower.

Whitley, R. (1990) 'Eastern Asian Enterprise Structures and the Comparative Analysis of Forms of Business Organization', *Organization Studies*. 11 (1), 47-74.

Zysman, J. (1983) *Governments, Markets and Growth: Financial Systems and the Politics of Industrial Change*. Ithaca, NY: Cornell University Press.

# 10
# The Societal Construction of Labour Flexibility: Employment Strategies in Retail Banking in Britain and France

## Jacqueline O'Reilly

Previous debates on labour market flexibility have paid scant attention to the institutional and cultural factors affecting employers' labour strategies. These debates have depicted labour usage in terms of a stark, dichotomous choice between core or peripheral forms of employment. Most discussions have implicitly assumed that the rationales for using different forms of flexibility are universal, and that there is a general process at work whereby most advanced industrial economies are moving in the same direction, in search of greater 'flexibility'. However, the panache of the proponents of flexibility has disguised the fact that, in reality, employers' labour market strategies are more complex and messy than these theories would have us believe.

This chapter examines how employers in the retail banking sector in Britain and France have developed their labour strategies in the 1980s. Comparative research of this nature is usually concerned with identifying commonalities and differences in industrial organisation characteristics across countries (Maurice et al., 1982; Gallie 1978; Lane, 1987; 1990; and Chapter 3 in this volume; Gregory, 1987; Nishida and Redding, Chapter 11 in this volume). The work of Maurice et al. (1982), for example, marked an important departure from the traditional, culture-free perspective of technological determinism developed by Kerr et al., (1964), stressing instead the importance of cultural variables and the 'societal effect' on the organisation of work in their study of France and Germany. Whitley (Chapter 1 in this volume) has carried these themes further and proposed a framework for the express purpose of comparative research, integrating an analysis of industrial organisation with the social institutions and cultural values which shape a specific society. This chapter will show how the use of diverse flexible labour strategies can be explained by drawing on the institutional features of specific countries.

**Theoretical Issues**

To a large extent, the flexibility debates have been a reformulation of the concepts developed by earlier dual labour market theorists applied to the level of the firm. Essentially, early theorists argued that the labour market was divided into distinct sectors of advantaged and disadvantaged workers, in the core and secondary market respectively (see Rosenberg, 1989; Gallie, 1988). However, these theorists had a tendency to overemphasise single-cause explanations, whether this be technology, training, or systems of managerial control (Doeringer and Piore, 1971; Berger and Piore, 1980; Edwards, 1979; Gordon et al., 1982). The growing interest in 'flexibility' emerged as concern moved away from a simple explanation of differentiation to ask how these boundaries are created and adapted in relation to changing product and labour market conditions (Rubery, 1988). This shift in interest has moved analysis away from looking at the divisions in the labour market at large, as dual labour market theorists did, to examining the firm as the centre of action and decision making around which these divisions are created and changed.

Discussions on labour flexibility have focused on the concepts of functional and numerical flexibility which are empirically examined in this research. Functional flexibility is a strategy used to broaden the range of skills amongst the permanent, core workforce to meet changing product market demands (Atkinson and Meager, 1986: 38). The concept of numerical flexibility, a strategy developed amongst secondary sector workers, explains how employers match workers to workload fluctuations. This can operate in either of two ways: they can bring in *additional workers*, with the assumption that they can get rid of them when work levels are low; or, employers can use their *existing workers* to reorganise working time to cover these fluctuations (Atkinson and Meager, 1986: 14). A diverse range of employment contracts can be used to achieve numerical flexibility: these include temporary work, part-time work, permanent staff working overtime and/or an alteration of shift patterns and flexible working time.

Despite the success of the model of the flexible firm in academic and commercial circles, it has come under considerable criticism for conflating diverse elements under generalised categories, and it suffers from the problems of comparing heterogeneous groups, allocated on the basis of functional or numerical flexibility, to the primary or secondary labour market respectively (Pollert, 1987; Gallie and White, 1991). It has also been criticised for concentrating on the problem of labour allocation and paying less attention to other issues with regard to product market competition, product design, retail and after-sales service (Rubery, 1988). The gendered construction of flexibility, which is seen for example in the use of part-time work which is predominantly female, has received sparse attention in these debates (Walby, 1989). The emphasis has focused wholly on the role of employers' policies (Robinson and Wallace, 1984), with limited consideration given to the differing characteristics of the people employed on these contracts, and how this may affect employers' ability to introduce flexible forms of employment. One further weakness of the flexible firm model is its neglect of the impact of institutional segmentation, and the role played by the unions and state intervention in employers' attempts to introduce flexibility and restructure the work force. In sum, it is a model which has been developed in a cultural vacuum.

In order to understand the circumstances in which employers use certain forms of numerical or functional flexibility, we need to have a broader appreciation of the economic and social pressures that formulate the context within which these strategies are developed. Gallie and White (1991) have argued that employers' policies need to be analysed in relation to structural factors such as the type of industry, its size and labour market location. Contextual considerations related to product market strategy and competitive pressures also need to be included. Whilst this is clearly useful, for cross-national studies we also need to encompass a wider perspective, as suggested in the business systems framework of analysis (Whitley, Chapter 1 in this volume). This will allow us to encompass factors which in single-nation studies can often be taken for granted, for example, the character of the industrial relations system, or the education and training system, and how these factors shape the way in which employers conceptualise their labour requirements. Whitley's framework sets up a wide range of possible configurations on different levels of analysis, which can allow us to understand where there are shared and divergent patterns of development, this allows us to break away from monocausal explanations and the strictly dualist or dichotomous model developed by early labour market theorists. It also allows us to incorporate an analysis of change by identifying the different levels from which change can develop. These levels of analysis are clearly elaborated in the introduction to this book, so for the purposes of this chapter let us turn first to look at the evidence collected in the case studies for the development of flexible strategies in Britain and France, before examining the explanations for difference and similarity.

**The Banking Sector in Britain and France**

One of the most practical ways to tackle these theoretical questions, from a comparative perspective, is to conduct research at the level of the sector. The retail banking sector was chosen here for a number of reasons. Firstly, information technology has had, and will continue to have, a radical impact on the provision of services, skill requirements and work organisation of the banks (Rajan, 1984; Bernoux et al., 1990; Bertrand and Noyelle, 1987; Moussy, 1989; Cossalter, 1989). Secondly, along side this 'information revolution', the banks have been subjected to considerable domestic and European competition (Burgard, 1988; de Quillacq, 1987; Frazer and Vittas, 1984; Graham, 1988; Lewis, 1987; Marsh, 1985). Thirdly, academic research has for a long time been dominated by studies of manufacturing industry, and an examination of the banking sector offers a fresh perspective. Coupled with this, the banking sector also offers the opportunity to examine some of the questions relating to the gendered organisation of work which have been raised in recent debates, because of the significant number of women employed in this area (Crompton, 1989; Strober and Arnold, 1987). These factors make the banking sector an apposite area of research for the questions raised by the flexibility debates.

The retail clearing banks[1] cater for the needs of personal customers offering loans, saving plans and money transmission services. For this research interviews were conducted with senior personnel managers in most of the main banks, and one major bank in each country was selected for detailed case study analysis. This selection was determined by size and market share to make the banks as comparable as possible. Data were collected from interviews with managers, supervisors, part-time and full-time employees, trade union representatives and by observational methods in each of the banks. Approximately 60 managers/supervisors were interviewed on several occasions in these two banks, and a total of 126 part-time and full-time female employees were interviewed using a structured questionnaire. Where obstacles to conducting these questionnaires were encountered, I had to rely on the access obtained to another comparable bank in France. Secondary documentation was provided by research departments in the banks and the trade unions.

Table 10.1  *The characteristics of the retail banking system in Britain and France*

| France | Britain |
| --- | --- |
| Nationalised for the most part, until 1986 | Independent companies |
| Tool of government economic policy – source of cheap loans to industry | City of London independent from government policy – *laissez-faire* philosophy |
| Lower capital/assets ratio, comparatively less secure | |
| Competition, perennial characteristic, from mutuals and *banques populaires* | Competition more recent from building societies |
| Several diverse players | A smaller number of competitors |
| More regionalised | More centralised |
| Saturated market | Market penetration less extensive although nearing saturation levels |

## The Characteristics of the Retail Banking System in Britain and France

Although the banks in both countries have been experiencing similar pressures in terms of competition and technological change, there are nevertheless important differences between the organisation of the two systems which suggest that the banks are likely to adopt different employment strategies. These differences concern ownership, relations to state policy, stability, competitive structure and market saturation, and these are summarised in Table 10.1.

In France much of the retail banking system was nationalised by de Gaulle after the Second World War and the banks were severely restricted in the services they could offer (Burgard, 1988; AFB, 1986; Green, 1986). Since the late 1960s these restrictions have progressively been lifted, and in 1986 Jacques Chirac privatised the Société Générale and some other smaller banks. The banks in France have traditionally been used as an instrument in government financial policy to provide a source of cheap funds to industry, although since 1983 there has been less pressure on the banks to do so (Marsh, 1985; Lewis, 1987; Shreeve and Alexander, 1991; de Quillacq, 1987). This involvement of the state has enabled the leading French banks to operate with a relatively low capital/assets ratio, which is a commonly accepted measure of a bank's economic stability. The close link between the banks and government can also be seen in the appointment of senior managers of the nationalised banks, who are often political appointments.[2] Despite common state ownership there is intense competition between these rival groups.

In Britain, by contrast, the fierce historical independence of the City of London together with a liberal political culture have acted as obstacles to state control and governmental direction of financial capital (Zysman, 1983). The retail banking sector in Britain has been dominated since the 1970s by the 'Big Four': Barclays, NatWest, Lloyds and Midland, although deregulation has increased the number of players contesting for business. Until quite recently one could distinguish between the Clearing Banks, which deal with transferral of funds, and the building societies, which finance house purchases. However, deregulation has now blurred these boundaries. Although the same degree of market segmentation between consumer credit and housing finance does not exist in France, there is a wider range of institutions active in the field of retail banking. These include deposit banks, credit banks, popular banks, agriculture credit banks like the Crédit Agricole, and mutual credit banks (Frazer and Vittas, 1984: 158–60). The Crédit Agricole is one of the largest banks in France and is somewhat exceptional compared to the other clearers. It was originally set up to provide cheap credit for the agricultural community. Although it benefits from offering preferential credit, like other mutualist banks, the state is active in its lending policy, and the government can nominate members for the national Management Board (*caisse*).[3] Green argues that 'Despite this control, the activities of the cooperative and mutual agencies have altered to such an extent that it is increasingly difficult to sustain the distinction between them and the commercial banks' (1986: 90). As the mutual and cooperative banks have expanded their services they have become the major source of competition to the main commercial banks like the Société Générale, the Crédit Lyonnais, the Banque Nationale de Paris (BNP), and the Crédit Industriel et Commercial (CIC).

Until quite recently the British system was concentrated in the hands of the major clearers, whereas in France there were a significantly larger number of players. For example in 1983 there were 13 clearing banks in Britain, which controlled 52 per cent of the personal accounts market; in France during the same period there were 406 companies defined as commercial banks, controlling 40.8 per cent of the market (Banque de Règlements Internationaux et La Banque de France, 1986). However, since the 1987 Banking Act a larger number of institutions in Britain can now offer banking services. In France competition between a larger number of financial institutions has been a perennial characteristic, whereas in Britain the cosy cartel status of the major clearers has only recently been broken up by government deregulation and fierce competition coming from the building societies and other financial institutions.

Compared to continental banking systems the British system is exceptionally centralised in its organisation (Child and Loveridge, 1990). In France we find not only important regional banks,[4] but the administrative clearance of cheques is also decentralised (Lasfargues, 1980), whereas in Britain all cheques have to pass through the London clearing centre. The impact of the decentralised system in France is that it reduces the intensity of weekly fluctuations in workloads and therefore imposes different labour requirements, which are discussed more fully in section three below.

There are also significant differences in levels of market penetration which affect the nature of competition in this sector in the two countries. In France the personal accounts market is completely saturated, whereas in Britain in the 1980s there remained a significant number of adults without a bank account. For example, in 1981 90 per cent of adults in France had a bank account compared to 60 per cent in Britain. By 1988 the gap had narrowed, with 99.3 per cent market density in France (Graham, 1988) compared to 80 per cent density in Britain in 1989 (Bailey, 1990). Competition has taken the form of offering a wider range of services: in Britain this has been a means of attracting new clients, and in France, where clients often hold more than one account, the banks compete for the principal account, that is the one into which their client's salary is paid.[5] Given the differences in the forms of ownership, control and competitive structure of the banking sector in each country, how does this affect the forms of flexibility the banks are interested in developing?

## Forms of Flexibility in Britain and France

The following section will outline the main findings for the labour strategies used in each country with regard to the use of functional flexibility, part-time and temporary work. It will then go on to look at the factors which can explain these differences.

### Functional Flexibility

There has been a more conscious strategy to develop functional flexibility in France than in Britain, which is reflected in the language used by the managers interviewed. In France managers continually referred to the importance of improving '*la compétence*' and '*la qualité*'; staff needed to adapt, they needed to be '*polyvalent*' and '*à l'écoute des besoins des clients*' (listening to the needs of the customers). The recurrent reference to these concepts in France invoked a discourse which did not appear to exist to the same extent in Britain. British managers were aware of the need to adapt and face the competition, but they did not use the same language to describe how they envisaged these changes. British managers were more likely to refer to the structural reorganisation of the bank, and the specialisation of services offered to business and private customers. The emphasis on changing the personal qualities of the staff employed by the bank was a major issue in France, whereas in Britain it was barely mentioned.

These attitudes were backed up by employees' experience of job variety. From evidence collected in the employee questionnaire, 78 per cent of the French staff interviewed described their job as varied compared to only 18 per cent in Britain. The British respondents were more likely to say that their job was routine and repetitive. To measure change and the development of functional flexibility the same staff were asked if they thought their task variety had increased. The difference between the two countries was less marked on this issue: 69 per cent of French staff and 61 per cent of the British respondents gave a positive response to this question. This might suggest that although employers are starting from a different base there has been a move to increase the variety of tasks performed by staff in both countries (O'Reilly, 1992a).

On the basis of detailed observations and in-depth discussions with cashiers in both countries, it was clear that in France they performed a wider variety of tasks compared to their British equivalents. This was facilitated by direct access to computer terminals in France. This technology did not exist in the British banks at the time when this research was conducted (1989), although it has been more popular with the Trustee Savings Bank and some of the smaller building societies. The use of technology was tailored to the different service policy in each country. In France, the banks were seeking to develop a more integrated service policy, so that one cashier could provide a wider range of services. In Britain, on the other hand, the banks had segmented their service policy by splitting up cashier jobs: cashiers worked on quick service tills (staffed Automatic Teller Machines) for transactions of less than £300; other cashiers, located at the back of the bank behind glass counters, offered more traditional services; and staff at the front of the bank dealt with enquiries and advice.

## Temporary Work

Temporary work is not a major source of labour flexibility in the banking sector, and has only increased marginally in recent years. In Britain the use of temporary work has increased from 1.5 per cent of all employment in this sector in 1984 to 2.4 per cent in 1989; in France temporary work in the financial services over the same period increased from 2.8 per cent to 4.5 per cent of total employment in this sector (INSEE 'Enquête sur l' emploi' and HMSO 'British Labour Force Survey'). Temporary work is more popular in France than it is in Britain. French employers were more likely to draw on temporary staff from the external labour market, whereas in Britain the banks made more use of former employees working intermittently (O'Reilly, 1992b, Chapter 5).

In both countries it is common for the banks to employ temporary staff to process mundane administration, for example in a privatisation shares issue. At the other end of the skills ladder the banks also use contract staff to provide highly specialised services, like those of computer systems developers. Temporary contracts were also used, in France more so than in Britain, as a testing period before offering permanent employment. Where relief teams[6] were in operation in France, they were used for the dual purpose of providing temporary cover and broadening the experience of the staff involved for future promotion.

## Part-time Work

Part-time work, at the national level, has been more popular in Britain than in France for a number of years. This pattern is mirrored in the financial sector where, in 1988, part-time work represented 14 per cent of all employees in Britain compared to 9.6 per cent in France. There has been a slight growth in the use of part-time work in both countries: in 1982 it represented 12 per cent of employment in the financial services in Britain and 7.3 per cent in France (Enquête sur l'emploi and British Labour Force Survey). In Britain a wider range of part-time contracts was offered: these ranged from 'week on week off' contracts, two- or three-day a week contracts, to morning or afternoon only contracts five days a week, and in the branches lunch-time cover was also offered. In France part-time work was defined as 80 per cent of full-time hours, usually interpreted as one day a week off, or 70, 60 or 50 per cent of full-time hours. British employers could change the type of part-time contracts they offered to new recruits more easily than French employers. For example, in the clearing department in Britain, after the advice of a management consultancy, the 'week on week off' contracts were gradually being replaced by two- and

Table 10.2   *A comparison of the flexible strategies adopted in Britain and France*

| Type of flexibility | France | Britain |
|---|---|---|
| Functional | More developed | Less important but increasing slightly |
| Numerical | 4.5 per cent of workforce | 2.4 per cent of workforce |
| Temporary work | More external temps | More use of former |
| | Fixed-term contracts more popular; | employees |
| | Used as a testing period before offering permanent employment | |
| Part-time work | 9.6 per cent of workforce | 14 per cent of workforce |
| | Less developed | More popular |
| | More recent | In operation for a number of years |
| | Strictly defined by law, offers less flexibility to employers | A diverse range of contracts used, very adaptable |
| | Has been relatively expensive | Relatively cheap, especially before improved benefits |

three-day a week contracts used for the busiest days. This was a move to match part-time hours to the weekly peaks in workload. In France part-time work was originally introduced in the 1970s to allow people to return to work after long-term illness. In the early 1980s it was seen as a means to combine demands for chosen working time with a possible solution to the problem of reducing unemployment. French employers have less flexibility in the use of these contracts compared to their British counterparts, which may be part of the reason this contract is not as popular in France. Table 10.2 provides a brief summary of some of these differences.

It is clear from this evidence that there are distinct differences in the flexible labour strategies adopted by the banks in each country, although these may not be as great as one would expect, given the differences outlined earlier (O'Reilly, 1992b, Chapter 6).

### Explanations

Explanations for these differences can be provided if we look at four key areas: the organisation of the firm and the intensity of fluctuations in work levels, labour market conditions in each country, the educational and training system, and finally the role of the state.

*Organisation of the Firm: Centralisation, Work Load*
*Fluctuations and the Division of Labour*
The regionalised organisation of clearing operations and the intensity of fluctuations in the volumes of work treated are important
factors accounting for the differences in labour strategies used. As
mentioned earlier, the British system of cheque clearance is centred
in London, whereas in France there are important regional clearing
centres located in large provincial cities. The regional organisation
of cheque clearing in France is attributable to regulations
introduced by La Banque de France. After conducting a study,
they found that over 90 per cent of cheques were written and
cashed within the same region (Lasfargues, 1980). Where the
operations are centralised, the variation in workloads are of a
greater intensity. For example, in Britain, on average, three and a
half million cheques pass through the clearing department on a
Tuesday, the busiest day, compared to two million on Friday, the
quietest day. For a comparable bank in France the volume of work
was less intense; they cleared 200,000 cheques on an average day
and 270,000 on a Tuesday. This difference in the volume of work
and intensity of fluctuations posed different labour requirements.
In France, staff employed in smaller work units were expected to
perform a variety of tasks, whereas in Britain there was a more
extensive division of labour and greater use was made of part-time
shifts to meet these fluctuations.

The development of functional flexibility is closely associated
with the size of the work unit in both the branches and the clearing
department. Where this is small it is more likely that staff will be
expected to perform a wide range of tasks;[7] in a large unit it is
likely that there will be a more extensive division of labour and
greater recourse can be made to part-time and temporary staff for
low-skill jobs. Thus, for example, the differences in the size of the
branches also explains why functional flexibility is more developed
in France, where the branches are on average smaller than in
Britain (Moussy, 1989). Clearly the size of organisations are not
independent factors and are a product of the society in which they
developed. In the case of Britain the centralisation of operations in
London is related to the historical importance of the City and the
centralisation of banking in the 1870s, whereas in France, as in
many other European countries, the decentralised system has
emerged in the process of industrialisation. (For a fuller discussion
of these developments see Zysman, 1983; Burgard, 1988; Morris,
T., 1986.)

The question of security is also relevant to the organisation of
work in the banks, and this has been handled differently in each

country. In France cashiers can perform a wider range of transactions from selling foreign exchange to paying out large sums of cash. In Britain services are more segmented; enquiries and low risk transactions are treated in the central lobby and high risk transactions are dealt with at the back of the branch, where the staff are protected behind glass panels. This difference in the two countries can be partly explained by the treatment of security issues: in France, due to a series of armed hold-ups in the 1970s, security arrangements in the branches were tightened to make it more difficult to enter a branch.[8] In Britain the same security question did not arise and it is much easier to walk in and out of the branch. Therefore, in France all cashiers could handle high risk transactions because the branch was more secure for the staff, which facilitated the policy of functional flexibility.

*Labour Market Conditions*
Another important factor which needs to be taken into account is the state of the labour market. At the end of the 1980s the labour market for white-collar jobs was relatively tight in the South of England because of the boom in financial services and the predicted decline in the number of school leavers entering the labour market, although this has since changed with falling profits and pressure to reduce jobs. In France the banks have been keen to reduce their overall staff numbers since the early 1980s. At the same time they have raised their recruitment age to attract more highly qualified staff, with commercial qualifications. Staff with higher qualifications are considered to be more adaptable and this recruitment policy is related to the development of functional flexibility. As a result, the banks in France have raised their standard recruitment age to 20 +, whereas in Britain it is still common for the banks to recruit school leavers from 17 +. The reason for these different recruitment policies is because the French banks wanted to change the profile of their personnel: they thought younger, better educated staff would be more adaptable to change, and better able to provide a more integrated service to customers. In France there was a greater emphasis on reducing low-grade administrative tasks and promoting commercial skills, compared to Britain where this has not developed to the same extent.

When the banks in France were keen to reduce staff numbers this had the effect of making staff more functionally flexible: staff were borrowed between departments to cover for staff shortages where staff had left and not been replaced. In Britain at the end of the 1980s, when there was a tight labour market, employers saw part-time work as a solution to these labour problems: former employees who had left to have children could be encouraged to come back to work part-time. This policy was also used when employers found it difficult to attract full-timers. For example, in the clearing department in London the 'week on week off' contracts were introduced to provide full-time cover when it was impossible to attract sufficient full-timers on the wages being offered.

In France employers were beginning to use part-time work as a way of reshaping their work force and reducing overall numbers. The banks in France were keen to squeeze out the generation of low-skilled staff, employed in the period of expansion in the 1970s, and replace them with new, younger, more commercially aware employees. Rather than enforcing redundancies, some banks in France have been offering part-time work contracts to their existing staff on the basis that they agree to work half time for 3–5 years.[9] This allows the bank to slim down the size of the labour force and reshape it. In this way part-time work in France is being used to move staff, particularly women, out of the workforce, whereas in Britain it is often seen as a means of re-entry into paid employment.

Employers' labour market policies are shaped in terms of who they perceive is available for work, together with the experience they have of successfully, or unsuccessfully, recruiting the type of staff they decide they need. Workers' preferences, an aspect which has received limited attention in the literature, can also affect the way employers construct jobs. In Britain the banks make greater use of part-time work than in France, where research on the issue (Maruani and Nicole, 1989) suggests that the demand from French women to work part-time is far less than it is in Britain. These differences in women's labour force participation at a national level could well affect the way employers formulate their labour market strategies.[10] This would mean that in Britain, where many women with young children leave permanent paid employment (Martin and Roberts, 1984), employers think, and in many cases rightly so, that these 'mums' will be willing to work occasionally or on a part-time basis. As a result, in Britain employers in the retail banking sector can successfully call on former employees to work temporarily, or offer a more diverse range of part-time hours than employers in France. In France, where women tend to work more continuously and take less time off after childbirth, the same pool of labour is not available, therefore employers do not offer similar part-time contracts because they do not expect anyone to accept them. However, in France, where some banks have made redundancies this has created a pool of qualified staff available for temporary work on the external labour market.

Table 10.3   *Young persons aged 14 to 24 in full-time and part-time education as a percentage of the active labour force in 1989*

|  | France | | | | Britain | | | |
|---|---|---|---|---|---|---|---|---|
|  | women | | men | | women | | men | |
| 14–18 | 15.6 | (1643) | 11.3 | (1531) | 11.3 | (1395) | 8.4 | (1377) |
| 19–22 | 5.6 | (593) | 3.7 | (496) | 2.2 | (266) | 1.8 | (302) |
| 23–24 | 0.9 | (96) | 0.6 | (85) | 0.6 | (73) | 0.6 | (97) |
| Active labour force | 43.8 | (10,531) | 56.2 | (13,531) | 42.9 | (12,310) | 57 | (16,372) |

*Source*: Eurostat Labour Force Survey 1989, tables 01 and 24; the numbers in brackets are the real numbers in thousands

### Educational Levels

French women have a notably higher level of education in general compared to their British counterparts (Barrere-Maurisson et al., 1989; Benoit-Guilbot, 1987). This is clearly brought out in Table 10.3 using the figures published by Eurostat.

More than twice as many women in France (5.6 per cent) were likely to stay on in some form of education between the ages of 19–22, compared to Britain where only 2.2 per cent of the female labour force were attending post-18 education; the same pattern is also true for men. In contrast to Britain, new labour market entrants in France were likely to be older and more highly qualified, which is reflected in the personnel policy of the banks in France.

This pattern was borne out in the samples selected for the case studies: in Britain just over 97 per cent of the women employees interviewed had left school by the age of 17, whereas in France, amongst women employees in similar jobs, over 50 per cent had gone on to post-18 education. This reflects the greater importance the French give to education (Zeldin, 1983). Apart from having a higher level of education, the French staff also had higher expectations of promotion compared to their British equivalents: only 55 per cent of all employees interviewed in Britain said they wanted promotion compared to 76 per cent in France. These two factors may contribute to an explanation of why French employers place greater emphasis on the development of functional flexibility than do employers in Britain. Functional flexibility served to increase the task variety and job interest of these staff in France. In Britain, where the women were less well educated and had lower career expectations, they appeared to be more willing to take up part-time work.

The education system also has another effect on female labour supply. In France part-time contracts on an 80 per cent basis are the most popular contracts because children do not go to school on Wednesdays, and a lot of part-timers prefer to have this day off. This makes French women part-timers less flexible than their British equivalents and emphasises the importance of taking domestic and social welfare constraints into account in order to understand the terms on which people participate in paid employment, and how this may in turn affect employers' policies.

*The Role of the State*
State ownership of the banks in France has affected their strategic choices more than their day-to-day operations. For instance, the government has recently sought to influence the banks' policies by encouraging the merger of GAN insurance with the CIC bank as a way of increasing the bank's capital and providing an outlet for insurance sales, to protect these sectors from the competition which will follow 1992. In this way the banks are being forced to reconsider and restructure their operations to make them more profitable.

Additionally, as for other industries, the state affects firms' employment policy through employment legislation. The most significant regulation which directly affects the use of part-time work in the banks in France is the 1937 decree on working time, which specifies that bank employees are entitled to two consecutive days off, one of which must be a Sunday. This means that branches are only allowed to open either Monday to Friday, or Tuesday to Saturday. The decree also forbids the banks to use overlapping or twilight shifts so that part-timers cannot be employed as they are in Britain to cover for lunch breaks.

Part-time and temporary work are more closely regulated, and part-time work is more expensive for employers, in France than in Britain (Thurman and Trah/ILO 1989). The limited protection and relative cheapness of part-time work for employers in Britain is often cited as one of the main reasons for its use in the UK. However, cost is not the only criterion in the banks: part-timers offer the banks a means of retaining skills as well as providing cover for busy periods. In 1986 the restrictions on the use of temporary staff were lifted by the Chirac government, although some limited attempts to restore protection for these employees has been reintroduced more recently. In general French employment law is more restrictive on employers than is the case in Britain. Also the costs of hiring new staff are higher because of the social security payments that employers have to make and the greater difficulty of making them redundant. Table 10.4 summarises

Table 10.4   *Explanations for the differences in flexible labour strategies developed in Britain and France*

| Type of flexibility | France | Britain |
| --- | --- | --- |
| Functional | Increasing use in small work units in both countries | |
| | French branches are smaller | |
| | Regionalised clearing in smaller work units | Centralised clearing in very large centre |
| | Educational levels are higher | Lower educational levels |
| | Increasingly older staff (20+) are recruited with higher level of education | Younger staff (17+) employed |
| | Integrated service policy | Segmented service policy |
| | Cashiers have direct access to computer terminals | Terminals are used selectively |
| | Security arrangements in branches make it more protected inside the branch | Open entry branches |
| **Numerical** | | |
| Temporary work | Less availability of women prepared to work intermittently | Women spend longer out of paid work to raise a family and are willing to come back to work intermittently |
| | Redundancies in other banks provide pool of available qualified temps on the external market | |
| Part-time work | More restrictions on use | Limited restrictions on use, relatively cheap |
| | Relatively expensive | |
| | Seen as a form of chosen working time and a solution to unemployment | |

these explanations in relation to the different forms of flexibility developed in each country.

## Implications and Conclusions

This chapter set out to examine how employers in retail banking were developing flexible employment policies, and to what extent these developments were similar or different in Britain and France. We have seen how the banks in each country employ distinctive forms of flexibility, but these developments are not as neat as the model of the flexible firm would suggest. The evidence presented from this research shows that the concepts constructed in the flexibility debates have been too simplistic in the motivations they attach to the use of different forms of flexibility.

More recognition needs to be given to the fact that a broad configuration of different institutional and societal factors shape the way in which labour requirements are constructed, and that there is no single rationale for the use of similar forms of flexibility which can be employed for different purposes. For example, we have seen functional flexibility on the one hand being used to upgrade the skills required from cashiers; at the same time staff shortages created by restructuring operations have led to the remaining staff having to take on a wider range of tasks to cover these gaps. These are quite distinct reasons for using functional flexibility. In the first case employers are keen to improve their service policy in the branches, whereas in the second this is a temporary stop-gap measure resulting from rationalisation. There is evidence for both strategies being used in each country but to varying degrees.

In France, despite state control the banking sector has been highly competitive, especially since the reforms of the late 1960s. Also employers have sought to develop functional flexibility because they want to offer an integrated service policy. This policy is facilitated by (a) the higher educational level of bank staff in France; (b) the cashiers having direct access to computer terminals; (c) the relatively small size of work units; and (d) security arrangements in the branches. In Britain this policy was not as developed, branches tended to be larger, and the centralisation of clearing involved an extensive division of labour. The female staff employed in Britain had lower levels of education and lower career expectations. The branches were organised on the basis of a segmented service policy and a more extensive use of part-timers which hindered the development of functional flexibility. The development of functional flexibility marked a significant move away from the traditionally administrative role of bank employees towards the development of more competitive and commercially orientated staff.

With regard to numerical flexibility, in both countries part-time work was more important than temporary work, and more popular in Britain than in France. One explanation put forward for this difference was attributed to the composition of available labour in each country. In Britain women's discontinuous labour market participation makes them a potential reserve of untapped labour, and the banks have been able to successfully fill part-time and temporary contracts, usually by employing ex-female employees who have left to have children. In France part-time work does not offer employers the same degree of flexibility as it does in Britain. Part-time work is comparatively expensive and women are less flexible in the hours they work because of the school timetable, where children do not attend school on Wednesdays.

From these observations we can conclude that where there is a highly qualified labour force, where competition is based on quality service rather than cost, where technology is used to widen the range of tasks an employee can perform, and where work units are relatively small, it is more likely that employers will develop a policy of functional flexibility. On the other hand, where there is an extensive division of labour, and jobs are relatively low-skilled performed by staff with limited qualifications, it is easier to substitute these employees with part-time and temporary workers. This analysis has aimed to show how employers' policies develop from a configuration of factors which can work in varying ways and which can change over time. Definitions of the type of flexibility required by employers varies in the way it is constructed in different countries. The flexibility obtained from similar contracts is dependent on the regulatory, economic and social context in which they are developed and this needs to be more fully recognised than it has been in the past.

## Notes

This chapter was based on research conducted for my PhD at Nuffield College, Oxford University. Financial support was provided by The Leverhulme Trust and the Economic and Social Research Council (ESRC).

1 Not all retail banks are clearers; some of the smaller banks use the services of the larger clearers for a fee (Wright and Valentine, 1988).
2 For example, the director of Société Générale was replaced after the 1986 election of Chirac, and the head of the BNP is considered to have kept his position only because of his close friendship with President Mitterrand.
3 Although the structure of the bank is decentralised and run on an independent regional basis, the national *caisse* can provide financial support for local *caisse* by issuing bonds in its own name (Green, 1986: 89).
4 Some of these banks have their headquarters located in provincial cities, for example Banque de l'Aquitaine at Bordeaux, Banque Cooperative et Mutualiste de Bretange at Brest, Banque Niçoise de Crédit at Nice, Société de Banque de Provence at Toulon, Société Générale Alsacienne de Banque (SOGENAL) at Strasbourg etc. . . . (AFB, *Liste des membres*).
5 For example, some banks, like the CCF, have been trying to eliminate low profit clients from their books by closing their accounts so that they can concentrate their services on more profitable clients.
6 Teams of full-time permanent staff who were moved around the branches to meet temporary need.
7 Although, as Lockwood (1989) pointed out, a large organisation is not synonymous with extensive bureaucratisation.

8 It is common in France to have to pass through two sets of locked doors, which can only be opened by the cashiers inside, before you can get inside the branch.

9 These employees are paid 60 or 70 per cent of their full-time salary if they agree to work half time for three or five years respectively. Unlike the policy of voluntary redundancies at the Crédit du Nord, this policy of part-time work was seen as a more effective way of reducing the workforce.

10 The sociological problem this presents here is one of causality: is women's labour force participation a product of employers' policies or women's preferences? This is an issue which cannot be fully treated here, but it should be noted that such patterns of behaviour cannot be reduced to monocausal explanations. See L. Morris (1990) for an interesting analysis of the diversity of women's labour force experience and the role of social welfare.

# References

Association Française des Banques (AFB) (1986) *La Banque: le système bancaire français*. Paris: AFB.

Atkinson, J. and Meager, N. (1986) *Changing Working Patterns: How Companies Achieve Flexibility to Meet New Needs*. London: National Economic Development Office.

Austrin, T. (1991) 'Flexibility, Surveillance and Hype in New Zealand Financial Retailing', *Work, Employment and Society*. 5 (2): 201–21.

Bailey, E. (1990) 'Banking on Everything but Money', *The Telegraph*. 23 April.

Banque de Règlements Internationaux et La Banque de France (1986) *Systèmes de paiement dans onze pays developpes*. Paris: BIS.

Baron, J. and Bielby, W. (1984) 'The Organization of Work in a Segmented Economy', *American Sociological Review*. 49: 454–73.

Barrere-Maurisson, M-A., Daune-Richard, A-M. and Letablier, M-T. (1989) 'Le Travail à temps partiel plus développé au Royaume-Uni qu'en France', *Economique et Statistique*. 220 (avril).

Beechey, V. (1989) 'Women's Employment in France and Britain: Some Problems of Comparison', *Work, Employment and Society*, 3 (3): 369–78.

Beechey, V. and Perkins, T. (1987) *A Matter of Hours: Women, Part-time Work and Labour Markets*. Cambridge: Polity Press.

Benoit-Guilbot, O. (1989) 'Quelques réflexions sur l'analyse sociétale: l'exemple des régulations des marchés du travail en France et en Grande-Bretagne', *Sociologie du Travail*. 2:

Berger, S. and Piore, M. (1980) *Dualism and Discontinuity in Industrial Societies*. New York: Cambridge University Press.

Bernoux, P., Cressey, P., Eldridge, J. and MacInnes, J. (1990) *New Technology and Employee Relations in a Scottish and a French Bank*. Summary report of a research project undertaken by the Department of Sociology and Social and Economic Research, University of Glasgow, and Groupe Lyonnaise de Sociologie Industrielle, Université de Lyon II, May 1990.

Bertrand, O. and Noyelle, T. (1987) 'L'Emploi dans les banques et assurances: comparison internationale et perspectives d'evolution', *Economie et Humanisme* (mai-juin):

Burgard, J-J. (1988) *La Banque en France*. Paris: Presses de la Fondation Nationale des Sciences Politiques/Dalloz.

Casey, B. (1988) *Temporary Employment: Practice and Policy in Britain*. London: PSI.

Child, J. and Loveridge, R. (1990) *Information Technology in European Services: Towards a Microelectronic Future*. Oxford: ERSC/Blackwell.

Cossalter, C. (1989) *Renouvellement des qualifications et gestion des ressources humaines dans les banques*. Working paper prepared at the Centre d'Etudes et de Recherches sur les Qualifications, ref: CC/OS/CEREQ, Départment Enterprises et Formation.

Cox, A. (ed.) (1986) *State, Finance and Industry: A Comparative Analysis of Post-War Trends in Six Advanced Industrial Economies*. New York: St Martin's Press.

Crompton, R. (1989) 'Women in Banking: Continuity and Change since the Second World War', *Work, Employment and Society*. 3 (2): 141–56.

Crow, G. (1989) 'The Use of the Concept of "Strategy" in Recent Sociological Literature', *Sociology*. 23 (1).

de Quillacq, L.M. (1987) 'Restructuring of French Banks', *Retail Banker*. 26 January.

Doeringer, P. and Piore, M. (1971) *Internal Labor Market and Manpower Analysis*. Lexington, MA: Heath.

Edwards, R. (1979) *Contested Terrain: the Transformation of the Workplace in the Twentieth Century*. London: Heinemann.

Frazer, P. and Vittas, D. (1984) *The Retail Banking Revolution: an International Perspective*. London: Michael Cafferty Publications.

Gallie, D. (1978) *In Search of the New Working Class: Automation and Social Integration within the Capitalist Enterprise*. Cambridge: Cambridge University Press.

Gallie, D. (ed.) (1988) *Employment in Britain*. Oxford: Blackwell.

Gallie, D. and White, M. (1991) *Employers' Policies, Employee Contracts and Labour Market Structure*. Paper presented at the 2nd Nuffield/PSI Conference, 11 January, Nuffield College, Oxford.

Gordon, D.M., Edwards, R. and Reich, M. (1982) *Segmented Work, Divided Workers: the Historical Transformation of Labor in the United States*. Cambridge: Cambridge University Press.

Graham, G. (1988) 'Stagnation on the Plateau', *Financial Times*. 18 May.

Green, D. (1986) 'The State, Finance and Industry of France', in A. Cox (ed.), *State, Finance and Industry: a Comparative Analysis of Post-War Trends in Six Advanced Industrial Economies*. New York: St Martin's Press.

Gregory, A. (1987) 'Le Travail à temps partiel en France et en Grande-Bretagne: temps imposé ou temps choisi?', *Revue Française des Affaires Sociales*. 3 ( juillet–septembre).

Hakim, C. (1987) 'Trends in the Flexible Workforce', *Employment Gazette*. 95 (11).

HMSO 'British Labour Force Survey', London: HMSO.

Hodson, R. and Kaufman, R. (1982) 'Economic Dualism: a Critical Review', *American Sociological Review*. 47: 727–39.

Hu, Y–S. (1975) *National Attitudes and the Financing of Industry*. London: PEP Political and Economic Planning Vol. XLI, Broadsheet No. 559.

Huws, U. (1984) *The New Homeworkers: New Technology and the Changing Location of White Collar Work*. Low Pay Unit, No. 28.

INSEE 'Enquête sur l'Emploi', Paris: INSEE.

Kerr, C., Dunlop, J., Haribson, F. and Myers, C. (1964) *Industrialism and Industrial Man: the Problems of Labor Management in Economic Growth*. Oxford: Oxford University Press. [First published by Harvard University Press, 1960.]

Lane, C. (1987) 'Capitalism or Culture? A Comparative Analysis of the Position in the Labour Process and Labour Market of Lower White-Collar Workers in the Financial Services Sector of Britain and the Federal Republic of Germany', *Work, Employment and Society.* 1 (1): 57–84.

Lane, C. (1988) 'Industrial Re-organization in Europe: the Pursuit of Flexible Specialization in Britain and West Germany', *Work, Employment and Society.* 2 (2): 141–68.

Lane, C. (1989) *Management and Labour in Europe: the Industrial Enterprise in Germany, Britain and France.* Aldershot: Edward Elgar.

Lane, C. (1990) *Industrial Re-organization in Europe: Patterns of Convergence and Divergence in Germany, France and Britain.* Paper presented at the Work, Employment and European Society Conference, Bath, 6–8 September 1990.

Lane, C. (1991) *Gender and the Labour Market in Europe: Britain, Germany and France Compared.* Paper presented to the Gender and Labour Market Seminar, Nuffield College, Oxford, 5 February 1991.

Lasfargues, R. (1980) 'La Compensation départementale des chèques: nouveau régime applicable à partir du ler octobre 1980', *Banque.* No. 399: 1103–6.

Lewis, V. (1987) 'French Banks Face Further Reforms', *The Banker.* May.

Lockwood, D. (1989) *The Blackcoated Worker: a Study in Class Consciousness.* 2nd edn, Oxford: Clarendon Press. [First published 1958 by Allen & Unwin.]

Lui, T.L. (1990) *'The Social Organization of Outwork: the Case of Hong Kong'.* DPhil Thesis, University of Oxford.

Marsh, D. (1985) 'Winds of Change: French Banking and Finance', *The Banker.* April.

Martin, J. and Roberts, C. (1984) *Women & Employment Survey: a Lifetime Perspective.* London: HMSO.

Maruani, M. and Nicole, C. (1989) *Au labeur des dames: métiers masculins, emplois féminins.* Paris: Syros Alternatives.

Maurice, M., Sellier, F. and Silvestre, J-J. (1982) *Politique d'éducation et organiza-tion industrielle en France et en Allemagne.* Paris: Presses Universitaires de France. Trans. 1986 as *The Social Foundations of Industrial Power: a Comparison of France and Germany.* Cambridge, MA: MIT Press.

Michon, F. (1981) 'Dualism and the French Labour Market: Business Strategy, Non-Standard Job Forms and Secondary Jobs', in F. Wilkinson (ed.), *The Dynamics of Labour Market Segmentation.* London: Academic Press.

Morgan, D. (1989) 'Strategies and Sociologists: a Comment on Crow', *Sociology.* 23 (1).

Morris, L. (1990) *The Workings of the Household.*

Morris, T. (1986) *Innovations in Banking: Business Strategies and Employee Rela-tions.* London: Croom Helm.

Moussy, J-P. (1989) 'L'Emploi au coeur de la mutation bancaire', Banque et Emploi, *Revue d'Economie Financière.* No. 7.

Nolan, P. (1983) 'The Firm and Labour Market Behaviour', in G.S. Bain (ed.), *Industrial Relations in Britain.* Oxford: Blackwell.

Nolan, P. and Edwards, P.K. (1984) 'Homogenise, Divide and Rule: an Essay on *Segmented Work, Divided Workers'*, *Cambridge Journal of Economics.* 8: 197–215.

O'Reilly, J. (1992a) 'Where do you Draw the Line? Functional Flexibility, Training and Skill in Britain and France', *Work, Employment and Society.* 6(3).

O'Reilly, J. (1992b) 'Banking on Flexibility: a Comparison of Employers' Flexible

Labour Strategies in the Retail Banking Sector in Britain and France', DPhil Thesis, Nuffield College, Oxford University.

Piore, M. and Sabel, C. (1985) *The Second Industrial Divide: Possibilities for Prosperity*. New York: Basic Books.

Pollert, A. (1987) *The Flexible Firm: a Model in Search of Reality or a Policy in Search of a Practice?* Warwick Papers in Industrial Relations. No. 19, December.

Rajan, A. (1984) *New Technology and Employment in Insurance, Banking and Building Societies: Recent Experience and Future Impact*. Brighton: Institute of Manpower Studies.

Reynaud, J-D. (1989) *Les Régles du jeux: l' action collective et la régulation sociale*. Paris: Armand Colin.

Robinson, O. and Wallace, J. (1984) *Part-time Employment and Sex Discrimination Legislation in Great Britain*, Department of Employment Research Paper, No. 43.

Rose, M. (1985) 'Universalism, Culturalism and the Aix Group: Promise and Problems of the Societal Approach to Economic Institutions', *European Sociological Review*. 1 (1).

Rosenberg, S. (1989) 'From Segmentation to Flexibility', *Labour and Society*. 14 (4).

Rubery, J. (1978) 'Structured Labour Markets, Worker Organisation and Low Pay', *Cambridge Journal of Economics*. 2: 17–36.

Rubery, J. (1988) 'Employers and the Labour Market', in Gallie (1988).

Savage, M. (1989) *Career Structures and Managerial Hierarchies: the Case of Lloyds Bank 1870–1950*. University of Surrey (July), mimeo.

Shreeve, G. and Alexander, J. (1991) 'My Heart Belongs to Daddy', *The Banker*. February.

Silverman, D. (1987) *The Theory of Organizations: a Sociological Approach*. Aldershot: Gower. [First published 1970 by Heinemann Educational Books.]

Strober, M. and Arnold, C. (1987) 'The Dynamics of Occupational Segregation amongst Bank Tellers', in C. Brown and J. Pechman (eds), *Gender in the Workplace*. Washington, DC: The Brookings Institution.

Thurman, J. and Trah, G./International Labour Office (1989) *Conditions of Work Digest: Part-time Work*. Vol. 8 No. 1. Geneva: ILO.

Upton, R. (1984) 'The "Home-Office' and New Homeworkers', *Personnel Management*. September.

Walby, S. (1989) 'Flexibility and the Changing Sexual Division of Labour', in S. Wood (ed.), *The Transformation of Work?* London: Unwin Hyman.

Wright, D. and Valentine, W. (1988) *Business of Banking*. 2nd edn, Plymouth: Northcote House.

Zeldin, T. (1983) *Les Français*. Paris: Librairie Arthème Fayard.

Zysman, J. (1983) *Governments, Markets and Growth: Financial Systems and the Politics of Industrial Change*. Oxford: Martin Robertson.

# 11
# Firm Development and Diversification Strategies as Products of Economic Cultures: the Japanese and Hong Kong Cotton Textile Industries

## J.M. Nishida and S.G. Redding

This chapter contrasts the development of the Japanese and Hong Kong textile industries as an example of how institutional contexts affect patterns of firm growth and market organisation along the lines suggested by Richard Whitley in his chapter in this volume. By studying the diversification strategies of cotton-spinning firms in Japan and Hong Kong we wish to illuminate the workings of the processes of determinancy proposed in the Whitley framework, and begin the process of operationalising the notion of 'embeddedness' proposed by Granovetter (1985).

In summary, distinct differences in the formation, operation and development of cotton spinning companies in Japan and Hong Kong can be identified. The Japanese cotton spinners have developed an oligopolistic structure and have successfully diversified into higher technologies. In contrast, the Hong Kong spinners are small family firms with a limited range of products and markets, if they remain in the textile business at all. The basic question to be addressed here then is: how have institutional differences led to these quite distinct patterns of firm development in Japan and Hong Kong? First we will summarise the major characteristics of the textile industry in the two economies and consider their crucial differences as business systems. Next the major institutional features which have contributed to these differences will be summarised and their consequences discussed.

## The Cotton Textile Industries of Japan and Hong Kong

The textile industries of East Asia provide a particularly interesting vehicle for the study of the development of economic cultures (Berger, 1986) because of their key role in the remarkably successful industrialisation of those economies. Each textile industry has developed distinctive business systems reflecting the differences both in the development of the institutional setting, and in the choices made by managerial elites.

The form in which each textile industry has survived is indicative of the way in which an economic culture has developed. One of the major means of survival has been the degree to which textile firms have diversified their products and markets, in order to maintain or develop their economic power.

The Japanese textile industry ranks second in the world to the United States in terms of output; it is export-oriented, and characterised by a small number of large spinning or 'upstream' companies which operate as an oligopoly and a large number of small weaving and apparel or 'mid-' and 'downstream' companies, many of which are allied to the large spinning or trading companies. The whole range of natural and man-made textile fibres is produced; the industry has diversified from its pre-war world dominance in cotton to become second only to the United States in the production of chemical fibres, which has enabled continued diversification into other end uses for textiles such as household furnishings and industrial materials. Uniquely in the world textile industry, the leading cotton-spinning firms of Japan have diversified into chemical fibres, competing with the specialist chemical fibre companies in Japan and elsewhere.

Textiles and apparel are a major industry in Hong Kong, accounting for 40 per cent of Hong Kong's total exports; the textile industry has no significant world ranking, but the apparel industry is seventh in the world in terms of value of output, and first in exports. A small number of larger firms have accounted for a considerable proportion of total textile production, alongside a large number of small firms making apparel for export. Export markets are narrowly focused on North America and Western Europe, which are protected by Multi-Fibre Arrangements under the auspices of GATT. Consequently around 75 per cent (by value) of Hong Kong's textile and garment exports to the United States and 95 per cent to the European Community are subject to quota restrictions (Cline, 1987: 160). One effect of the quota system is that it has 'trapped' Hong Kong in maintaining its position as a dominant supplier of apparel to the United States and European markets. It has encouraged Hong Kong textile companies to diversify by forward integration into manufacture of high-value apparel and into retailing. Diversification into property has been virtually the only non-textile business into which they have ventured. For some cotton-spinning firms property has become the dominant business activity. Noticeably lacking in Hong Kong has been diversification into synthetic fibre production and textile-related

Table 11.1 *Cotton spinning firms of Japan and Hong Kong*

| | | Japan | Hong Kong |
|---|---|---|---|
| Founding of modern cotton spinning mills | | 1880s | Late 1940s |
| No. of mills and spindles | 1950 | 4.4 mill. spindles | 10 mills/132,000 spindles |
| | 1970 | 11.8 mill. spindles | 31 mills/896,000 spindles |
| | 1988 | 8.6 mill. spindles | 15 mills/284,000 spindles |
| | 1990 | 7.8 mill. spindles | 9 mills/264,000 spindles |
| Characteristics of production | 1950 | Mainly cotton, some rayon and wool yarns | Low count cotton yarns |
| | 1970 | Cotton, wool and synthetic yarns | Low/medium count cotton and some cotton/polyester blends |
| | 1990 | High count cotton, high quality synthetic and wool yarns | Low/medium count cotton yarns |
| Structure of the industry | | Big spinners have diversified textile and non-textile operations. New spinners concentrate on spinning, or spinning and weaving. Medium and small spinners concentrate on production of high quality yarns, forward integration and some non-textile diversification | Most spinners have weaving and apparel interests, and have diversified into property; most have overseas investments in textiles and property |
| Main markets for yarn | | | |
| Fabric | | Domestic weavers. Cotton to domestic apparel companies, some exports; 40 per cent synthetic fabric exported | Domestic weavers, mainly denim. Domestic apparel companies |
| Apparel | | Domestic market | Exported mainly to USA and Germany |
| Business trends | | Comparative advantage of fibre production is moving to Taiwan, S. Korea and China; therefore strong emphasis on high quality yarns, automated production, forward integration to apparel and non-textile diversification | Spinning operations closing down, weaving and apparel sectors import yarns and fabrics from China, S. Korea, Taiwan and Japan |

*Sources*: Hong Kong Cotton Spinners' Association (1988); *Monthly Report of the Japan Spinners' Association*, various issues

Table 11.2   *Nature of the firm*

| Firm characteristics | Cotton spinning firms | |
| --- | --- | --- |
| | Japan | Hong Kong |
| Managerial discretion from owners | High | Low |
| Range of activities and resources | High | Low/medium |
| Degree of radical change in growth | Low | Medium |
| Externalisation of risk through mutual dependence | Medium | Low |

businesses such as household fabrics and new industrial materials.

Excess capacity worldwide means that textile companies in industrialised countries need to consider diversification into new uses for textiles and into non-textile businesses, or else they face closure. A comparison of the main characteristics of the Japanese and Hong Kong cotton-spinning industries is given in Table 11.1, which illustrates the success of the Japanese in diversifying into a wide variety of high quality textiles, while the Hong Kong industry has been more conservative in its development, almost to the point of cessation.

**Business Systems**

The major characteristics of firm type and development to be considered here can be described in terms of Whitley's (1990; 1991) summary of the key characteristics of the nature of firms and of market organisation. Comparing first the nature of the firm in the Japanese and Hong Kong textile industries, the four key characteristics are listed in Table 11.2, together with an assessment of how they apply to the leading cotton-spinning firms.

*(i)   The Nature of the Firms*

*Managerial discretion from owners*   The shareholding of the leading Japanese cotton-spinning companies is diffused and based on cross-shareholdings among a number of companies (Ballon and Tomita, 1988: 51–2). The senior management of Japanese cotton-spinning companies are generally 'proper' employees. (The word 'proper' has been incorporated into the Japanese language to indicate those who have served all their working lives with the company.) Once a 'salaryman' achieves directorship most are capable of being president, but the choice is often in the personal gift, subject to political manoeuvrings, of the outgoing president or chairman on personalised rather than objective criteria. The composition of board members in the large companies has a tendency to change significantly once a new president is appointed. Most presidents have powers equivalent to an owner and there is a reluctance by subordinates to challenge decisions, middle management seeing their role as supporting the president. Odaka (1984: 1) termed this '*omikoshi* management'. (An *omikoshi* is a small Shinto shrine which is carried by a number of young men through the streets at festivals.) Provided the company continues to make a profit, there is no alternative source of power to control the president and senior management (Ballon and Tomita, 1988: 187). Hence the diversification strategies adopted by the big companies often reflect the preference of particular presidents in the timing of a company's diversification, and on the path chosen (Yonekawa et al., 1991).

In contrast, although a handful of the Hong Kong cotton-spinning firms are listed on the Hong Kong Stock Exchange, they are all essentially family-owned and managed (Nishida, 1990: 145). The senior managers of the spinning companies are often members of the same family or represent an alliance between families, and even though the company may be publicly listed, the board of directors' membership remains in the control of the family or families. Decisions concerning diversification therefore will be based on family interests. Protection of family capital during the transition of Hong Kong from a British colony to a Special Administrative Region of the People's Republic of China in 1997 is one of the reasons for the steady decline in the number of active spinning mills since 1980; by the end of 1992, it is expected that there will be only seven mills retaining membership of the Hong Kong Cotton Spinners' Association in comparison with 28 in 1980. (Hong Kong Cotton Spinners' Association, 1990).

*Range of activities and resources coordinated through authority hierarchies* The leading Japanese cotton-spinning firms have, over the past century, become more diversified from specialist cotton-spinning firms reliant on trading firms for the development of markets for yarns and fabrics, to fully integrated operations, including spinning, weaving, finishing, apparel-making, and retail for a range of natural and synthetic fibres. Kanebo and Toyobo, for instance, have produced a wide range of textiles – cotton, wool, silk, nylon, rayon, and polyester. Furthermore, they have developed non-textile businesses often based on chemicals. Increasingly, the larger companies are carrying out their own marketing and sales activities in order to respond more quickly to rapidly changing market trends, especially in apparel fashion-related products. They have their own research and development institutions which have been instrumental in the development of new business linked in some way to current expertise: for example, Kanebo has a cosmetic business, ranked third by sales turnover in Japan. In 1940 they diversified from textiles to cosmetics through their silk business which started in 1930. (Kanebo, 1988: 1015–16). The silk worm produces an oil which was used in the production of soap, which led to cosmetics, and is now leading to an important biotechnology business.

Most of the Hong Kong cotton-spinning companies have had ownership links to weaving and apparel-making factories and to textile trading companies. All have property interests in Hong Kong and/or overseas. They have made few changes to their spinning operations apart from regular upgrading of their equipment, which has enabled better-quality yarns to be produced, and a greater emphasis on the production of knitting or combed yarn (Hong Kong Cotton Spinners' Association, 1988: 23). The number of cotton-spinning firms is declining rapidly as second- or third-generation family members choose to emigrate from Hong Kong, mainly to North America. A few are relocating their operations to Malaysia and Thailand where they are setting up integrated spinning, weaving and finishing operations, based on similar medium-weight types of yarn produced in their Hong Kong mills.

Overall, then, the variety of activities and skills coordinated by the spinning firms is greater in Japan than in Hong Kong, although families in the latter have moved opportunistically into new business areas.

*Degree of radical change in skills and activities during growth*   This refers to preferred growth patterns and the way of organising growing activities. The Japanese spinning companies conform to Kono's (1984: 78) findings that Japanese corporations follow a trend of moving from being a single-product company to a dominant-product company by adding new products, and from there to a diversified products company. Japanese cotton-spinning firms can be classified into these three categories. First, the three big general textile firms have diversified into a wide range of textile and non-textile businesses; second, there are those companies which have concentrated on the production of distinctive cotton textile products with limited diversification into non-textiles. The third category is the 'new spinners', who restarted or entered the cotton-spinning business after the war. These firms concentrate on the production of yarn and cloth, and two of them now have top ranking in terms of the number of spindles in Japan. The first and second categories have the more diversified non-textile operations at between 30 per cent and 50 per cent of sales turnover, and are continuing to reduce the number of spindles and close down mills (*Senken Shinbun*, 8 May 1991). The first category use their experience of synthetic fibre production technology as a base for diversification into related industries such as new industrial materials, pharmaceuticals and biotechnology. Only a few large companies have followed diversification strategies which do not originate in textile products or technology, for example Nisshinbo has successfully diversified into anti-skid brake production, Kanebo into food and Shikibo into reinforced ceramics through a joint venture. Most of the large companies continue to research developments in textile technology; for example, Nittobo has developed a super-fine cotton yarn of 260 counts (the highest count produced in Hong Kong is 80s, but most are in the 20s to 40s range). The large companies are also following strategies of inter-nationalising their production operations with a particular focus on the ASEAN countries of Malaysia, Thailand and Indonesia, but also to the United Kingdom and United States. The medium-sized companies are following a variety of approaches – either concentrating their resources on developing spinning techniques and technologies, or gradually abandoning spinning and focusing on developing strong forward links to apparel operations, or diversifying into non-textiles. Diversification has been assisted by the generation of surplus assets in land as the size of spinning operations has reduced over the years due to advances in technology.

The Hong Kong spinning companies are much smaller than most of their Japanese counterparts; reluctance to assign authority to non-family members has been an overriding constraint on size and their ability to extend their product range. The largest cotton-spinning company has one mill, in comparison with 15 for the equivalent in Japan. As the Hong Kong companies have not invested in the research and development of new textile products, their failure to develop new products has made their textile operations vulnerable to the increasing competitive power of other Asian textile industries. Those that maintain textile operations in Hong Kong are on a reduced scale, with an emphasis on trying to produce the same product more efficiently. Some have relocated operations to lower wage-cost economies such as Malaysia. All have diversified into the non-textile interests of property and investment, and in one case, also into joint venture arrangements in the People's Republic of China for the manufacture of food and health products, reflecting the opportunistic interests of the owning family.

*Externalisation of risk*    The risks in undertaking new diversified operations are modified by the huge assets from retained earnings that the large Japanese spinning companies have at their disposal, and by the long-term support they enjoy from banks, *sogo shosha* (general trading companies) and their *keiretsu* companies (a loosely knit organisation of independent companies based on a bank, or as in this case a major manufacturer), who participate in risk sharing. New operations are often launched by the formation of a subsidiary or a joint venture company. The subsidiary may be incorporated into the main company or the joint venture disbanded once the new business and its new technology is fully established. The separation of a new venture from the main body allows independence of action from the bureaucracy of the mother company, which is also protected from any losses and from incurring fixed costs in support of the new business. The *sogo shosha* play a particularly important role in joint ventures set up to manage overseas operations.

The Hong Kong cotton spinners have demonstrated a strong preference for high risk avoidance through flexibility over risk sharing largely due to the absence of risk sharing institutions. Thus in the Hong Kong companies, the management of risk is dependent on the skill and connections of family members. For new ventures, the risk is shared through joint venture arrangements with personally trusted individuals. The low level of industrial diversification and the avoidance of its attendant risks is a response to the following factors which all have risk management implications: the small domestic market, weak marketing and sales functions, reluctance to delegate power to non-family members, and an institutional environment based on the *laissez-faire* government policy. Thus, in the early 1960s, when the cotton spinners began to face protectionist pressures against their exports of yarn and fabric, their response was to diversify forward to a growing domestic apparel manufacturing market which has maintained its premier position in US and European export markets through the protection of the quota system.

## (ii)    Market Organisation

Turning now to consider market organisation, only two characteristics are selected for discussion; these are the extent of long-term relations between firms, and dependence on personal trust and ties as shown in Table 11.3.

*Extent of long-term cooperative relations between firms*    In Japan the *sogo shosha* (general trading companies) and *tonya*

Table 11.3  *Market organisation*

| Characteristics of market relationships | Cotton spinning firms | |
|---|---|---|
| | Japan | Hong Kong |
| Extent of long-term cooperative relations between firms | High | Medium |
| Dependence on personal ties and trust | Medium | High |

(wholesalers) have played a significant role in the development of the Japanese textile industry. After the Second World War, the trading companies supported the large spinners in their diversification into synthetics by developing markets for them (Clairmonte and Cavanagh, 1981: 60). However, since the 'oil shocks' of the 1970s, the large spinners have concentrated on developing integrated weaving and finishing operations within their own operations and within their *keiretsu* companies. Medium and small spinners still continue to sell their yarn to trading companies and wholesalers, who supply small weaving and finishing firms in the *sanchi* or production districts based in provincial cities. Those weavers and finishers who are not part of a large spinning company's *keiretsu* are supported by the trading companies and wholesalers through the provision of yarn or fabric financing, design and marketing information, and sales of their products in Japan and overseas. For example, C. Itoh has a group of 100 weaving companies in the Fukui province *sanchi* (*Senken Shinbun*, 9 May 1991). These cooperative relationships also foster technical updating. The Japanese textile industry can thus be characterised by its long-term cooperative relations between firms within the industry.

The comparatively simple structure of the Hong Kong textile industry and its ethnic divisions between Shanghainese and Cantonese have led to quite a different pattern of relations between firms. The absence of strong Chinese general trading companies, and of marketing and sales functions within the companies, has resulted in a narrow range of markets to which access is controlled by import restrictions or quotas. The industry is responding by making some attempt to diversify markets with the help of the Hong Kong government, but the favoured response is to diversify production locations to lower labour cost countries such as Malaysia and Thailand and continue to compete with the same, but cheaper, product in existing markets. However, most cotton-spinning-mill owners, who are Shanghainese, like other Hong Kong entrepreneurs are leaving the industry and emigrating from Hong Kong. Their absence does not have any particular adverse effect on the mid- and downstream companies because those dealing in low count yarns and fabrics can now obtain cheaper supplies from China and ASEAN countries, and the companies who are upgrading their production can obtain yarns and fabrics from Korea, Taiwan and Japan. In 1990, 54 per cent of Japan's cotton yarn exports were to Hong Kong to meet an increasing demand for imported casual and sportswear yarns, and special yarns. Hong Kong's clothing industry continues to respond to the demand for high quality fashion goods, and is now producing a great variety of clothing items (*Hong Kong 1991*: 82).

As has already been discussed, the Hong Kong spinners set up integrated spinning and weaving operations from the 1950s when they began to face difficulties in exporting their yarn due to the rise of protectionism in their main markets. When the same difficulties were faced in the export of fabric, the clothing industry emerged, becoming the leading exporter of apparel in the world by the late 1970s. Most of Hong Kong's manufacturing exports are heavily dependent on Original Equipment Manufacturing (OEM) or private label manufacturing for consumer product companies in the United States and Europe, and apparel is no exception. The industry is now characterised by three main features: first, the large manufacturers tend to hold quotas and small companies become dependent on obtaining them; second, the mass of small manufacturers have individually very little bargaining power with end-product buyers; third, when forward integration has occurred it has normally been into subsidiaries owned and managed by family members. When orders are received requiring a larger production capacity than that available in the family-controlled firms, the excess will be sub-contracted on short-term commercial arrangements. Thus cooperative relations are structured differently in Hong Kong because of the different institutional arrangements; relations which are kin-based will be long-term and stable, and those with non-kin will be more opportunistic.

*Dependence on personal ties and trust*   Trust based on personal ties has much stronger significance in Hong Kong than in Japan. Trust relations feature in Whitley's schema as a 'background social institution' and as such will be discussed later in this account. The personal tie basis in Hong Kong not only limits the size of companies, but also the nature of inter-firm relations. The situation is exacerbated for the cotton spinners by ethnic differences between themselves as Shanghainese, and the majority of the Hong Kong population which is Cantonese (Wong, 1988: 14). The textile and apparel industries are split between the two groups: most of the spinners and the larger weavers and dyers and finishers are Shanghainese, and the Cantonese predominate in the apparel industry. In addition the status of Hong Kong as a British colony has resulted in a third ethnic group, the British, dominating the managerial ranks of the leading banks and trading companies. The Shanghainese spinners have attempted more self-reliance by incorporating long-term inter-firm relations through some degree of ownership, hence the large number of subsidiary companies evident in their structures.

In Japan, inter-firm linkages are less dependent on personal ties. The large spinning firms and trading companies are bureaucracies with large internal labour markets, and the building of an institutionalised link with other firms is not dependent on individuals. A spinning company's *keiretsu*, its long-term relationships with the small downstream weaving and finishing companies in the *sanchi* is based on mutual business benefits over the long term; any change or break in the relationship will not arise from personal relationships, but because of policy changes made by the senior managing group in the companies.

## Conclusion

Our discussion of the nature of the firm and market organisation has focused on the main characteristics shown in Tables 11.2 and 11.3. The crucial differences in the business systems evident in the Hong Kong and Japanese textile industries can be summarised as follows. Firm development and market organisation in the Japanese industry is characterised by incremental diversification, high managerial discretion and obligational contracting and risk sharing. In the Hong Kong industry, firm development is opportunistic, family-controlled, and features low investment in capital-intensive related industries. Market organisation is weak. How the institutional contexts have affected these patterns of firm growth and market organisation is shown in Figures 11.1 and 11.2, in which we propose the processes of determinancy by the institutional contexts on firm development. We will discuss first the 'background institutions' of Whitley's (1991) schema relating to trust, commitment, individualism and authority, and then the 'proximate institutions' of the state, financial systems and educational and training systems.

## Background Social Institutions

Many of the background social institutions of significance to this analysis are commonly referred to in the literature under the

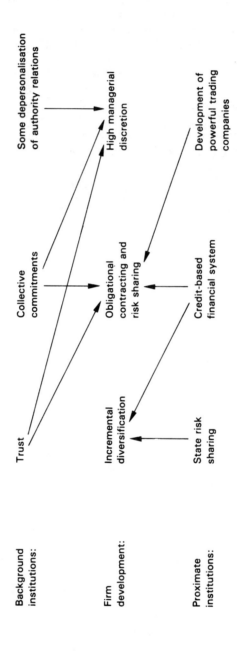

Figure 11.1 *Institutions and diversification strategies in Japan*

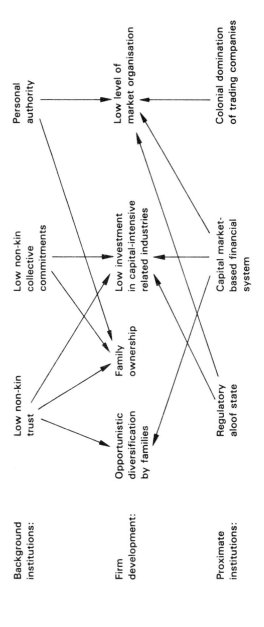

Figure 11.2 *Institutions and diversification strategies in Hong Kong*

heading 'culture'. The values and norms of a society, which are the currency of most cultural analysis, predispose a member of that society to conform to certain tendencies and exhibit certain behaviours. It is not our purpose here to enter into a semantic argument as to whether these factors are cultural or institutional, but simply to note that they are analysable in either category or both. Here we treat them as institutions.

### (i)  Trust

The first of these features to be considered is trust, more specifically the degree and basis of trust between *non-kin*. The centrality of this feature for determining the nature and subsequent success of economic structures has been argued by Harrison (1985) in an analysis of the failure of South American economies, and its workings have been analysed in detail by, among others, Dasgupta (1988), Luhmann (1979) and Eisenstadt and Ronigar (1984).

For a market to work, a certain minimum level of trust is required as a means of dealing with risk and uncertainty. The growth of a strong civil society and its attendant institutions normally serves to provide a set of guarantees of transactions. Without such institutions businesses resort to reputational, ascriptive and personal means of trust-bonding, often buttressed by ethics supporting mutual obligation and the idea of trustworthiness (Zucker, 1988).

In the case of Japan, the longstanding existence of a strong civil society contrasts with the situation in China, and until recently in Hong Kong. The administrative infrastructure of Japan was traditionally denser than that of China, and during the Tokugawa period, the *samurai* class responsible for such structure was roughly five times the proportional size of the degree-holding gentry class in China, resulting in *han* (feudal domain) governments which were broadly-based bureaucracies, rather than narrow aristocracies (Fairbank et al., 1965: 185). Village organisations in Japan stressed inter-family cooperation and trust as well as loyalty to local leadership (Rozman, 1991a: 175). The legitimacy of such leadership rested in turn on the expression of obligation to subordinates (Nakane, 1970) and on behaviour which was essentially nurturing (Pye, 1985: 163). In the higher reaches of the social fabric, elite legitimacy was based on competent performance of duties to society (Fairbank et al., 1965: 181; Collcutt, 1991: 126), and entry to the elite was relatively open due to an opportunity structure which improved markedly during the Tokugawa period and eroded the traditional elite class barriers (Rozman, 1991b: 29). Vertical loyalty was highly structured and integrated and fostered much decentralisation of power from the seventeenth century onwards (Fairbank et al., 1965: 181–8).

In such circumstances, it became possible for economic power and state power to work separately but in consort. Economic growth in the Tokugawa period was unhampered by mistrust of government, or fear of feudal expropriation, with the result that 'Japanese merchants were able to make long-range investments with greater security than were their counterparts in most of Asia' (Fairbank et al., 1965: 191). The cooperation of government and business which followed the Meiji Restoration was a development from a long tradition of trust.

Thus in the case of the Japanese textile industry it was possible for large firms to emerge and for their industrial associations to work with government in pursuing policies which assisted them. Firms could also be integrated in complex ways and could include much technical and product complexity, as the issue of cooperation both inside and between firms appears not to have acted as a handicap. Such tendencies are visible in the formation of the pre-war *zaibatsu* and their post-war successors.

In Chinese society, by contrast, trust is a fundamental problem, and can only be handled interpersonally, not societally. The absence of a developed civil society prevented the emergence of ways to reduce uncertainty (for example: commercial law, accounting, professionalisation) and hindered the decentralisation of decision-making power. The result is a tradition of self-sufficiency, small business, separation of the political and economic arenas, and coordination via interpersonal networking (Feuerwerker, 1984; Elvin, 1973; Jacobs, 1958). One of the consequences is a textile industry of family businesses, relatively small in scale, and directed strategically in the interests of family wealth. One of the outcomes of scale limitation is dependence on others for technical innovation, and for functions such as marketing.

*(ii) Commitment*

Commitment and loyalty to collectivities beyond the family are extensions of the general issue of trust, but they throw light on other contrasts between the *kaisha* and the Chinese family business. If the Chinese family business is a family, or for many employees a paternalistic surrogate family, and succeeds on those terms, then the large Japanese corporation is a large village, with its strong local loyalties, its tribal sense of belonging, and its chosen elders. The psychological attachment of members is different: in the Chinese case it is a matter of connection to and dependence on a person who is, or represents, ownership; in the

Japanese case the connection and dependence are much more to an institution than a person, and such attachment outside the family circle is entirely normal.

### (iii) Individualism

The importance of individual identities, rights and commitments, commonly analysed under the general category 'individualism', is argued by Whitley to have a strong influence on social organisation. In particular, at the level of the firm, if organisations are nothing more than temporary alliances between utility-maximising individuals, then cooperation and coordination cannot rely on common loyalties and identities. A further impetus also exists towards formal specification of specialised roles and tasks for individuals.

In the East Asian context, however, it is the other end of the continuum which is of interest. This is the collectivist or communitarian end, and it begins to bifurcate according to what kind of collectivity a person psychologically belongs to. Here a strong contrast emerges between Japanese and Chinese society. In Japan the collectivity is that which centres on work, the old traditional '*ie*' now transferred to the modern corporation. In consequence the cooperation of Japanese workers with their often very large organisations operates with a naturalness which flows from a long-established institution of work-group bonding and dependence (Pye, 1985; Rohlen, 1974; Doi, 1973; McMillan, 1989).

For the Chinese, by contrast, the collectivity has always been the family, specifically one's own family, and this results in: (a) the persistent overlap of family ownership and control in the Chinese firm; and (b) the problem of building workforce loyalty when competing with the countervailing pull of the worker's ambitions for and duties towards his own family's success (Redding and Wong, 1986). This is especially crucial for key employees, either technically skilled or managerially competent, and will affect a firm's willingness to invest in them via training, or to expand on the assumption of their availability.

The result is that Hong Kong's spinning companies remain relatively small and highly dependent on the availability of family-based managerial resources. They are now moving out to places like Malaysia for reasons which have much to do with the protection of family capital, and they are suffering the leaching away of rare talent in the brain drain. Japan's equivalent industry is professionally managed and able to accumulate the technical and managerial skills needed in depth to sustain the high level of technical sophistication, organisational complexity and variety now being displayed.

## (iv)   Authority

Authority relations are seen here on a continuum from personalistic to depersonalised/formalised. Although the classic Western bureaucracy is the prototype manifestation of the latter, our concern here is not so much with an East/West contrast as with a further East/East contrast. In Chinese authority patterns, personalism is the key. Japanese tradition provides much more for the institutional role to take precedence over the incumbent as person (Pye, 1985: 169). Thus the Chinese organisation remains constrained by the limits of personalistic authority – it can only be stretched so far – and the decentralisation of decision-making power is hampered. The Japanese organisation finds no such limits and authority based on competence can proliferate within the Japanese equivalent of bureaucracy and produce very large and complex organisational forms.

An implication here is that the 'Japanese equivalent of bureaucracy' is not the same as the Weberian ideal type. The differences lie in (a) the inclusion of loyalty along with competence as a determinant of a boss's legitimacy, (b) the nature of leadership as representation rather than domination, (c) the *gemeinschaft* context of many organisational interactions and (d) the avoidance of too obvious a connection between *individual* performance and the judgement of worth, in favour of a more collective definition of effort.

A stable society with a strong and clearly defined elite and uncoordinated political power in lower strata tends to accord authority to that elite in ways which perpetuate the differentiation between strata. Traditionally in China, the ruling mandarins were allowed to claim superior moral status based on education, and their claim to authority never needed to be justified in terms of 'performance' or the delivery of welfare (Pye, 1985: 198). Criticism of policy from below was stifled as essentially against the prevailing moral order, and still is. The transfer of this ancient authority structure into the context of modern industry has been illuminated by Silin (1976), who describes the nature of Chinese business leadership as essentially moral. For the leader to retain authority over employees, the rights which flow from the strong legitimising force of ownership must be exercised with dignity, benevolence, responsibility, probity and a paternalistic concern for welfare. One of the outcomes of this is the highly centralised firm in which all key decisions remain the province of the owner, again a feature which inhibits the scale of operations and allows for narrow interests to dictate strategy.

In Japanese history, by contrast, power was competed for

aggressively over a wider front and was never the complete monopoly of a self-perpetuating elite claiming moral superiority. The Tokugawa state was divided into 265 feudal domains, as *han*, many of whose *daimyo* (lords) were capable of displaying quite high degrees of independence from the shogunate. In response to such dividing of political authority, central control was maintained via an elaborate structure connecting village government, town government and central government. But within this the towns retained much autonomy and fostered the growth of the economic and political power of the merchant industrialists (Jacobs, 1958: 88) throughout the Tokugawa period. The expectations about participation to which this gave rise are met today in the typical Japanese corporation's use of consensus decision-making, widespread consultation, extensive communications and, at least partly in consequence, workplace commitment.

The textile industry in Japan shows evidence of an ability to handle increasingly complex production technology, worker variety and organisational complexity, all of which require from any individual company high degrees of institutional differentiation and integration. Such features of institutions are normally easier to achieve if the membership works with shared superordinate goals and also with a clear sense of common identity. These in turn are normally enhanced by processes of participation in the establish-ment of common purposes. Thus the Japanese corporation, in diffusing authority, at the same time enhances its capacity to respond to environmental complexity in ways not accessible to the Chinese equivalent.

The use of reciprocity in the exercise of political power is well understood in East Asia, and well documented as part of the Japanese system of state influence on the economy (Johnson, 1982; Vogel, 1978). Over time, a system of balancing out ensures that the government pays its debts to industry and vice-versa so that the accommodation between the two is essentially cooperative rather than confrontational and the developmental state progresses. The primary result of this filtering down into the economy is the reduc-tion of risk by the elimination of areas of uncertainty, and the firm is thus able to take a longer view, invest more capital, and assume larger scale.

The absence of this process in Hong Kong, where business is left essentially to fend for itself, is that risk and uncertainty remain high, and investment remains consequently short-term, small-scale or consciously high-risk.

**Proximate Social Institutions**

Proximate social institutions are those which constitute the more immediate business environment. Institutions representing the role of the state, financial systems and education and training systems will be examined here in relation to their impact on the development of Japanese and Hong Kong cotton textile firms.

*(i) Role of the State*
The characteristics of a 'developmental state' (Johnson, 1982) are very evident in the relations the Japanese government has with the textile industry (see Dore, 1986: 221–4). Since 1956 the government has enacted a number of measures to reform the structure of the textile industry, primarily aimed at the small and medium firms in the mid- and downstream segments of the industry. In addition, spinning companies through the auspices of the Japan Spinners' Association have organised production cuts through anti-depression cartels. Although there are no formal import quotas, the Japanese government through MITI sponsors an import surveillance scheme conducted by the Japan Textile Importers' Association, and issues 'administrative guidance' to the dozen or so top members of this Association to delay deliveries or refrain from new contracts when imports rise above an agreed level (Yamazawa, 1988: 416–17). Another MITI concern is the future survival of the textile industry. The Textile Industry Council and the Textile Industry division of the Industrial Structure Council have identified three strategies for the revitalisation of the Japanese textile industry: first, the promotion of technological change and inventiveness accompanied by business switch-overs and closures of the less efficient firms; second, a closer integration of the interrelationships existing in the industry; and third, the internationalisation of the industry. The leading spinning companies and the Japan Cotton Spinners' Association have fully endorsed these strategies.

In Hong Kong, the government's traditional role of *laissez-faire* became one of 'positive non-interventionism' in the late 1960s in order to respond more effectively to the challenges from other newly industrialising economies. The government promotes and protects the industry's interests in Multi-Fibre Agreement (MFA) and bilateral negotiations, and has set up institutions to help develop new markets and products. The Hong Kong Trade Development Council (HKTDC) was set up in 1966 in order to assist in the development of market opportunities in Hong Kong's traditional markets of the USA and Europe, and to promote new markets. It plays a very important role in identifying and assisting in the penetration of markets for companies who are expected to seize the opportunities presented and organise and manage them according to their own business objectives.

Other institutions set up to promote industrial and economic development are, for example, the Hong Kong Productivity Council (1967), the Vocational Training Council (1982) and – under the auspices of the Trade Department – the Textiles Advisory Board, which administers textiles quota. Lobbyists and other governmental efforts in the quota negotiations are paid for by the general taxpayer. More recent government action in Hong Kong is leading to an upgrading of support for technology, and to an active search for new investment, but the basic 'hands off' approach to the firm itself remains unchanged.

In Japan the state plays a distinctly stronger facilitating role by creating an appropriate infrastructure of laws and institutions to assist the development of the cotton textile industry in maintaining an internationally competitive role. The Japan Cotton Spinners' Association also plays an important part in collecting industry views and lobbying government. It provides to its members a great deal of information on trends in the domestic and overseas markets, including analyses of close competitors such as the Korean and Taiwanese spinners. In the past, the Hong Kong Cotton Spinners' Association has held a similar role to that of the Japanese, in representing industry views to the government and disseminating information. However, the significant decline in the number of spinning mills still operating in Hong Kong indicates that, in spite of governmental actions to support the industry, the impending change in sovereignty to the People's Republic of China in 1997 is an overriding concern for the Shanghainese spinners, who, considering what they lost earlier in Shanghai, would rather close their mill operations in view of this uncertain future.

*(ii)   Financial Systems*

The 'developmental' rather than 'regulatory' role of the Japanese government (Johnson, 1982: 19–23) is also evident in financial matters. The main actors are MITI, the Fair Trade Commission, the Bank of Japan and the Ministry of Finance. 'Administrative guidance' initiated by officials is an important tool for helping and encouraging private initiative within government guidelines (Dore, 1986: 26–7).

A distinctive feature of large Japanese firms is their financial stability and long-term view which supports diversification into higher technologies. This is enhanced by their symbiotic relationships with banks, trading companies and their *keiretsu* companies.

For example, Kanebo's return to profit in the late 1970s after a period of regular losses was clearly assisted by the support of Mitsui Bank, which attached its deputy president to oversee its diversification strategy.

The *sogo shosha*, in particular C. Itoh and Marubeni, and the *sen'i senmom shosha* (textile trading firms) play a vital role in the textile industry by providing raw materials and credit to the weaving and processing firms. Their role as financial intermediaries arises from their provision of financial arrangements with suppliers and customers. Their most important protection against losses is their knowledge of their clients' markets; in comparison, the banks are more conservative in their lending policies to small companies because they do not have such detailed understanding of companies' operations and attendant risks (Ballon and Tomita, 1988: 65).

The industrial groupings or *keiretsu* are also an important aspect of the financial system. Mutual shareholdings, interlocking directorates, presidents' meetings and transfer of personnel bind a group together and stabilise corporate performance substantially (Nakatani, 1988: 188). These also support the adoption of long-term growth perspectives rather than short-term financial performance as indicators of success.

The small scale of Hong Kong manufacturing enterprises (average size is 14 employees) simplifies financing needs. Most of the family businesses have a strong preference for raising funds from within the family and retaining the form of a partnership or private company. Although industrial output is 20 per cent of GDP, only 8 per cent of bank loans are currently to manufacturing firms (Ho, 1991). Hence in Hong Kong, the combination of the British colonial elite's policy of non-interventionism in business affairs, and the concern of Chinese entrepreneurs for secrecy and independence from potential government interference, have resulted in a great deal of self-reliance by firms for the provision of finance, and little assistance from government for diversification.

*(iii) Education and Training Systems*
Factors which influence the ease with which firms acquire or develop new skills for new business developments are shown in Table 11.4. It is apparent that the only advantage enjoyed by Hong Kong companies is the dual education system in which there is state provision of technical and professional training and education, largely by the polytechnics and technical institutes, with the universities concentrating more on the provision of academic education.

Table 11.4 *Education and training systems*

|  | Cotton spinning firms | |
|  | Japan | Hong Kong |
|---|---|---|
| Provision of basic education as reflected in literacy rates | High | Medium |
| Provision of technical and professional training and education by the state | Low | High |
| Provision of in-company training | High | Low |
| Flexibility of job boundaries | High | Low |
| Trade union support for re-skilling | High | Low |
| Introduction of new skill by mid-career hiring | Low | Medium |

In the unitary system of Japan, the state focuses on the provision of academic education, leaving firms to organise their own technical training. The Japanese education system produces highly disciplined and literate school, college and university graduates who have faced severe competition in achieving entry into the higher-ranking schools and universities. Their selection into leading companies is on the basis of the rank of their school and/or university, their academic achievements and their character. High school graduates are recruited for technical and clerical work, university graduates for technical and administrative work. The technical training and education received by Japanese employees is therefore entirely firm-specific. The employee development systems require employees at all levels to acquire over time experiences in different aspects of the business. Most of this training and development is on the job, but visiting experts will be asked to give short courses, and employees will be seconded to associated or joint venture companies in order to learn new technologies.

When large groups of employees face redundancy in the declining cotton textile industry, every attempt will be made to place them in other subsidiary, associated, *keiretsu* or supporting companies where they will be assimilated and retrained. For example, in November 1991 Toyobo announced the closure of a cotton-spinning mill affecting the employment of 259 employees (*Senken Shinbun*, 14 November 1991). All have been guaranteed continued employment in subsidiary and related companies, and discussions with the company's trade union have commenced to discuss the arrangements for the transfers. A number are expected to transfer to the company's new film business which is expanding. The low levels of mid-career hiring in Japanese companies are offset by the flexibility of employees towards learning new skills and the depth and breadth of skill they have already acquired in the company's operations. This is a very important factor in the high success rate of incremental improvements and adaptations of existing technologies to new products and processes. Mid-career hiring is, however, now being implemented in company research institutes as they put more emphasis on aspects of basic research, which require entirely new knowledge and skills. In these instances, the companies look to the universities and government research institutes for the hiring of experienced researchers.

In Hong Kong standards of education achieved in the general population reflect the historically weak provision of education by the colonial government and the large influx of migrants from the People's Republic of China. This situation has been exacerbated by poor provision of training in companies. The Cantonese weaving and garment factories have earned a reputation for little investment in the training of their labour force, except for family members. Workers themselves have no expectations of a long commitment to one particular company, preferring to job-hop to gain new knowledge and skill, and build sufficient know-how and connections to set up their own businesses. In contrast, the Shanghainese spinners introduced extensive education and training programmes in their mills on their arrival in Hong Kong from Shanghai in the early 1950s, and founded a technical school. They also attempted to establish internal labour markets, following the example of the Japanese spinners in pre-war Shanghai (Nishida, 1990). The emphasis on training employed by the Shanghainese spinners in Hong Kong enabled them to achieve the highest rates of machine productivity in the world from the 1950s to the early 1970s (Burkman, 1977: 199), but the companies remained small and their rate of technical change low.

In conclusion to this discussion on the proximate social institutions in Whitley's schema, the Hong Kong experience reflects a combination of British colonial policy and Chinese antipathy to governmental 'interference' in the running of their businesses, and a workforce which is more concerned with its own family fortunes than with those of the companies in which they are employed. Under these circumstances, any attempt by Hong Kong companies to diversify into higher technologies has faced severe institutional obstacles. In contrast, the Japanese benefit from the mutual dependence between Japanese state institutions and business, and a workforce with life-long expectations of a career with one company.

## Conclusion

The development of the textile industries of Japan and Hong Kong has clearly followed two different tracks. There is substantial homogeneity within each type but substantial variation between them. This variation is exhibited especially in organisation size, but it is also manifest in organisational complexity, in forms of relationship with the market, in relations with government, in technical sophistication and in finance-related fields such as investment in research and development. Perhaps its most crucial variation, however, is in the aspect of ownership structure, with the large professionally managed and publicly owned corporations of Japan contrasting with the closely held family networks of the Overseas Chinese.

It has been our contention that these two clusters are representative of distinct economic cultures, and that those cultures have formed as a result of the influence of the forces pointed to by Whitley. The peculiar combinations of institutional and/or cultural elements which have historically shaped modern industry are distinct because of the localised nature of certain key ones within national boundaries.

We have indicated connections between the background and proximate social institutions and the characteristics of organisations in one industry. These connections are not explored in detail to track the process of determinacy, but that analysis is clearly a further necessary stage for future work. In carrying out that work it is essential to be reminded that determinacy is influenced by two considerations: first, the institutional elements are interconnected among themselves and single causes cannot be isolated easily, or perhaps at all; second, the interactions between societal institutions and economic structures are reciprocal and in a constant state of flux.

## Note

The research reported here has been supported by the Institute for the Study of Economic Culture, Boston University, and the Citicorp Doctoral Program, University of Hong Kong Business School.

## References

Ballon, R.J. and Tomita, I. (1988) *The Financial Behaviour of Japanese Corporations*. Tokyo: Kodansha International.
Berger, P.L. (1986) *The Capitalist Revolution*. New York: Basic Books.
Burkman, J.H. (1977) 'Measurement of Technological Change and Productivity

Growth in the Textile Industries of Japan and Hong Kong: 1950–1974'. PhD thesis, University of Pittsburg.

Clairmonte, F. and Cavanah, J. (1981) *The World in their Web: Dynamics of Textile Multinationals*. London: Zed Press.

Cline, W.R. (1987) *The Future of World Trade in Textiles and Apparel*. Washington, DC: Institute for International Economics.

Collcutt, M. (1991) 'The Legacy of Confucianism in Japan', in G. Rozman (ed.), *The East Asian Region: Confucian Heritage and its Modern Adaptation*. Princeton, NJ: Princeton University Press. pp. 111–56.

Dasgupta, D. (1988) 'Trust as a Commodity', in D. Gambetta (ed.), *Trust: Making and Breaking Co-operative Relations*. Oxford: Blackwell. pp. 49–72.

Doi, T. (1973) *The Anatomy of Dependence*. Tokyo: Kodansha International.

Dore, R. (1986) *Flexible Rigidities: Industrial Policy and Structural Adjustment in the Japanese Economy 1970–1980*. London: Athlone Press.

Eisenstadt, S.N. and Ronigar, L. (1984) *Patrons, Clients and Friends*. Cambridge: Cambridge University Press.

Elvin, M. (1973) *The Pattern of the Chinese Past*. Stanford: Stanford University Press.

Fairbank J.F., Reischauer, E.O. and Craig, A.M. (1965) *East Asia: the Modern Transformation*. Boston: Houghton Mifflin.

Feuerwerker, A. (1984) 'The State and the Economy in Late Imperial China', *Theory and Society*. 13 (3): 297–325.

Granovetter, M. (1985) 'Economic Action and Social Structure: the Problem of Embeddedness', *American Journal of Sociology*. 91 (3): 481–510.

Harrison, L.E. (1985) *Underdevelopment is a State of Mind*. Cambridge, MA: Harvard University Center for International Affairs.

Ho, R.Y.K. (1991) 'The Banking System: an Overview', in R.Y.K. Ho et al. (eds), *The Hong Kong Financial System*. Hong Kong: Oxford University Press. pp. 3–30.

*Hong Kong 1991* Hong Kong: Government Information Services.

Hong Kong Cotton Spinners' Association (1988) *Forty Years of the Hong Kong Cotton Spinning Industry*. Hong Kong: Hong Kong Cotton Spinners' Association.

Hong Kong Cotton Spinners' Association (1990) Interview with the Secretary of the Association, 22 August 1990.

Jacobs, N. (1958) *The Origin of Modern Capitalism in Eastern Asia*. Hong Kong: Hong Kong University Press.

Japan Spinners' Association *Monthly Report of the Japan Spinners' Association*. Osaka: Japan Spinners' Association.

Johnson, C. (1982) *MITI and the Japanese Miracle*. Stanford: Stanford University Press.

Kanebo Company Ltd (1988) *Kanebo Hyakunen Shi* (The Hundred-Year History of Kanebo). Osaka: Kanebo Co.

Kono, T. (1984) *Strategy and Structure of Japanese Enterprises*. London: Macmillan.

Luhmann, N. (1979) *Trust and Power*. New York: Wiley.

McMillan, C.J. (1989) *The Japanese Industrial System*. 2nd edn, Berlin: de Gruyter.

Nakane C. (1970) *Japanese Society*. Berkeley, CA: University of California Press.

Nakatani, I. (1988) *The Japanese Firm in Transition*. Tokyo: Asian Productivity Organization.

Nishida, J.M. (1990) 'The Japanese influence on the Shanghai textile industry and implications for Hong Kong', MPhil dissertation, University of Hong Kong.

Odaka, K. (1984) *Japanese Management: a Forward Looking Analysis*. Tokyo: Asian Productivity Organization.

Pye, L.W. (1985) *Asian Power and Politics: the Cultural Dimensions of Authority*. Cambridge, MA: Harvard University Press.

Redding, S.G. and Whitley, R.D. (1990) 'Beyond Bureacracy: Towards a Comparative Analysis of Forms of Economic Resource Co-ordination and Control', in S.R. Clegg and S.G. Redding (eds), *Capitalism in Contrasting Cultures*. Berlin: de Gruyter. pp. 79–104.

Redding, S.G. and Wong, G.Y.Y. (1986) 'The Psychology of Chinese Organizational Behaviour', in M.H. Bond (ed.), *The Psychology of the Chinese People*. Hong Kong: Oxford University Press. pp. 267–95.

Rohlen, T.P. (1974) *For Harmony and Strength: Japanese White-Collar Organizations in Anthropological Perspective*. Berkeley, CA: University of California Press.

Rozman, G. (1991a) 'The East Asian region in Comparative Perspective', in G. Rozman (ed.), *The East Asian Region: Confucian Heritage and its Modern Adaptation*. Princeton, NJ: Princeton University Press. pp. 3–44.

Rozman, G. (1991b) 'Comparisons of Modern Confucian values in China and Japan', in G. Rozman (ed.), *The East Asian Region: Confucian Heritage and its Modern Adaptation*. Princeton, NJ: Princeton University Press. pp. 157–203.

*Senken Shinbun*. 8 May 1991; 9 May 1991; 14 November 1991.

Silin, R.H. (1976) *Leadership and Values*. Cambridge, MA: Harvard University Press.

Vogel, E.H. (1978) 'Guided Free Enterprise in Japan', *Harvard Business Review*. 56 (3): 161–70.

Whitley, R.D. (1990) 'East Asian Enterprise Structures and the Comparative Analysis of Forms of Business Organization', *Organization Studies*. 11 (1): 47–74.

Whitley, R.D. (1991) 'The Social Construction of Business Systems in East Asia', *Organization Studies*. 12 (1): 1–28.

Wong, S.L. (1988) *Emigrant Entrepreneurs: Shanghai Industrialists in Hong Kong*. Hong Kong: Oxford University Press.

Yamazawa, I. (1988) 'The Textile Industry', in R. Komiya et al. (eds), *Industrial Policy of Japan*. Tokyo: Academic Press. pp. 395–423.

Yamazawa, I. (1990) *Economic Development and International Trade: the Japanese Model*. Honolulu: East-West Center.

Yonekawa, S. et al. (1991) *Sengo Nihon Keieishi*. Vol. 1 (Postwar Japanese Management History), Tokyo: Toyo Keizai Shinposha.

Zucker, L.G. (1988) 'Where Do Institutional Patterns Come From? Organizations as Actors in Social Systems', in L.G. Zucker (ed.), *Institutional Patterns and Organizations: Culture and Environment*. Cambridge, MA: Ballinger.

# CONCLUSION

## 12

## The Comparative Study of Business Systems in Europe: Issues and Choices

### *Richard Whitley*

The contributions to this book have focused on the relationships between dominant social institutions and patterns of economic organisation in different societies and shown how variations in firm–market relations arise from institutional differences. They clearly demonstrate that effective forms of economic organisation vary considerably across European countries and that they are deeply embedded in their particular institutional contexts. Thus, the structure of firms and markets in Britain is different from that in Germany because of differences in key proximate institutions and in the pattern of industrialisation in the two countries. Similarly, the highly successful Finnish forest sector developed in different ways from the Swedish pulp and paper industry because of variations in its institutional environment, and the Danish metal working industry has successfully established a distinctive pattern of coordination and control as the result of the craft-educational complex and other institutional features. No single economic logic or efficient mode of organising economic activities dominates European economies and the paths to economic success both vary between institutional contexts and are clearly dependent on dominant institutions.

These studies of European business systems have also emphasised the varied nature of the relationships between business system characteristics and institutional features in Europe, as well as the greater heterogeneity of both institutions and forms of economic organisation within national boundaries compared to East Asian countries. Additionally, some have drawn attention to issues of social and economic change and to the internationalisation of European economies. These points raise a number of issues about the comparative analysis of business systems, especially in Europe, which I shall briefly discuss in this concluding chapter. First, I shall consider the question of the most appropriate unit of analysis and, in particular, the relations between national and sectoral business systems. Second, the extent to which business systems are stable, cohesive phenomena which change only slowly and severely restrict individual firms' choices will be discussed. Third, the implications of the growing internationalisation and interdependence of national economies for the analysis of business systems and the transfer of managerial technologies will be covered. Finally, I shall consider the different ways in which comparative studies of firm–market configurations can be carried out, in Europe and elsewhere.

## Firm–Market Configurations in Europe: National, Sectoral or Cultural?

The pluralism and differentiation of many institutional arenas in European countries, together with the considerable degree of interaction and interdependence between them, mean that the internal homogeneity and integration of institutions within nation states, and their distinctiveness between states, are not as strong as in East Asia (cf. Whitley, 1992). This has led Lilja et al. and Räsänen and Whipp to suggest that national business systems may be less significant and stable than sectoral ones and, indeed, are better regarded as the contingent outcome of competing sector logics than as the 'natural' unit of firm–market relationships. Together with the success of the Chinese family business in different East and Southeast Asian states, which Redding (1990) has attributed to the strength of a distinctive economic culture, this suggestion highlights the different levels at which business systems can develop and requires some further discussion.

Strictly speaking, there is no single level or social order in which distinctive and cohesive business systems can necessarily be expected to become established. As particular combinations of firm–market characteristics and connections they develop wherever dominant social institutions and cultures are sufficiently integrated and mutually reinforcing to generate separate patterns of economic organisation which reproduce themselves as effective socio-economic structures. In principle, these could be, and empirically have been, national, sectoral or cultural. To a considerable extent, then, it is an empirical matter which depends on the cohesion and distinctiveness of particular institutions in particular contexts. Where states and cultures overlap and are quite distinct from neighbouring ones, for instance, we would expect quite separate business systems to develop as in, say, Japan. Where states contain many ethnic groups which manifest quite distinct cultures it seems unlikely that a single, nationally different business system will emerge, unless one ethnic group is able to dominate others economically, as in post-colonial Malaysia (Jesudason, 1989).

There are, however, two important theoretical points to be considered. First, business systems are particular combinations of firms and markets which have become established in particular institutional contexts and so develop at the level of collective organisation which contains key institutions. Second, the level at which distinctive forms of economic organisation should be analysed depends on the characteristics which are of interest, in this case it is the broad pattern of forms of economic coordination and control which is being considered.

The major institutions which constrain and guide forms of economic organisation in market economies were divided into two types in the first chapter in this volume: background and proximate. The former can be summarised as those covering trust relations, collective loyalties to non-kin, individualism and authority relations. The latter concern the availability of, and conditions governing access to, financial and labour resources, together with the overall system of property rights and political control. In brief, proximate institutions comprise the political, financial and labour systems.

Background institutions may be conceived as predominantly 'cultural', although they are also interdependent with state institutions such as the legal system and the means by which political power is legitimately acquired. As largely cultural phenomena they can be specific to particular ethnic groups which need not overlap greatly with individual state boundaries and so can generate distinctive business systems across countries where cultural identities are strong and persistent and national institutions are heterogenous and weakly integrated. This is arguably the case for the expatriate Chinese in Southeast Asia (cf. Redding, 1990; Wu, 1983).

In considering the level at which background institutions generate distinctive business systems, it seems unlikely that they will be restricted to particular sectors, although it is sometimes suggested that South Asian immigrants to the UK have an affinity with the retailing sector. While sector-specific business systems derived from distinctive background institutions and cultural preferences may emerge among some disadvantaged groups for a time, these will tend to remain peripheral to the dominant business system as long as the major institutions and dominant culture retain their central position in the society. Indeed, such ethnically specific forms of economic organisation are usually restricted to minor niches in the established market economies, and further growth often requires adaptation to the dominant pattern of firm–market relations.

In general, sector- and industry-specific ways of organising firms and markets in Europe are not derived from distinctive background institutions dealing with trust, loyalty and authority relations but rather reflect particular beliefs and preferences about the dominant rules of the game which have developed in the course of the sector's becoming established in different countries. They are better conceived as distinct business 'recipes' which summarise dominant beliefs of industry leaders about effective business behaviour rather than broad systems of firm–market relationships coordinating economic activities throughout an economy.

Similarly, most proximate institutions are national rather than sectoral, although there may be some variations in how labour markets and skills are organised between industries. Obviously the state and the overall political system are national institutions and affect business systems at that level, even if the degree of central state control and coordination of political economic institutions and activities does vary considerably between European countries, as the discussion of corporatism shows (e.g. Streeck and Schmitter, 1985). Again, while financial systems also vary in their degree of national centralisation and regulation, they are usually quite nationally distinct and governed by national legislation that has a substantial impact on the structure and practices of financial institutions, as Knights et al. and O'Reilly show in this volume. Education and training systems, skill certification and collective labour organisations are also predominantly nationally specific and typically generate distinctive industrial relations systems and ways of organising work, as Maurice and his colleagues have so clearly shown (1980; 1986; see also Baglioni and Crouch, 1990).

Overall, then, most of the institutions that structure broad configurations of firm–market relations are cultural and national rather than sectoral. The patterns of economic organisation which are here described as business systems are thus the outcome of processes operating at quite general levels of social organisation. As emphasised above, this need not mean that distinctive business systems are always national or that each nation state generates its own separate way of structuring economic activities. The extent to which national institutions do produce sharply different business systems depends on their integration, mutual interdependence and identification with particular cultural beliefs and values. What this point does emphasise is that many of the key institutions which guide and constrain systems of economic organisation develop at the national level and are often quite specific to particular countries. Consequently, any comparative analysis of business systems has to consider the nation state and deal with the relations between national institutions and firm–market relations in market economies. Sector-specific ways of organising economic activities will only become established if distinctive social institutions exist to structure them within each sector. The sorts of institutions seen here as critical to business system development are rarely specific to particular sectors and so it is difficult to see how discrete and coherent sector-focused business systems could develop.

This discussion highlights the importance of clarifying the nature of the phenomenon being considered and the characteristics of economic organisation which are to be explained. This is the second theoretical issue mentioned above. In emphasising that the socially constructed nature of economic phenomena implies the institutionally variable nature of economic organisation and paths to economic success, so that different institutional contexts generate equally effective but distinctive ways of structuring economic activities between market economies, the study of business systems focuses on how firms and markets are constituted differently in different environments and form distinctive systems of economic coordination and control.

Business systems are thus seen here as rather general patterns of economic organisation which deal with the three basic questions that arise in any market economy: how are activities to be coordinated, how are markets to be organised and how are economic activities within authority hierarchies to be structured and controlled? Clearly these are very broad questions and not all economies are characterised by a single, tightly integrated configuration of firm–market relations. Nonetheless, I would argue that dominant institutions in all societies structure processes of industrialisation such that particular kinds of firms and markets become established and form a distinctive system of economic relations that reproduces itself interdependently with political etc. institutions. Given the considerable importance of the state, and of state-regulated and supported institutions, in coordinating industrial processes and maintaining social boundaries, it seems reasonable to consider market economies initially as bounded by states. Sectoral differences in the size of firms and degree of market organisation do, of course, develop in some countries, but these are often combined with cross-sectoral similarities in the management of risk and growth patterns, as well as in authority relations and the dominant pattern of work organisation, because of the strong influences of national political, financial and legal systems and related institutions.

Consequently, sectoral variations in some characteristics of business systems rarely constitute distinct and cohesive business systems as a result of the non-sector-specific influences of national and cultural institutions. The Swedish pulp and paper industry may, for instance, have changed its dominant 'recipe' for growth in the 1980s without any corresponding change in national institutions, and so exhibited a limited autonomy from those institutions, but it still differed in certain important respects from its Finnish counterpart because of differences in patterns of industrialisation, land ownership and the actions of the state. It is not at all clear, then, that a single international configuration of firm–market relations has come to dominate this industry irrespective of national institutional differences.

This example highlights the differences between the general analysis of firm–market relations in an economy and the specific study of firms' strategic choices and 'industrial wisdom', as discussed by Hellgren and Melin in this volume. The former focuses on the dominant logic governing, for instance, the degree of discontinuity in firms' growth patterns which derives from the institutional environment, as outlined in the first chapter in this book. The latter deals with the development and change of particular beliefs and actions of industrial leaders within the broad framework of the overall business system, as modified by influences from other business systems and foreign institutions.

Thus, the comparative analysis of business systems is concerned with the explanation of how different patterns of firm–market relations develop and change in different institutional contexts while the study of sector recipes and corporate strategies considers how these emerge and alter within the broader logic of the dominant business systems. This logic structures the general pattern of beliefs and rationalities in an economy, so that individual firms that pursue highly 'deviant' paths to success are unlikely to emerge as dominant economic agents, but does not specify particular 'recipes' or how they change. Obligational or 'relational' contracting is a general characteristic of connections between firms in Japan, for example, but this does not mean that all market relations are highly organised in this sense or that the particular ways in which such obligations are developed and fulfilled are the same in all sectors. This discussion is linked to the second set of issues to be considered in this chapter: how do business systems change and how do firms and markets develop novel patterns of economic organisation?

## Business System Change and Cohesion

A number of the chapters in this book discuss significant institutional changes in European societies and their impact on firm–market configurations. Others emphasise the continuity of some institutional and/or cultural features and of their associated business system characteristics. These contrasts highlight the problem of determining when and how alterations in some characteristics effectively lead to a significant change in the nature of particular business systems as a whole and, relatedly, how novel forms of firms and markets can develop and become institutionalised as new business systems.

Business systems are conceived here as relatively stable and cohesive configurations of firms and markets whose characteristics are, to a considerable extent, mutually interdependent and reinforcing. By definition, then, they do not change frequently or rapidly. Furthermore, since they become established in particular institutional contexts and are interdependent with dominant institutions, substantial changes in business systems are unlikely to take place in the absence of major institutional changes, such as those implemented by the occupying powers in Germany and Japan after the Second World War and by the French state at the same time. Even here there were substantial continuities, so that it would be misleading to claim that wholly new business systems had emerged in these economies (Berghahn, 1986; Clark, 1979; Johnson, 1982). Once established as distinctive and integrated forms of economic organisation, then, business systems rarely undergo wholesale change and their characteristics alter interdependently with those of connected institutions. Major changes in business systems thus imply related changes in critical institutions.

However, within this broad conception of business systems there are obviously varying degrees of cohesion and stability manifested by different configurations and, as we have seen in Europe, of the ability of firms and industries to develop novel forms of economic organisation within particular systems. The more interdependent, integrated and distinctive are major social institutions in an economy, the more integrated and cohesive will be its business system and the lower the likelihood of its changing unless most of these institutions also change substantially. Conversely, where institutions are quite differentiated and interdependence is relatively weak, a single homogeneous and strongly integrated business system is unlikely to become established and particular characteristics may well change as particular institutional features alter without the whole pattern altering. It is questionable, for example, whether there is a single dominant business system in post-war Italy or rather three overlapping but distinct configurations of firm–market relations in the North-West, the North-East and Centre and the South. Certain characteristics of the Italian industrial districts, it could be argued, changed as a result of the growth of regional government in the 1970s (Nanetti, 1988) while others remained the same. The extent to which business system characteristics change, then, depends on their degree of integration and close interdependence with major social institutions.

Similarly, the degree to which firms' actions and practices are subject to the dominant business system logic throughout an economy varies according to its integration and cohesion, which in turn reflect institutional homogeneity and interdependence. While some firms in peripheral sectors can, and often do, pursue 'deviant' policies in terms of the prevailing business system in many economies, growth and continued success involve adaptation to dominant practices, albeit to varying degrees. For instance, much of the small-firm sector in Japan practices different employment policies from most large firms. However, as they become more successful and seek to rise in the 'society of industry' (Clark, 1979: 95–7), they increasingly have to follow the norms and practices of that society if they wish to recruit high quality labour and elicit higher levels of commitment from employees. Despite frequent claims over the past decade or so that these policies were becoming too costly and would be replaced by more 'efficient' external labour markets, it seems that they remain solidly entrenched in the Japanese business system, except in certain specialist fields like securities trading, and it is difficult to become a large firm in Japan without adopting them (Dore et al., 1989; Whittaker, 1990).

In less integrated and cohesive business systems it is, of course, easier to develop and maintain 'deviant' structures and practices, sometimes to the extent of institutionalising distinctive patterns of firm–market organisation as in the case of Italy. More commonly, some different characteristics of business systems become established in particular regions or sectors while others remain common throughout the economy, as is arguably the case in the contrast drawn by Herrigel (1989) between the autarkic firm based industrial order and the decentralised region-based industrial order in post-war Germany. As Lane argues in her chapter in this volume, there are a considerable number of business system characteristics which are manifested throughout the German economy as a result of institutional commonalities and which constitute a distinctly German form of economic organisation, but there are also some that vary and these can be reconstructed as varied subordinate orders within the overall system. Similarly, in Britain the high level of institutional differentiation has enabled internal, organisation-based labour markets and considerable investment in training to be developed in some firms and sectors, but the overall constraint of the market for corporate control which applies to all firms, together with the lack of state involvement and commitment to industrial development, nonetheless limit the extent of employer–employee commitment. Thus, business systems do not preclude firms developing deviant characteristics, especially in pluralist societies, but they do typically set limits to such deviance, especially where related institutions are dominant and firmly establish particular rules of the game.

Overall, then, while the autonomy of firms to develop novel structures and practices varies between business systems which differ in their degree of integration and interdependence with dominant social institutions, the general patterns of firm–market relations that have become established in a particular economy limit the extent and longevity of such novelty. Such limitations are weakened when major institutions do not reinforce each other so that firms can enlist the support and legitimacy of one in defying another, as is arguably the case in some German regions where firms and unions have been able to obtain the support of the provincial government in pursuing network forms of economic organisation (Herrigel, 1989).

Equally, when state agencies follow divergent policies and/or political pressure can be mobilised by a variety of interests, economic actors are able to acquire resources and develop their own distinctive forms of economic organisation in the face of official attempts to rationalise the economy according to currently fashionable conceptions of efficiency, as Kristensen suggests has happened in Denmark. Finally, the growing internationalisation of European economics could provide external sources of support for firms wishing to develop novel activities and practices, especially in the more 'corporatist' economies, although the recent financial crises in some countries suggest that recourse to international capital markets as a means of transcending national financial systems does not always lead to effective alternatives. This point leads to a more general consideration of how the internationalisation of firms and markets is affecting business systems and its implications for their comparative study.

## The Internationalisation of Firms and Markets

It has become a journalistic cliché to see the 'globalisation' of firms and markets as heralding the demise of the nation state and the growth of worldwide competitive arenas. Similarly, the proposals for removing tariff and other barriers to the movement of capital and goods within the EC on the 1st of January 1993 have been seen as major steps towards the creation of 'European' firms and the decline of nationally specific forms of economic organisation. Relatedly, internationalisation of firms and markets could lead to the easier transfer of managerial structures and practices across political and culture boundaries so that a single 'recipe' of effective management becomes institutionalised internationally.

It is important to emphasise here that just as national institutions and cultural phenomena structure forms of economic organisation in particular market economies, so too are international firms and markets socially constructed and changed by national and international institutions. There is no innate competitive logic in global markets that determines efficient strategies and patterns of organisation which all successful firms have to follow if they are to remain effective. Rather, effective forms of economic organisation in world markets reflect the outcome of competition and conflict between those established in national economies, and so, indirectly, the result of institutional competition. While such conflict usually generates novel features because it would be unusual for any one organisational pattern to so dominate international markets that it effectively determined their operation, it is obviously structured by existing business systems and so the result will reflect the characteristics of those that come to dominate international markets.

As Hellgren and Melin suggest, it is the combination of worldwide oligopolistic firms operating in all major markets with worldwide competition which has become a significant factor in some industries in the past few decades. These 'transnational' (Bartlett and Ghoshal, 1989: 25–9) firms increasingly compete with each other on a global scale and are developing distinctive 'rules of the game'. However, it is unclear how these companies change their structures and practices from predominantly national to transnational ones and many MNCs seem to transfer their established practices from their home markets to overseas ones, especially the USA and Japan (Egelhoff, 1988: 226–9). Especially where the home market is large and firms have dominant positions in them, it seems likely that they will try to replicate their successful recipes elsewhere rather than create a new set of structures and relationships for the whole organisation in all the economies it operates in. Thus, Japanese firms in Britain have developed long-term relations with many suppliers and negotiated single union agreements – or sometimes excluded unions altogether (Oliver and Wilkinson, 1988).

The extent to which such a transfer of business system characteristics to host economies occurs does, of course, depend on the openness of dominant institutions in those economies to novel forms of economic organisation and the relative strength of established business systems in them. The more open and pluralistic an economy is, the more likely it will be to accept – or at least acquiesce in – the transplanting of new firm–market relationships. Conversely, where institutions are cohesive, integrated and have generated a distinctive business system, it is more likely that MNCs will have to adapt their mode of operation to the prevailing pattern. This is especially so where the host economy is powerful and large, as in the case of Japan since the 1960s.

A further point to bear in mind when considering the transfer of business system characteristics between economies, particularly in already industrialised societies, is its dependence on their similarity to those current in host economies and their centrality to the established business system, together with the importance of the specific sector to dominant institutions. Thus, the transfer of financial management techniques and accounting procedures between the Anglo-Saxon economies – especially the USA and the UK – is easier than it would be between British and French firms because of the common importance of capital market financial systems and of the 'professional' mode of organising accounting principles and skills in the former countries and their absence in France.

Similarly, transferring novel labour management practices to countries where trade unions are weak and there are few legal constraints is obviously more straightforward than introducing them to subsidiaries in states with strong unions and/or where there is a distinctive and systematic legal framework governing labour relations, as in many Scandinavian countries. Additionally, introducing novel financial practices and structures to countries with a powerful financial services sector, such as the US and the UK, is much more difficult than modifying established practices in sectors which are more peripheral to the dominant institutions. In sum, the transfer of managerial structures and practices between countries and cultures by multinational firms depends on the institutional structures of host societies and the relative balance of power between firms and institutions in home and host countries.

Thus, the institutionalisation of a single form of economic organisation across all industrialised societies through the agency of transnational firms is most unlikely as long as market economies continue to display a variety of dominant institutions and of their integration.

Turning to consider the implications of this discussion for the development of distinctive and separate European business systems, there are a number of points to be made. First, the considerable variety of institutional arrangements between European states limits the extent to which a single 'European' pattern of firm–market relations is likely to become established. Second, if pan-European political and financial institutions which are quite distinct and separate from national ones do develop, they will encourage, eventually, the development of novel forms of economic organisation. However, these will not supplant national business system characteristics unless, and to the extent that, nationally distinct institutions decline in importance and are replaced by pan-European ones. Third, the more national institutions become standardised around common European conventions and policies, the more similar will the business system characteristics most closely interdependent with those institutions become – as, perhaps, may happen with some features of the 'social charter'. However, such standardisation is by no means easy to accomplish, as the tortuous negotiations over common accounting standards shows, and in any case political agreements over broad issues do not always lead to the transformation of nationally specific practices and procedures into standard European institutions. Fourth, the progressive replacement of national powers and institutions by European ones – if it does indeed take place – may well be accompanied by a growth in regional variations of important institutions, as is arguably already the case in Italy, and so while some business systems characteristics may become more similar across Europe, others may become more differentiated between European regions. Finally, the institutionalisation of relatively free movement of goods and services through the European Community will not, in itself, lead to a pan-European business system as long as major institutions, such as financial systems, education and training systems and state structures, remain nationally distinct. Facilitating the development of a European market may enable some economies of scale in production and marketing to be realised on a European scale in some sectors, but firms will remain predominantly 'national' in their structures and practices as long as key institutions are predominantly national.

As the chapters in this book show, and the recent history of cross-national mergers in Europe has often dramatically demonstrated, important characteristics of firms and markets are highly interdependent with dominant institutions in different countries and do not change readily. The development of Europewide competitive strategies does not imply that national business systems are necessarily less important than they were, since such competition remains typically between firms from them and as long as their top management and key functions are still nationally specific and interdependent with national institutions, these firms are not going to change their procedures and structures substantially. While employer–employee relations, for instance, in factories in different European countries have to adapt to the prevailing legal systems and labour market patterns where these are strongly entrenched, such adaptation will take place in the framework already established in firms in their own domestic economies and hence will reflect their different institutional contexts. Similarly, firms may raise some capital from international financial markets and thus have to adapt to their exigencies, but as long as they remain closely linked to domestic banks in credit-based systems they will continue to follow the financial policies and management patterns which have become established in their home economy. The historically greater degree of interaction and competition between European societies and institutions has meant that nationally distinct and integrated business systems are less strongly established in Europe than in East Asia, but important institutional differences remain and limit the institutionalisation of new European business systems.

## Institutions and Business Systems in Europe: Forms of Comparative Research

These points have a number of implications for the sorts of comparative research of European business systems that can be carried out and how it could be organised. In particular, they highlight three major dimensions for contrasting alternative objects of analysis. First, comparisons either contrast general patterns of economic organisation, covering all or most components of business systems, in different institutional contexts, as in the study of East Asian economies (Whitley, 1992), or else focus on particular characteristics, such as work organisation or typical patterns of firm growth or market organisation. Correlatively, institutional contexts can be considered as relatively integrated and distinctive wholes, as by Christel Lane in this volume, or else particular institutions, such as the financial or education systems, could be compared across market economies and their consequences for specific aspects of economic organisation in each economy analysed.

Second, comparisons can either contrast whole economies or focus on particular sectors in different institutional contexts. Again, sectors can either be analysed as a whole, interdependent systems of firm–market characteristics, or else particular components may be highlighted for comparative purposes. For example, in this volume O'Reilly focuses on labour management practices in the retail banking industry while Nishida and Redding consider both the nature of firms and their development and of market relations in the textile industry as representative of general characteristics of the post-war Japanese and Hong Kong business systems. A third contrast is between analyses which focus on major changes in business system characteristics and associated institutions and those which concentrate on reconstructing the relatively stable and underlying properties of business systems to be explained in terms of enduring features of their institutional contexts. This distinction can obviously be applied to whole business systems, to particular components of them or to individual sectors. These three dimensions can be summarised as differences in the level of analysis, the scope of analysis and the dynamic focus which generate various types of comparisons. These are shown in Table 12.1 together with some examples.

The first dimension reflects the extent of business system decomposability. As a number of contributors to this book have shown, European patterns of economic organisation are more pluralistic within nation states and exhibit more similarity between them than do East Asian ones. The identification of cohesive and distinct business systems within national boundaries is therefore not easy and the degree of mutual interdependence and reinforcement between component characteristics is lower than in, say, Japan. As a result, the study of how particular institutions vary across European economies and affect particular business system components, or of variations in those components between countries, is more appropriate in Europe. This does, however, assume that institutional contexts and business systems can be broken down so that their elements can be analysed in isolation, an assumption which may be perfectly reasonable for relatively peripheral institutions but may not be for more central ones or where national and cultural boundaries are coterminous. Such decomposability clearly varies between societies and system components and so the appropriateness of comparing complete business systems or

Table 12.1    *Types of comparative analysis of business systems*

| Scope of analysis | Level of analysis | |
|---|---|---|
| | Component characteristics | Whole systems |
| Sector | Comparisons of sector components, e.g. labour management practices in banking | Comparison of sector organisation, e.g. the structure and development of the textile or paper industries in different economies |
| Economy | Comparisons of components between economies, e.g. work organisation across European countries | Comparisons of business systems between economies e.g. Britain and Germany, East Asia |
| Dynamic focus | Comparisons of underlying patterns of economic organisation, e.g. growth and risk management practices in countries with different political and financial systems | Comparisons of changing business system characteristics and institutions, e.g. emergent business systems in East-Central Europe |

particular component characteristics of them depends on their cohesion and integration, as well as on the precise focus of concern.

Similarly, the second dimension reflects the extent to which market economies may be decomposed into separate sectors or studied as integral wholes in reconstructing distinctive business systems. Where there are general characteristics of firm–market relations which seem to be reproduced in all major sectors and exemplify a broad logic of economic organisation, there seems little point in focusing on individual sectors, except as representative of the dominant pattern. For instance, the textile industry is useful for comparing Chinese and Japanese patterns of economic organisation because it has played a major role in the industrialisation of both Hong Kong and Japan and exemplifies many key characteristics of their distinctive business systems.

On the other hand, where sectors manifest distinctive forms of economic coordination and control, and so constitute separate business systems, they can clearly form the basic unit of analysis for drawing comparisons across economies. However, it seems improbable that the same sector would form identifiable, distinct firm–market configurations in all European economies for the reasons mentioned above, indeed it is precisely an interesting characteristic of these economies that they vary in the extent to which industries and/or sectors do exhibit distinctive patterns of economic organisation. Sector differences, then, are to be better viewed as properties of economies than as implying the need to compare the characteristics of individual sectors in different European societies, except where particular patterns of firm–market relations appear to be more effective in certain industries. For example, networks of small firms in industrial districts or similar forms of 'flexible specialisation' (Hirst and Zeitlin, 1991) appear to be quite competitive in the machine tool industry (Friedman, 1988), as well as in some other sectors, and so it would clearly be interesting to find out which conditions encourage this form of economic organisation in this industry in different countries. Additionally, the different forms that flexible specialisation assumes as a distinctive system of production in varied institutional contexts would be worth studying, just as one could analyse variations in 'Fordism' across economies.

A further reason for comparing the organisation of the same sectors in different economies is because they are thought to be closely connected to key institutions and/or play a leading role in structuring other parts of the economy. Thus, a detailed analysis of their organisation and functioning in different contexts should reveal significant relationships between institutions and firm–market configurations, especially if they are studied over time. An example would be the financial services sector, which is closely linked to the state in many capitalist societies, although the degree of overt regulation and centrality to the political system does, of course, vary. Similarly, in some economies, such as those dominated by the primary sector, particular industries in that sector may be so central to the economy that their pattern of organisation can be taken to exemplify the dominant one in those economies, as seems to be the case of the forest sector in Finland.

In considering the issue of dynamic focus, it is important to note that the analysis of business system change presumes substantial alterations in dominant patterns of economic organisation because the comparative study of business systems deals with general patterns of firm–market relationships which are unlikely to change frequently. An obvious instance of such change is the current set of transformations in Eastern and Central Europe which are likely to generate distinctive forms of economic coordination and control because of the different ways in which market economies are being established and the different institutional and economic/industrial inheritances in each country. Similarly, significant institutional changes occurred during the Allied occupations of Germany and Japan after the Second World War. By comparison the deregulation of some financial markets in the 1980s seems likely to have had only limited long-term effects on many business system characteristics, although of course these will have been more marked in economies where the financial markets play an autonomous and leading role, such as the UK. The more attention is focused on particular firms and sectors, the more significant will short-term changes appear, but these should not always be assumed to herald significant alterations to established patterns of firm–market relations.

## Conclusions

In this chapter I have tried to deal with a number of issues that have arisen from the contributions to this book. By way of conclusion I would like to summarise the key points about the comparative analysis of business systems. First, it assumes that the nature of firms and markets are socially structured so that variations in major social institutions, such as cultural patterns and those governing access to economic resources, result in significant differences in the ways that market economies are organised. Second, key characteristics of firms are interdependent with the ways that markets are structured and risks are shared between economic actors so that distinctive business systems have become established in different economies which combine growth and ownership patterns with particular kinds of inter-firm connections and authority patterns. Third, once established, these develop interdependences with their institutional contexts so that major changes in business system characteristics are unlikely in the absence of substantial alterations in related institutions. Fourth, because the nation state contains many of the key institutions which affect the sorts of business systems that develop in market economies, important business system characteristics are often nationally bounded and distinctive, although strong cultural systems can also generate sharply distinct patterns of economic organisation in some circumstances. Finally, the institutionalisation of separate international business systems depends on the emergence of strong and separate international political and other institutions. Until that happens, particular patterns of firm–market relations across national boundaries are likely to reflect those of the dominant economy and its institutions, albeit modified by the competitive struggle with other economies.

## References

Baglioni, G. and Crouch, C. (eds) (1990) *European Industrial Relations*. London: Sage.

Bartlett, C.A. and Ghoshal, S. (1989) *Managing Across Borders: the Transnational Solution*. London: Hutchinson Business Books.

Berghahn, V.R. (1986) *The Americanisation of West German Industry 1945–1973*. Leamington Spa/New York: Berg.

Clark, R. (1979) *The Japanese Company*. New Haven: Yale University Press.

Dore, R., Bounine-Cabalé, J. and Tapiola, K. (1989) *Japan at Work: Markets, Management and Flexibility*. Paris: OECD.

Egelhoff, W.G. (1988) *Organising the Multinational Enterprise: an Information Processing Perspective*. Cambridge, MA: Ballinger.

Friedman, D. (1988) *The Misunderstood Miracle: Industrial Development and Political Change in Japan*. Ithaca, NY: Cornell University Press.

Herrigel, G. (1989) 'Industrial Order and the Politics of Industrial Change: Mechanical Engineering', in P.J. Katzenstein (ed.), *Industry and Politics in West Germany*. Ithaca, NY: Cornell University Press.

Hirst, P. and Zeitlin, J. (1991) 'Flexible Specialisation versus Post-Fordism: Theory, Evidence and Policy Implications', *Economy and Society*. 20: 1–56.

Jesudason, James V. (1989) *Ethnicity and the Economy: the State, Chinese Business and Multinationals in Malaysia*. Singapore: Oxford University Press.

Johnson, C. (1982) *MITI and the Japanese Miracle*. Stanford: Stanford University Press.

Maurice M., Sorge, A. and Warner, M. (1980) 'Societal Differences in Organising Manufacturing Units', *Organization Studies*. 1: 59–86.

Maurice, M., Sellier, F. and Silvestre, J.J. (1986) *The Social Foundations of Industrial Power*. Cambridge, MA: MIT Press.

Nanetti, R.Y. (1988) *Growth and Territorial Policies: the Italian Model of Social Capitalism*. London: Pinter.

Oliver, N. and Wilkinson, B. (1988) *The Japanisation of British Industry*. Oxford: Blackwell.

Redding, S.G. (1990) *The Spirit of Chinese Capitalism*. Berlin: de Gruyter.

Streeck, W. and Schmitter, P.C. (1985) 'Community, Market, State and Associations? The Prospective Contribution of Interest Governance to Social Order', in W. Streeck and P.C. Schmitter (eds), *Private Interest Government: Beyond Market and State*. London: Sage.

Whitley, R.D. (1992) *Business Systems in East Asia: Firms, Markets and Societies*. London: Sage.

Whittaker, D.H. (1990) 'The End of Japanese-Style Employment?', *Work, Employment and Society*. 4: 321–47.

Wu, Y-Li (1983) 'Chinese Entrepreneurs in Southeast Asia', *American Economic Review*. 73: 112–17.

# Index